THE MAKING OF THE BACKWARD PUPIL
IN EDUCATION IN ENGLAND
1870–1914

Woburn Education Series
General Series Editor: Professor Peter Gordon

For over 20 years this series on the history, development and policy of education, under the distinguished editorship of Peter Gordon, has been evolving into a comprehensive and balanced survey of important trends in teaching and educational policy. The series is intended to reflect the changing nature of education in present-day society. The books are divided into four sections – educational policy studies, educational practice, the history of education and social history – and reflect the continuing interest in this area.

For a full series listing, please visit our website: www.woburnpress.com

THE MAKING OF THE BACKWARD PUPIL IN EDUCATION IN ENGLAND 1870–1914

Ian C. Copeland

University of Reading School of Education

WOBURN PRESS
LONDON • PORTLAND, OR

First published in 1999 in Great Britain by
WOBURN PRESS
Newbury House
900 Eastern Avenue
London IG2 7HH

and in the United States of America by
WOBURN PRESS
c/o ISBS
5804 N.E. Hassalo Street
Portland, Oregon 97213-3644

Website: http://www.woburnpress.com

Copyright © 1999 I. Copeland

British Library Cataloguing in Publication Data
Copeland, Ian C.
   The making of the backward pupil in education in England,
   1870–1914. – (The Woburn education series)
   1. Special education – England – History
   I. Title
   371.9′0472′0942

ISBN 0 7130 0216 6 (cloth)
ISBN 0 7130 4037 8 (paper)

Library of Congress Cataloging-in-Publication Data
Copeland, Ian C., 1937–
   The making of the backward pupil in education in England,
   1870–1914 / Ian C. Copeland.
     p.   cm. – (Woburn education series)
   Includes bibliographical references and index.
   ISBN 0-7130-0216-6 (cloth). – ISBN 0-7130-4037-8 (paper)
   1. Handicapped children–Education–England–History.
   2. Education, Elementary–Social aspects–England–History.
   3. Mainstreaming in education–England–History.
   4. Special education–England–History. I. Title.
   II. Series.
   LC4036.G72E544   1999
   371.91′0941–dc21
                                                                        98-30483
                                                                        CIP

Printed in Great Britain by
Creative Print and Design (Wales), Ebbw Vale

'There are four kinds of people in this world: cretins, fools, morons and lunatics.'

'And that covers everybody?'

'Oh, yes, including us. Or at least me. If you take a good look, everybody fits into one of these categories. Each of us is sometimes a cretin, a fool, a moron, or a lunatic. A normal person is just a reasonable mix of these components.'

Umberto Eco, *Foucault's Pendulum*
(London, Secker & Warburg, 1989, p. 61)

For Jane, Emma and Jo

Contents

Contents

Appendices:

Tables and Figures

TABLES

FIGURES

Foreword

Historical accounts of special education have tended to focus on children with physical or sensory impairments and, to a lesser extent, the 'mentally handicapped'. Far less attention has been paid to that sizeable group of children whose learning is simply slower or more difficult than that of peers. Commonly termed 'backward' or 'feeble-minded', they exist in an educational twilight: the main thrust of policy and provision has paid scant regard to them; and academic enquiry has virtually ignored them.

Quite apart from the educational loss and the diminution of life chances experienced by so many young people, our understanding of human learning and of key societal forces has been impoverished because of this academic neglect. Sarason and Doris's (1979) seminal book on mental retardation was one of the first studies to subject mental retardation to a detailed social historical critique. They document plainly how mental retardation is a socially invented concept, and neither provision nor professional practice can be properly understood outside of prevailing sociocultural forces.

The social construction of disability and learning difficulty is now quite familiar and is beginning to move into everyday discourse. It is far from well established, however. Within education, for instance, there are big differences between and within countries over the extent to which pupils' difficulties in school are seen to result from an interaction between environmental and innate factors. In some places the traditional discourse of special education is alive and well, as evidenced in widespread use of special schooling and remedial education, whereas elsewhere inclusive education is the prevailing discourse and there is negligible use of special schooling.

When these opposing discourses co-exist in the same education system, as in contemporary England, the tortuous progress of social ideas is clearly exposed. Social progress is seldom linear, of course, and it would be unrealistic to expect conceptions of school failure or learning difficulty to move ahead in a straight line.

This does not mean that the current confusion of ideas and practice is inevitable. Social progress or the lack of it draws from many sources. One salient feature, which this book addresses, is the extent to which guiding ideas are clearly understood. This means a historical perspective but, more than that, an analytical one, whereby concepts and the practices in which they are embedded are deconstructed, related to one another and located within appropriate theoretical frameworks.

Backward pupils were a creation of universal compulsory education. In Britain the Foster Education Act of 1870 was a decisive moment. In this book, Ian Copeland focuses on the time between the Foster Act and the outbreak of war in 1914. In scrutinising the historical documents of the period, he conducts a penetrating and at times revelatory analysis of the making of the backward pupil. Some of the historical detail he presents is fascinating – and soberingly prescient of later tensions, such as the conflicting weight of medical opinion already evident even then – but the fundamental achievement of this book is to make explicit how educational backwardness was socially constructed.

SEAMUS HEGARTY
Director, National Foundation for Educational Research
October 1998

REFERENCE

Sarason, S. B. and Doris, J. (1979) *Educational Handicap, Public Policy and Social History: A Broadened Perspective on Mental Retardation,* London, Collier-Macmillan.

Acknowledgements

First, the generosity of the University of Reading and its resources made this study possible. Second, I am grateful for the support of my colleagues in the Education Department by reason of their discussions, encouragement and example. Third, my thanks to the library staff at Bulmershe Court, who have tracked down texts diligently in their own stacks and those of other libraries; also the help and knowledge of staff in various Public Record Offices have been appreciated. Fourth, I am much indebted to my colleague Kevin Brehony, who has been a particular source of critical comment and encouragement. Finally, I acknowledge the enduring indulgence and tolerance of my immediate family members.

Abbreviations

BoE	Board of Education
COS	Charity Organisation Society
CSI	Centres for Special Instruction
DCDEC	Departmental Committee on Defective and Epileptic Children, 1898 (Education Department)
DES	Department of Education and Science
DFE	Department for Education
EE(DEC) Act	Elementary Education (Defective and Epileptic Children) Act, 1899
HMI	His/Her Majesty's Inspectorate/Inspector
LEA	Local Education Authority
LSB Min.	Leicester School Board Minutes
PD	Parliamentary Debates (Hansard)
PP	Parliamentary Papers
RCBDD	Royal Commission on the Blind, the Deaf and the Dumb, &c., 1889
RCCCFM	Royal Commission on the Care and Control of the Feeble-Minded, 1908
RCEEA	Royal Commission on the Elementary Education Acts, 1886, 1887, 1888

Introduction

The prime category of the analysis which follows is that of children regarded as dull, backward or feeble-minded. The time frame is the period which starts in 1870, when Elementary education began to include all children and ends in 1914, when educational provision for pupils ascertained as mentally defective became compulsory. Conventionally, the dull and backward pupil is considered alongside the blind, deaf and/or dumb and each is regarded as an exceptional or special category. That approach is rejected in this instance; the aim is to comprehend the case of the pupil judged dull or backward within the overall structure and organisation of prevailing education. To this end, an analytical framework is constructed which draws upon a combination of Max Weber's concept of status group and Pierre Bourdieu's theory concerning the social reproduction through time of sets of advantages and disadvantages. However, the heart of the study identifies the irrational, contradictory and inconsistent ideas upon which policy and practice for special classes for the dull and backward were established and persisted with. The challenge thus became to comprehend the irrational by the rational. Some formulations by Michel Foucault are developed to this end.

The methodical approach to historical data and their interpretations has been through a combination of 'narrative' and 'analysis'. 'By narrative I mean an account of some process or development in terms of a story in which a series of events are depicted chronologically ... By analysis I mean the explanation of concrete cases by the direct application of abstractions or theoretical models of what are believed to be widely replicated structures and mechanisms. As such it tends to abstract from particular historical sequences' (Sayer, 1992, p. 259). Although it is recognised that strictly 'narrative' is itself a form of 'analysis', the major advantage of this approach is that it permits enquiries to begin by cutting through protracted debates concerning the nature of historical facts, historical positivism and the relationship between theory in sociology and history (cf., Abrams, 1982, pp. 1–17; Goldthorpe, 1991, 1994; Bryant, 1994; Jenkins, 1995; Evans, 1997).

OUTLINE OF THE BOOK

Chapter 1 lays out the main consequence of the co-existence of two Royal Commissions on Elementary education and examines how historians have treated this phenomenon in particular and the growth of special education in general. Chapter 2 discusses the theoretical framework drawn from the formulations of Max Weber, Pierre Bourdieu and Michel Foucault.

Two questions underlie the organisation of the empirical and theoretical work of this study: why did special schools and classes for children judged variously dull, backward and mentally defective come into being in England at this time and why did they take the form that they did?

Certain preliminary considerations were necessary, however, before these questions could be broached, because the position was taken that the special schools and classes were not organised by chance and the children's lives were, in part at least, products of social circumstances. First, some account of the social, economic, industrial and demographic features which prevailed together with an analysis of the elementary education system embedded within this context was necessary. An investigation of the creation and control of policy and practice for elementary education in general was also needed. These considerations form Chapter 3. Second, examination of legislation for disabled children, the blind, deaf and dumb, was necessary as was an inquiry into how the difficulties which faced dull, backward or mentally defective children were conceived. The conception of the reason for children's difficulties is regarded as crucial because of its role in determining the provision thought appropriate and possible. Chapter Four tackles these issues.

After these preliminary considerations, Chapter 5 describes the background to the establishment of the first seven classes for mentally defective children. Each of these seven accounts is constructed from witnesses' oral evidence to the Departmental Committee on Defective and Epileptic Children in 1898.

The question of educational provision for mentally defective children had been first raised in the Royal Commission in 1889 alongside that for other disabled children such as the blind and deaf. However, because the question at that time could not be resolved, further consideration of the issues was referred to a specially constructed Committee of the Education Department. Chapter 6 examines that Committee's dispositions and deliberations, which are important because its recommendations became the basis for subsequent legislation.

In Chapter 7, there is discussion of certain conceptual inadequacies and contradictions which persisted through the deliberations from 1889 but nevertheless became the basis for legislation. A theoretical scheme to comprehend inadequacies and contradictions is proposed.

Finally, Chapter 8 draws these themes together.

1

A Pivotal Event in the Making of the Backward Pupil

INTRODUCTION

> More has been researched and written about education in Victorian England than in any other period. Yet we have neglected it. (Silver, 1983, p. 17)

Thus opens an extensive summary and critique of the relevant literature upon education in Victorian England (ibid., pp. 17–34). The main focus of writers has been upon the formation of policy and legislation, upon administration in terms of provision and of control, upon the changing elements of the constituent parts of the system – Board and Voluntary schools, Elementary and Technical schooling – and upon commissions and committees. However, 'The underlying pattern ... is one of neglect of questions relating to educational realities, to the impact of education, to its role in cultural and social processes' (ibid., p. 21). Educational provision for the pupil judged dull and/or backward is a precise example of such neglect.

The co-existence of two Royal Commissions, the Cross and Egerton Commissions, in the period 1886–89 proved a defining moment for the education of such pupils. The circumstances surrounding the establishment of each of the commissions were, however, very different.

The general background to the establishment of the Royal Commission on the Elementary Education Acts (RCEEA) under the chairmanship of Sir Richard Cross, subsequently Lord Cross, in the early days of 1886 was, first, Forster's Education Act of 1870 which permitted non-denominational School Boards to found schools to supplement the existing places provided by the church schools and, second, Mundela's Education Act of 1880 which compelled children to attend school. Thus Elementary education became comprehensive but schools for the first time contained children who had previously received no formal teaching and who came from families whose members had not attended school. As

1

a consequence, 'the lower classes (in schools) were thronged ... by unwilling and ignorant victims' (Smith, 1931, p. 307). The number of pupils in Elementary schools expanded rapidly from 1.7 million in 1870 to 4.8 million in 1891 (Board of Education (BoE), 1901, p. 104). Class sizes were also very large; if pupil-teachers who had recently completed their own school lessons and were subsequently apprenticed to teaching are included in the calculations, then there was a pupil:teacher ratio of 60:1 in 1870 and 48:1 in 1891 (BoE, 1901, p. 105). In addition, the teaching regime in Elementary schools was policed by Robert Lowe's Revised Code of Practice with its central principle of payment by results. In accordance with this principle, the amount of grant which a school was paid was determined in small part by each pupil's general merit and attendance rate but in larger part by the pupil's performance in examinations of the three Rs. Thus classes were large, teaching methods were mechanical and primarily directed towards preparing the pupil for the examination (cf., Smith, 1931, pp. 254–61; Wardle, 1976, pp. 68–89). These circumstances became the focus of the Cross Commission.

A few days after the establishment of the Cross Commission, the membership of a Royal Commission to examine the education of the blind, deaf and dumb, etc. (RCBDD), under the chairmanship of Lord Egerton was announced (RCBDD, 1889, p. 2). The establishment of this latter Commission had been tortuous and incremental. In 1885, a Royal Commission had been set up to inquire into the education of the blind. However, some few months later and following a lobby on behalf of the deaf and dumb by Lord Egerton, its terms of reference 'were extended by the inclusion of the deaf and dumb and of such other cases as from special circumstances would seem to require exceptional methods of education' (RCBDD, 1889, p. xi).

The creation of a category of 'such other cases as from special circumstances would seem to require exceptional methods of education' and the co-existence of the two Commissions had profound and far-reaching consequences for pupils judged backward. Early in its deliberations, the Cross Commission decided that pupils with special circumstances requiring exceptional methods of education fell into the domain of the Egerton Commission's concerns. 'The RCEEA having suggested that the case of feeble-minded children would come more appropriately within the terms of reference, we have received evidence that there are a great many backward children in our Elementary schools who require a different treatment to that of the ordinary children' (RCBDD, 1889, p. civ). Two profound consequences flow from this judgment: first, the 'exceptional cases', being divided off, cease to be regarded as 'ordinary children'; and, second, a search for the solution to the difficulty is directed away from scrutiny of mainstream pedagogic practices and organisational structures. In this way the seeds for segregated special provision are sown.

HISTORIANS' TREATMENT OF THE EVENT

For the most part, historians treat the event with the neglect identified by Silver. Following a close search through leading writers, a pattern emerges of a discussion of the main features of the Cross Commission's final report. The features discussed are usually the religious issue underpinning the division between board and church schools, the ill effects of the system of payment by results, the need to raise the school exemption age, the improvement of schools' facilities and the enlargement of the teacher-training system (cf., Adamson, 1930; Smith, 1931; Barnard, 1947; Curtis, 1948; Peterson, 1952; Jarman, 1953; Armytage, 1964; Eaglesham, 1967; Selleck, 1968; Dent, 1970; Morrish, 1970; Murphy, 1971; Digby and Searby, 1981). There is no discussion or even mention of the Egerton Commission. Several of these works were reprinted many times and ran to numerous editions. From that evidence alone, their extensive influence may be assessed. Despite the omission of reference to Egerton, some authors boldly insert words such as 'landmarks' or 'foundations' in their titles. The neglect of Egerton appears to have travelled confidently over a period of some half a century. A small number of sociologists, who offer a historical perspective on the growth of special education, present the problem in reverse, so to speak. In other words, a discussion of the Egerton Commission is divorced from a consideration of the impact of the Cross Commission (cf., Ford, Mongon and Wheelan, 1982; Tomlinson, 1982).

THE GROWTH OF SPECIAL EDUCATION IN THE LITERATURE

An outline of the inadequacies of existing sociological paradigms to account for historical developments in special education has been published elsewhere (Copeland, 1993, pp. 1–13). Briefly, there are two main sources for these inadequacies: first, the assumption that special education is an unproblematic, homogeneous category in which measures impact equally on all children with disabilities; and, second, the failure to develop sufficiently ideas such as safety-valve, social control and the pursuit of professional interests as explanatory devices.

An apt, if a little dated, bridge between the accounts of development produced by sociologists and historians who do include discussion of Egerton is the work of Owens and Birchenall (1979). Although this is intended as a sociological account, it nevertheless reproduces the features of historiographic works. 'Historiography' and 'sociography' are terms intended to denote studies which are essentially descriptive rather than analytical (cf., Andreski, 1964, pp. 64–6). The following is an example of a passage intended to explain the origins of a sub-committee of the Charity Organisation Society (COS) established to inquire into the care and education of the mentally deficient: 'It is fortunate that, whenever a group of people appear to society to be underdogs, there is always someone to champion them ... in 1887 a member of COS began a vociferous campaign ... his agitations bore fruit' (Owens and Birchenall, 1979, pp. 59–60). In this example, a contentious assertion is used to explain a particular event whose outcomes are identified metaphorically.

August Comte introduced the term 'positivism' to the social sciences: positivism insists, first, that science should only examine entities that are observable and known directly to experience, and, second, that the social world is subject to rules just as there are laws which operate in the natural world. The aim of positivism is to build general laws or theories which express relationships between phenomena. Thus the central tenets of positivism are the search to establish and accumulate facts together with the belief that facts speak for themselves to tell their own story through their interrelationships. The Report of the Ministry of Education (1951a, pp. 64–85) on the growth of the school health service from 1890 to 1950 is an example of historiography based upon positivism. Historiography aims to establish the details of events and proceeds in a smooth manner from the establishment of committees, proposals to commissions, bills in Parliament and their legal outcomes. It describes the establishment of systems and records the results of debates. The main theoretical difficulty arises as much from what is excluded by historiography as from what is included. Thus, while it may be important to know what a committee decided, it may be equally important to know what it rejected and the grounds for rejection.

Pritchard's (1963) work is an outstanding example of a historiographic account of the growth of special education in Britain from the eighteenth century until the middle of the present one. It draws upon a very extensive range of primary and secondary sources and is quite rightly used as a first resource by other writers (cf., Department of Education and Science, 1978, pp. 8–22; Cole, 1989, p. 2). It is examined in several places in the subsequent text.

Ted Cole read History at Oxford and is Principal of an independent residential school for children with learning and behavioural difficulties. He is author of *Apart or A Part? Integration and the Growth of British Special Education.* Pritchard's history of the handicapped child had concluded with the date 1960, which marked 'the period of consolidation [of] the 1944 Act' (1963, p. 207). Pritchard welcomed the advance embodied in the 11 categories of handicap which the Act brought in train but overlooked the contradiction that an Act intended to offer an education to all children in accordance with their 'age, aptitude and ability' (Education Act, 1944, Ch. 31, 5.1) simply passed over responsibility for the education of handicapped children to the Health Services (Ministry of Education, 1945). To be fair to Pritchard, however, it must be added that the sociology of education was largely in its infancy in Britain at that time. Cole, in contrast, was able to bring the history of special education up to the threshold of the Education Reform Act of 1988. As the subtitle suggests, his narrative focuses upon the extent to which children with disabilities were included within mainstream education.

Cole's historiography is at a higher level than Pritchard's, however, because he always seeks to introduce a particular period of change in special education with a larger summary of major political events and enactments for mainstream education. The time-span from 1870 to 1988 is broken up into five periods and the period 1893–1918, entitled 'To the End of the Great War', for example, is preceded by three pages which summarise 27 references to political events (1899, Second Boer War, Cockerton Judgement; 1902, Education Act) and 33 references to events in special education (1893, Blind and Deaf Education Act; 1899, Elementary Education (Defective and Epileptic Children) Act). In addition, the early paragraphs of description about each period identify the main characteristics within which events are embedded. Thus 1893 to 1918 is described as containing

> the Indian summer of Liberalism, with its increasing collectivist and socialist tendencies. It also saw the emergence of the Labour party as a significant Parliamentary force. It was an era of outward assurance, witnessed by the continued expansion of Empire but inner doubts caused by the Boer War, uncertainty over whether France, Russia or Germany was our real enemy, a worsening arms race, stiff economic and agricultural competition from the New World and domestic troubles with militant trade unions, aggressive employers, suffragettes ... (Cole, 1989, p. 36)

This attempt to provide a structure and historical framework is most commendable. However, when it comes to a description of changes in special education, there is no reference to these contextual factors and the account consists, like Pritchard's, of the actions of individuals, the work of committees and the enactment of legislation.

What of Cole's craft as a historian? The facts that the name of the chairman of a key sub-committee of the London School Board is misspelt throughout and his former rank in the army misreported are perhaps trivial (cf., Cole, 1989, pp. 38, 186). However, at another point he maintains that 'space alone prevents a detailed critique of [an author's] account of the history of special education [and] ... her major points rest upon a selective view of ... history' (ibid., p. 170). Cole puts forward the view that 'so many local education authorities did not provide for feeble-minded pupils until the 1914 Education Act forced them to [because] the sources do not suggest there was a problem' (ibid., p. 37). The reason such pupils were not a problem is explained by a reference to Lawson and Silver (1973, p. 329) that, in Cole's words, 'payment by results largely ended in 1890'. Lawson and Silver in fact argued that, although there had been important changes in the Code in 1890 which were potentially very liberating, teachers' former practices persisted for many years simply because no alternatives had been or were available. An important factor in this inertia was the fact that local authority inspectors were largely recruited from the ranks of headteachers in the authorities. Thus their skills and predilections had been shaped by a previous prevailing regime (cf., Smith, 1931, p. 328).

In addition, Cole's own account of the establishment of the first special classes contradicts the claim that there was no perceived problem, when he states that the Education Department granted permission for their establishment, being 'aware of more general complaints about the feeble-minded clogging up the Standards' (1989, p. 38). Finally, Cole reproduces Pritchard's (1963, pp. 119–20) account of the establishment of special classes in London and, although it later becomes clear that he is drawing from the same original source material, he nevertheless omits mention of London's false start and retraction of the first scheme for special classes. This is made more curious by virtue of the emphasis Pritchard accords the false start in his narrative (1963, p. 119).

J. S. Hurt is the author of *Outside the Mainstream: A History of Special Education* (1988). The time-span of the book is from the mid-eighteenth century up until the Education Act of 1981. The definition of special education adopted by the author is broader than a concern for the physically or mentally disabled child and includes 'the special arrangements ... made for those seen as posing a threat to social order: the pauper child and the socially deviant child' (p. 9). These two latter categories had been intended originally as the book's prime focus, but the author implies that his publishers obliged him to leave this part unfinished – having reached a point in the mid-1930s when the Home Office assumed responsibility for these categories – and devote the second half to 'what is more traditionally seen as within the sphere of special education' (ibid.). A part of one of the chapters in this second half discusses provision for dull, backward and mentally defective children.

Hurt, like Pritchard, was a university teacher and in the works of both there is a rich panoply of references to primary and secondary sources. While the range of sources is one consideration, a more important one is the use to which they are put. Hurt's opening sentence to the chapter entitled 'The Defective Child, 1888 to 1918' states that 'In response to the Egerton Commission's promptings a number of School Boards began making provision for feeble-minded children' (1988, p. 127). He then lists the eight Boards which had formed classes by 1898. Given the very much larger number of School Boards which did not respond to the prompting, would not a more appropriate stance be to ask why? Again, how could Hurt assess the Egerton Commission's role? First, General Moberly gave evidence to the Commission in his capacity as chairman of the London Board's sub-committee on the instruction of the blind, deaf and dumb. Moberly's evidence revealed that there were already pupils described as 'idiots' in the Board's schools and the Board was already addressing the question of provision (RCBDD, 1889, vol. II, p. 867). Second, all the eight Boards listed gave evidence to the Departmental Committee on Defective and Epileptic Children (DCDEC) established in 1896. All except Nottingham, which submitted written evidence, were asked about the origin of their special classes for feeble-minded pupils. None volunteered a mention of the Egerton Commission's report.

Eco suggests that written works may be subjected to at least three dimensions of analysis: the intention of the text *per se* and the intentions of the writer and of the reader (1992, p. 25). Hurt's intention in the sentence quoted above was doubtless to assist the reader's comprehension of historical events. This reader's intention, however, is to treat Hurt's text critically, and with access both to Hurt's text and the source(s) of a part of that text another dimension of analysis emerges which is overlooked by Eco – the omissions, the silences, the author's text makes from the original sources. Hurt has a lengthy discussion of physical stigmata and their link with imbecility and idiocy. He rationalises the medical profession's stance in this regard as follows: 'one must remember that medical men [*sic*] had only limited means of diagnosis at their disposal, while psychiatry and any form of mental testing were still in their infancy'

(1988, pp. 129–30). This form of rationalisation glosses over and omits mention of the important debate which took place between different branches of the medical profession and which was at the heart of the Egerton Commission's recommendations concerning provision for the feeble-minded and which was repeated in the opening stage of the Departmental Committee's inquiry. The details of the debate will be expanded upon in Chapters 4 and 6 when the work of the Egerton Commission is examined. Hurt's stigmata discussion also omits two other facts: first, the figure most prominently associated with the link between physical stigmata and mental deficiency was James Kerr, medical officer of the Bradford Board, who gave extensive evidence to the Departmental Committee and had published papers on the topic (DCDEC, 1898, vol. II, pp. 18, 22). Second, Dr A. Eicholz, who became the Education Department's Chief Inspector for Special Schools, reported from a European conference that stigmata were not taken as linked with mental deficiency on the Continent. Curiously, of the several members of the medical profession who gave evidence to the Departmental Committee, all mentioned stigmata and feeble-mindedness in some way in their evidence, but Hurt chooses to link the topic exclusively to Francis Warner (1988, pp. 126, 129), and also omits to mention that this was a single feature of a complete battery of practical tests developed by Warner for teachers' use in school. Again, this topic will be pursued further in this text. Finally, Hurt chooses to link George Shuttleworth's evidence to the Departmental Committee to the eugenicist movement in his statement that idiocy is transmitted through generations by 'marriages of persons of the same morbid tendencies' (DCDEC, 1898, vol. II, p. 96). On the contrary, Shuttleworth's main concerns arguably were not aetiological but those of classification and treatment.

The form of explanation for particular historical events which Hurt adopts may be described as an appeal to intellectual common sense or rationalisation. Thus his explanation for the permissive nature of the Elementary Education (Defective and Epileptic Children) Act, 1899, runs as follows:

> Apart from the difficulties of determining whether a child was merely backward, mentally defective or an imbecile, other considerations must have included the poor prognosis usually offered for all forms of mental defect … The social obloquy attaching to sufferers, the lack of suitably trained teachers, the sheer numbers of children involved, and doubts about the cost-effectiveness of teaching mentally defective children, also militated against compulsory legislation. (1988, p. 134)

By inference, if these factors were claimed to militate against compulsory provision, then there must also have been factors pointing in the opposite direction. In addition, the point concerning 'sheer numbers' is contentious within the original source and turned upon whether Warner's or Shuttleworth's evidence was given priority. Again, this issue is taken up later in this book.

In his concluding chapter, Hurt proposes two overarching explanations for developments in special educational provision: the first links the desire for 'a more orderly society' with 'a genuine concern for the ... disadvantaged'; and the second, a search for 'social control'. Thus, '[p]ioneers of education "outside the mainstream" were motivated by a desire for a more orderly society and a genuine concern for the socially, physically and mentally disadvantaged ... At the same time this humanitarian conviction has been entwined with considerations of social control' (1988, p. 189). The inadequacies of theoretical explanations which mix promiscuously different types of disability are stated in Copeland (1993, p. 3), as are those of the social control thesis (ibid., pp. 2–3). Since that was written, a devastating and extensive critique of the 'fantasies of social control' theory has been published (Sumner, 1994, pp. 139–249).

Two further criticisms can be directed at Hurt: the first is theoretically based and the second empirically based. In his introduction, Hurt stated that his concerns included the 'special arrangements ... made for those posing a threat to social order' (1988, p. 9). Given that the original thesis involves those posing a threat to social order, then it follows necessarily that there must be a search for 'a more orderly society' and some form of social control thesis in the outcome. Put in a different way, if a threat is posited as the starting point, then the logical conclusion is a reduction of that threat. The finish was built teleologically into the start.

The empirical criticism derives from Hurt's claim that '[p]ioneers ... were motivated by a ... genuine concern for the socially, physically and mentally disadvantaged' (Hurt, 1988, p. 189). Cole also accepts that point and declares that 'after trawling deeply through the annals, I am left agreeing with Hurt that early special education pioneers ... generally seemed imbued with a deep concern for the interests of special children' (Cole, 1989, p. 169). Pritchard, however, records that Thomas Braidwood established the first academy for the deaf and dumb in Edinburgh in 1760. The simple facts of its establishment were that Braidwood's original school for the teaching of mathematics was in decline through its failure to attract sufficient pupils. In 1760, he was approached by a wealthy merchant with a request to teach his deaf son. Braidwood's Academy thrived, began advertising in the *Scots Magazine* and by 1769 was turning pupils away through lack of accommodation. In 1783, Braidwood moved an enlarged Academy to London. Throughout, the academy was run as a business employing family members and jealously guarding outsiders' access to its pedagogical practices. Pritchard reports that critics regarded it as 'an unethical monopoly and possibly a racket' (1963, p. 14).

If this illustrates a financial motive, another person who worked with the blind also demonstrated that his concerns were partial if not biased. Thus the Egerton Commission's enlarged terms of reference to comprehend all major forms of sensory disability were criticised by him as 'unfortunate in that it gave stark recognition to a vicious bracketing of blind with deaf' (Ritchie, 1930, p. 35).

If there is a case to be made for humanitarian concern for children with disabilities as a motivating force, then evidence suggests that it may be linked with female membership of the School Boards. In the initial stages, the Boards' attentions were primarily quantitative in terms of the numbers of school places, teachers and buildings which were needed. Gradually, however, children began to be disaggregated and were seen to have special needs within differing groups. While it may be the case that in the first place women stood for election to School Boards 'not as educationalists devoted to children, but as feminists to advance the claims of women to public life' (Hollis, 1987, p. 87), they employed their suffragist skills to argue for the general improvement of children's lot. For example, '[t]hey pressed for school feeding, physical exercise, adequate playgrounds, and swimming baths, all designed to improve child health' (ibid., p. 141). The disaggregating process perhaps started with female Board members' recognition of the younger children's need for a kindergarten approach in their education and the need for an equal and relevant curriculum for girls. From this starting point, many examples are cited of female Board members' pressure and initiatives for the education provision for the physically disabled and the dull and backward child (ibid., pp. 124–5, 141, 183–4). There is also a detailed account of a particular suffragist's involvement as a School Board member in measured proposals for the provision of school meals and the medical inspection of schoolchildren (Steedman, 1990, pp. 53–7, 138, 170–1).

That aside, however, this review of the main features of the current literature on the growth of special education in Britain, points to the need to develop an alternative format to examine the provision for dull, backward and feeble-minded children.

The main source of difficulty for historiographers, and one which is perfectly understandable, is that in the aim to accumulate historical data, omissions and inaccuracies seem almost inevitable. The other source of difficulty is 'the result of historians treating sociological literature as a kind of academic potting shed containing a set of handy tools' (Smith, 1982, p. 287). Smith goes on to argue that historians reach for a sociological concept such as social class as a device to give a sense of order to data which are rampant (cf., Burke, 1980, pp. 32–3).

2

The Emergence of Classes
for the Dull Pupil:
Towards an Alternative Theory

The preceding discussion has identified both the neglect of the co-existence of the two Royal Commissions by historians and the inadequacies of attempts to explain the growth of special education. What follows is an attempt to establish an alternative framework, drawing initially upon the work of Max Weber, Pierre Bourdieu and, subsequently, Michel Foucault.

The following section sets out the reasons for using a combination of extracts from the works of Weber and Bourdieu as the theoretical background to the first part of the analysis.

Durkheim defined education teleologically thus: 'Education is the influence exercised by the adult generations upon those that are not yet ready for social life. Its object is to arouse and to develop in the child a certain number of physical, intellectual and moral states which are demanded of him by both the political society as a whole and the special milieu for which he is specifically destined' (1956, p. 71). Durkheim argued that educational practice serves jointly the demands of 'society as a whole' and 'each special milieu' or social group. The former provides the homogeneity necessary for society's survival and the latter the diversity necessary for social co-operation. Putting the functionalist assumptions aside, Durkheim omitted to explore whether the phrase 'society as a whole' was, in fact, an expression which legitimated the dominance of particular forces within society. In a similar vein, he did not consider the part played by ideology in the maintenance of consensus. Rather, what he elsewhere termed 'the moral consciousness of societies' (1952, p. 149) was not considered biased or working systematically in the interests of some groups and against those of others.

The idea that education is partly determined by the 'special milieu for which [the individual] is specifically destined' also forecloses the debate about the extent to which the education which an individual experiences determines social destination. Durkheim regarded education as a form of adaptation to national and occupational demands in modern societies. He overlooked the part education may play in predetermining and/or restricting life-chances. 'He saw [education] as adapting to an independently generated occupational diversity, not as helping to constitute and perpetuate social divisions' (Lukes, 1975, p. 133). Consequently, he did not examine the relationship between the technical and the social division of labour, that is, the relationship between the demands of the occupational structure for skills which may be inculcated by education and the perpetuation of social hierarchies.

There was a time when economic functionalism was the dominant theoretical mode which accounted for the differences between schools and their curricula. 'Despite idiosyncrasies of national history, political structure, and social tradition, in every case the development of education bears the stamp of a dominant pattern imposed by the new ... pressures of technological and economic change' (Halsey, Floud and Anderson, 1961, p. 1). The claim has been argued in detail for the development of school systems in England, France and Germany during the second half of the last century (Locke, 1984; cf., Green, 1990). Moreover, economic functionalists regard the economy and the school system as symbiotic. Thus Locke argued that high rates of economic advance towards the end of the nineteenth century in Germany arose in large measure because of the quality and quantity of training offered at the German technical institutes. These institutes were both larger and more practically oriented than was the Ecole Polytechnique in Paris and, at the same time, had a more scientific approach to knowledge than France's *écoles nationales d'arts et métiers*. However plausible on the surface, economic functionalism faces theoretical and empirical problems which must be resolved. First, if the central premise is that formal education furnishes the job skills demanded, then this may be questioned in two ways: on the one hand, there is the question whether vocational skills are learned at school or elsewhere and, on the other, there is the question whether more highly educated employees are also more productive. Both of these questions contain theoretical problems such as separating the effects of school experience from other experiences, and what is to count as productive labour. Empirically, both questions receive little support (Collins, 1971, pp. 1004–6). Secondly, there is the need to demonstrate that particular curricular experiences are useful for particular positions in industry or business. Finally, it has been argued that the approach of economic functionalism is fundamentally flawed by virtue of being embedded in a functionalist theory of social stratification such as that espoused by Davis and Moore (1945) or Goode (1967).

Allied to the economic functionalist case is the idea of the democratisation of education. This idea embraces the argument that the enlargement of the pool of students for whom education is provided implies an improvement of the access chances of less advantaged social groups to the different layers of education within the system. Thus the requirement for places in Elementary schools to be made available for pupils in the 1870 Education Act and the requirement for pupil attendance at the schools in the 1880 Act could be seen as a democratic enlargement of the education system. While this aspect of democratisation may be intelligible in terms of the establishment of Elementary schools, it becomes less tenable when the examination shifts to the establishment of higher Elementary schools which tended to syphon off centrally the more able pupils and the growth in secondary and tertiary education. As research on social mobility has suggested (Glass, 1954; Westergaard and Resler, 1976, pp. 279–314), the idea of democratisation tends to mask the process of the relatively uneven distribution of relative educational opportunities between social groups. Thus the relative educational gains of pupils of working-class origins remained virtually insignificant compared with the gains of the lower middle-class and propertied middle-class pupils (Westergaard and Resler, 1976, pp. 284–6). Ironically, the wider availability of academic credentials actually undermines the basis of such credentials as a mark of distinction.

The concept of social reproduction proposed by Pierre Bourdieu (Bourdieu, 1977; Bourdieu and Passeron, 1977) has a different focus. The concept of social reproduction implies the creation anew from generation to generation, from parental to filial generations, of hierarchical social relationships. Bourdieu makes distinctions between social, cultural and economic capital. Social capital consists of families' relationships, interrelationships, connections, friendships and so on. Cultural capital consists in the degree of familiarity with the dominant cultural modes. Some cultural forms such as music, poetry and drama become objectified and celebrated by social conventions which, in turn, are objectified in artefacts such as special buildings for artistic performances and further legitimised by becoming the objects of study in institutions of higher education. There is a degree of arbitrariness concerning the content of dominant cultural capital because it expresses the preferences and interests of particular social groups. As such interests change, however, so does the content of cultural capital. Thus new musical, literary or dramatical forms emerge with the initial support of a minority. The content of the school system, that is, subjects of study and modes of assessment, is a distillation of the dominant cultural capital. The school system is simultaneously the expression and the legitimation of dominant cultural capital. The legitimation of the particular selection of culture from the potentially available range is usually historically based. In this sense, schools may be regarded as 'museums of society' (Waller, 1965, p. 34).

Children who inherit a measure of cultural capital, by virtue of their families' immersion in it, have their inheritance further enhanced by virtue of the schools' foundation in a selection from that same capital. This congruence is likely to lead such children to success in the school system and the gaining of valuable credentials which, in turn, may provide access to valued social and occupational positions. In this way, educational credentials are a confirmation of familial cultural capital and, at the same time, present scope for the renewal and enlargement of social and economic capital.

The system is not perfect nor as straightforward, for example, as all the children of university graduates themselves becoming graduates. Rather, Bourdieu's emphasis is not upon the reproduction of precise quantities of economic, social and cultural capital but upon the reproduction of a set of relative advantages and disadvantages which produce a set of class relationships. In this light, Robert Lowe's cynical comment written in 1867 (quoted in Reeder, 1980, pp. 102–3) on the extension of the franchise, with the injunction that we should educate our masters, becomes more intelligible. The injunction has a twofold aspect: on the one hand, the man (literally) in the street is to be sufficiently literate to be economically productive and politically compliant; on the other, he must be capable of recognising the basis for his masters' social, cultural and economic superiority. Thus the intention was to reproduce a set of relative advantages and disadvantages which underpinned a set of class relationships.

Ideas such as Bourdieu's seem very fruitful for exploring the differentiation which occurred between different parts within the education system in the second half of the nineteenth century. For example, the emergence of higher Elementary schools, the distinctions between secondary schools and their enlargement and the nature of technical and higher education institutions. However, Bourdieu's concept of social reproduction is largely ahistorical and it may be necessary to turn to the sort of distinction which Max Weber made between class and status to inform historical analysis. 'The term "class" refers to any group of people ... (who have the same) typical chance for a supply of goods, external living conditions, and personal life experiences, in so far as this chance is determined by the ... power ... to dispose of goods or skills for the sake of income in a given economic order ... Class situation is, in this sense, ultimately market situation' (Gerth and Mills, 1948, p. 181). For Weber, as for Marx, the basic condition of class rested in the unequal distribution of economic power and from that, the unequal distribution of opportunity. However, this economic determination in Weber's view did not exhaust the conditions of group formation. What was needed was a concept which would encompass the influence of ideas upon the formation of groups without overlooking economic conditions.

> In contrast to the economically determined class situation, we wish to designate as status situation every typical component of the life fate of men that is determined by a specific, positive or negative, social estimation of honour ... In content, status honour is normally expressed by the fact that a specific style of life can be expected from all those who wish to belong to the circle ... Stratification by status goes hand in hand with a monopolisation of ideal or material goods or opportunities. Beside the specific status honour ... we find all sorts of material monopolies ... The decisive role of a style of life in status honour means that status groups are the specific bearers of all conventions. (ibid., pp. 186–91)

As 'bearers of conventions', status groups conduct their social affairs in accordance with the dictates of specific sets of ideas. For example, there may be an abhorrence of common physical labour among privileged status groups. Again, literary and artistic activities may be regarded as degrading as soon as they are pursued for income.

Class situation and status situation are antithetical. Thus the market is not based upon personal distinctions: stock exchange transactions are reduced to standardised formulae and the distinctions between stockbrokers is their respective credit rating. Economic actions are oriented towards 'a rationally motivated adjustment of interests' (ibid., p. 183). Class position may change rapidly in accordance with market conditions. In contrast, with a status order where human beings are grouped on the basis of social standing and way of life, all actions based upon considerations of status are oriented towards the 'feeling of the actors that they belong together' (ibid.). The status group opposes the suggestion that wealth as such is a valid basis for status because, if wealth were the basis, then the rich could claim higher status or honour than others with distinguished family lineages. Hence, in contrast to class, status groups act to support and maintain their social conventions. For these reasons, while material and economic conditions may bring about social change, status groups may continue to bolster and cherish conventions whose foundations may precede the social change. Thus elements of the past become manifest in the present.

Weber employed the distinction between class and status group in his examination of religions. In the first instance he examined group formation on the basis of shared religious beliefs, in which ideas work to shore up group cohesion, are a mechanism for status distinction, and may be the basis to monopolise economic opportunities. Thus conventions may initiate and determine market situation. He then examined ideas from a different starting point by taking particular social groups, such as feudal knights or craftsmen, to explore the religious dispositions which may be engendered by their class situation and status interest. In this instance, ideas are regarded as a reflection of material interests.

By making joint use of Bourdieu's and Weber's propositions, a framework may be set out, first, to explore the origins of special schools and/or classes for children judged feeble-minded and, second, to explore the shift in the basis of the criteria used for admitting pupils to these schools or classes. The criteria for admission changed quite rapidly and radically over a brief period of time from the schools' inceptions. The criteria also may be regarded as a reflection of the social groups which support them. Thus the background to the establishment of Elementary schooling for the whole of the relevant age group may be understood in Bourdieu's terms of the social reproduction of hierarchical social relations, which entails the reproduction of a set of relative social advantages and disadvantages. On this basis, the nature of Elementary schooling can be examined as can the emergence of the organisational pressure for the establishment of special schools or classes for feeble-minded pupils. Weber's distinction between class and status group can then be used to examine the ideas which lay behind the conventions which controlled the organisation of special schools and classes. From this general scheme a number of specific questions emerge. First, what was the nature of Elementary schooling in the period 1870–90 and what were the factors which produced the demand for special units? And, second, what were the criteria for admission of pupils to special units and in what way did they change?

FOUCAULT'S GENEALOGY

Genealogy is gray, meticulous, and patiently documentary. It operates on a field of entangled and confused parchments, on documents that have been scratched over and recopied many times ... Genealogy ... requires patience and a knowledge of details, and it depends on a vast accumulation of source material. (Foucault, in Rabinow, 1991, p. 76)

17

Foucault openly acknowledged his debt to Nietzsche in developing his concept of genealogy, which he intended as a radically different conception of historical analysis. The central idea is that 'The forces operating in history are not controlled by destiny or regulative mechanisms, but respond to haphazard conflicts' (ibid., p. 88). The ideas of descent and emergence provide the orientations for analysis. Thus:

> Genealogy as the analysis of historical descent rejects the uninterrupted continuities and stable forms which have been a feature of traditional history in order to reveal the complexity, fragility and contingency surrounding historical events ... the analysis of historical emergence [is] conceptualised not as the culmination of events or as the end of a process of development but rather as a particular momentary manifestation of the hazardous play of dominations or a stage in the struggle of forces. (Smart, 1983, pp. 56–7)

In Foucault's own words, 'An examination of descent ... permits the discovery, under the unique aspect of a trait or concept, of the myriad events through which – thanks to which, against which they were formed' (Rabinow, 1991, p. 81). And 'emergence is the moment of arising ... [and is] always produced through a particular stage of forces' (ibid., p. 83).

Elsewhere Foucault set out his main reason for this form of historical analysis:

> I would like to write the history of this prison ... Why? Simply because I am interested in the past? No, if by that one means writing the history of the past in terms of the present. Yes, if one means writing the history of the present. (Foucault, 1977, pp. 30–1)

Foucault is thus concerned to identify the present's antecedents and antecedents which figure in the present.

Finally, if genealogy is a history of the present which is specifically concerned with the complex, haphazard antecedents of a socio-intellectual reality, then this contrasts with an archaeology 'which is concerned only with the conceptual structures subtending the reality. *Discipline and Punish* is the fullest expression of genealogy ... since it ... is concerned with practices and institutions rather than experiences and ideas' (Gutting, 1994, p. 12).

FOUCAULT AND EDUCATIONAL STUDIES

The aim of the following section is to review the ways in which Foucault's work has been used in an analysis of matters educational. Until recently, there have been very few Foucauldian analyses, so this review can aim to be comprehensive. The reviews are presented chronologically in accord with dates of publication, but they could also have been presented in terms of how Foucault's own work developed. Thus there is the early adoption of the idea of archaeology as an organising principle (cf., Rose, 1979; Jones and Williamson, 1979; and Donald, 1985). In contrast, Sarup's brief account (1982), Skeggs (1991) and Meadmore (1993) can be organised around the concepts emphasised in Foucault's later work: objectification, subjectificaton and normalisation, which are described in the next part of this analysis. The chronological order, however, probably best reflects Foucault's work because although his cross references to his own publications are conspicuous by their absence, later concepts and problematics are nevertheless immanent in early publications.

An early example of the use of Foucault's concepts is found in Rose's article, 'The Psychological Complex: Mental Measurement and Social Administration' (1979). In strict terms, this may not be classified as an educational study, since its prime aim is to demonstrate how the concept of the feeble-minded became a tool to resolve the ideological debate between proponents of different solutions to the perceived problems of degeneracy and pauperism. On this terrain, according to Rose, there emerged the social practice of tests of individual's mental capacities, under which guise the debate concerning degeneracy and pauperism was transformed from what was regarded as a moral to a medical basis. Rose claims that his enterprise is characteristic of what Foucault termed a genealogy, by which he denoted a study of past beliefs and practices intended to shed light upon current practices. Rose hardly attempts this as his analysis draws to a close at the time of the start of the First World War. It is, however, a very fine example of what Foucault termed an archaeology, that is, a study of a set of interrelated beliefs and practices which supported social actions. Foucault's emphasis was upon the form of the beliefs and practices rather than their truth or validity.

In the same year, Jones and Williamson used Foucault's concept of archaeology as a framework to examine the formulation of pedagogy in popular schools in the first half of the nineteenth century in England. The central tenet in their analysis is that the form of popular schooling is not to be understood simply as 'traces of a last age' but rather as 'monuments, objects describable in themselves' (Jones and Williamson, 1979, p. 104). Their discussion is articulated around the question 'What made it possible for popular education to be formulated as a necessity?' (ibid., p. 62). The answer turns upon Foucault's concept of bio-power and describes, in the period in question, how the individual as a person and the population as a species became subject-objects of the state's concerns.

These concerns centred upon the problems of poverty, poor relief, the cost of labour, criminality and the idea of the dangerous class which provided a link between poverty and criminality and was also regarded as a political threat. The early regulation of town populations into districts in accordance with the establishment of police and health authorities yielded the basis for a topography of the population. From statistical records there quickly emerged an apparent link between morbidity, criminality and the living conditions of the unemployed, poor labourers and other segments of the population. The questions (and answers) which surrounded the issues of unemployment, poverty and criminality were conceived discursively in a personal, moral vein. The belief in the necessity of education was present in the discourses of all these issues and was constructed in terms of the ability of school instruction to lay down for the child correct moral principles, which, in turn, would inform the child's actions. Thus there emerged the impetus for the transformation of the pedagogy of popular schooling from the mechanical structure of the monitorial system based upon the efficient acquisition of skills and facts to that of the individual classroom where the teacher became the precept and model for the pupil. Here were taught object lessons which the pupil was intended to understand rather than merely echo or repeat. This understanding, informed by moral principles, was intended to guide the child. Hence the poor would gain the basis for an improved domestic economy, the 'perishing class' would be insulated from the contagion of the criminal class, and this latter would come to realise the folly of its erstwhile amoral pursuits and have some device to turn away from these pursuits to seek a living in a different manner.

The archaeology, according to Jones and Williamson, showed that the conceptualisation of social problems in terms of a history and topography of records of the poor, the unemployed and the criminal, also presented the state with a conceptualisation of their solution in terms of changes in pedagogy in schools. The state worked, therefore, through bio-power to achieve the necessary conditions in the individual and the species. The discourses on pauperism, criminality and political unrest united in a common concern to moralise those perceived as the amoral. The conduit of this morality was the newly created school classroom and its attendant teacher.

Sarup (1982, pp. 15–23) offers a brief account of modern schooling as essentially a disciplinary and grading mechanism in which the role of examinations was central. Although Sarup mentions surveillance and panopticism, he treats normalisation as their equivalent rather than as a component subsidiary.

Walkerdine (1984) draws upon Foucault's concepts of objectification and subjectification to argue the case that the precepts of developmental psychology effectively created both the young child-pupil and the teacher jointly as the subjects of a child-centred pedagogy and continues to do so.

In 1985, Donald produced a very detailed archaeology of the ideologies which surrounded the inauguration of the Elementary school system in the last century. Again, the facts of the Code of Practice for education, the creation of standards for age-cohorts of pupils and the institution of the examination by inspectors, operated to produce pupils as subjects. Unlike Walkerdine's thesis, however, the teacher does not also figure as a subject in the process.

A collection of articles published in 1990 claims to be 'the first [book] to explore Foucault's work in relation to education' (Ball, 1990). Its intention was expressly to explore the application of Foucault's work to the field of education. Three of the articles are set within the genealogical framework, which aims to excavate the past to illuminate the present. Here there is an account of the historical background to the urban schoolteacher (D. Jones), a more esoteric analysis of the relations between education practice and scientific knowledge in post-revolutionary France (R. Jones), and an exploration of the development of psychiatry in France and the discipline of geography in England as an exposition of the relationships between the modern state and professionals (Goodson and Dowbiggin). Three further pieces are cast in the archaeological mould to explore, first, conflicts within the policies for multicultural education (Knight *et al.*), second, the component ideological elements of the New Political Right (Kenway) and, third, the idea of managerialism as a moralising technology (Ball). Here the confessional as a mechanism which objectifies the subject, is explored in its migration from religion and the monastery, to psychiatry, social work, management and teacher appraisal.

Skeggs (1991) has employed some of Foucault's concepts in an ethnographic study sited in a college of further education to demonstrate how the discursive forms of sexuality may be used as regulative and tactical devices. The study focuses upon young working-class women taking 'caring' courses under the direction of male teachers. 'It demonstrates how, on the basis of the normalisation of masculinity, male teachers are able to regulate female students through the sexualising of situations' (Skeggs, 1991, p. 127). Discourse operates through actions and ideas and is not absolutely coercive. On the contrary, '[t]he resentment generated by being forced to confront their educational and feminine powerlessness leads the female students to develop a number of different coping tactics' (ibid.).

Ball (1994) draws extensively upon Foucault's ideas to argue that aspects of recent reforms in education in England and Wales, such as the introduction of market forces, managerialism, the national curriculum and tests, have operated to objectify pupils and teachers alike as subjects.

Foucault's thinking about the nature of power and his concept of dividing practices in the creation of individuality have been used to examine the cases in Australia of the Queensland State Scholarship Examination and the practice, prevalent from the 1930s onwards, of the use of psychological tests for entry to special schools for the backward (Meadmore, 1993). Both cases are illustrative of dividing practices in that the examination and the psychological tests are devices which effectively separate particular groups of children from their peers and identify them as subjects. In one case, the group is selected for a high-status form of education and, in the other, for a special form of instruction. In both cases, in popular discourse the examinations assumed a status which was taken for granted. The author argues that her position is that of 'taking a poststructuralist approach to the sociology of assessment [which] had sought to change the emphasis ... from the notion of power as a top-down repressive force to power as a capillary, productive force' (ibid., p. 71). This accorded with Foucault's view that power was ubiquitous in formal and informal social relationships. While this view of power as ubiquitously immanent in the examination as a dividing process is very convincing, the explanation for the origin of the academic examination is less so. Here it is argued that the examination 'was a reflection of the power base of the landowners, known as the "squatters", who dominated both houses of parliament and who were anxious for secondary schools to be set up in the British tradition for their sons' (ibid., p. 63). Here the structuralist view of power appears foremost, although this does not necessarily preclude the Foucauldian view of power.

FOUCAULT, SPECIAL PUPILS, SCHOOLS AND CLASSES

Foucault declared that the objective of his work 'has been to create a history of the different modes by which, in our culture, human beings are made subjects' (Foucault, 1982, p. 208). He proposed three modes of the objectification of the subject. The first mode he called 'dividing practices'. Here '[t]he subject is either divided inside himself or divided from others' (ibid.). The process of division may be spatial or social and combines the mediation of science or pseudo-science and the practice of exclusion, again in a spatial or social sense. *Madness and Civilisation, The Birth of the Clinic* and *Discipline and Punish* focus upon dividing practices. The second mode of objectifying the subject is related to the first but independent of it. It has been characterised as 'scientific classification' (Rabinow, 1991, p. 8). This springs from

> the modes of inquiry which try to give themselves the status of sciences: for example, the objectivising of the speaking subject in *grammaire générale*, philology and linguistics ... [or] ... the objectivising of the productive subject, the subject who labours in the analysis of wealth and of economics. Or ... the objectivising of the sheer fact of being alive in natural history or biology. (Foucault, 1982, p. 208)

Foucault's *The Order of Things* demonstrates how the discourses of language, labour and life became structured into disciplines. Each achieved a high degree of internal coherence and autonomy but each changed abruptly at several historical junctures. Thus the disciplines which appear to be concerned with the universals of human social life, and which appeared to progress logically to refine themselves in the course of history, displayed a conceptual discontinuity at different points.

The third mode of objectification can be termed 'subjectification'. Here, Foucault 'sought to study ... the way a human being turns him- or herself into a subject' (Foucault, 1980a, p. 208). The domain of sexuality was chosen for this study. The three modes of objectification are brought together in the idea of 'bio-power'. In the course of the growth and development of the modern state, the study and control of the population, the family and the economy became a central area of concern to administrators and rulers. In this process the state created the demand for 'statistics ... the collection, classification and discussion of facts bearing on the condition of a state or community' (*Oxford English Dictionary*). This development, to Foucault, constituted bio-power, which 'brought life and its mechanisms into the realm of explicit calculations and made knowledge-power an agent of the transformation of human life' (Foucault, 1980a, p. 143). Bio-power is organised around two dimensions. The first is the human species where scientific categories such as species, population, fertility etc., replace legal categories to become the objects of political attention and intervention which is sustained and systematic. The other dimension is the human body, not approached directly in a biological frame but rather as an object which may be manipulated and controlled. The joining of power and knowledge produce a 'disciplinary technology' whose aim is the forging of 'a docile body that may be subjected, used, transformed and improved' (Foucault, 1977, p. 190).

The dividing practices are evident in the disciplinary technologies by the organisation and separation of individuals in space. The scientific classification presents an explanation and justification of the type of organisation and the degree of separation. Surveillance, however, lies at the heart of disciplinary technology. Foucault identified Jeremy Bentham's plan of the panopticon as the paradigm for disciplinary technology. The panopticon contains a central tower encircled by a series of buildings which are divided into levels and cells. Each cell has two windows: one admits light from outside and the other faces the tower. From the central tower large observatory windows permit the surveillance of each individual cell. In turn, the cells

> are like so many cages, so many small theatres, in which each actor is alone, perfectly individualised and constantly visible. The panoptic mechanism arranges spatial unities that make is possible to see constantly and to recognise immediately. (ibid., p. 200)

The inmate is visible to the supervisor alone and separate from his peers. The disciplinary technology is both continuous and anonymous. The power apparatus operates effectively whether the surveillance is present or not, since the inmate cannot know that. Hence inmates behave as if surveillance were perpetual and total. Anyone may occupy the central tower. The inmates may be patients, criminals, workers or schoolchildren. The panopticon creates a hierarchy of subjects: surveillance both of inmates and of those responsible for them is possible. Hence supervision of doctors, nurses, overseers, teachers and patients may occur simultaneously. Each becomes a subject in their own location (ibid., p. 204).

The process of normalisation draws upon the modes of objectification. A norm is the centre of normalisation which produces a system of finely gradated and measurable intervals around which individuals can be distributed. The norm both organises the intervals and exemplifies them. Surveillance supervises the process of normalisation. 'An essential component of technologies of normalisation is the key role they play in the systematic creation, classification and control of anomalies in the social body' (Rabinow, 1991, p. 21). This supervision of social anomalies derives from the promoters' claims that anomalies can be isolated (and insulated) through their technologies and that corrective or therapeutic procedures may return them to the social field. The technologies of normalisation claim to be impartial techniques to handle dangerous social deviations. However, the advance of bio-power in the nineteenth century coincides with the appearance and proliferation of the categories of anomaly such as the delinquent, the moral imbecile, etc., which the technologies were supposedly designed to eliminate.

Some of the cutting-edge of Foucault's concept of normalisation has been lost in translation from the original French and in the editing of his work. Unlike English, French has an adjective meaning 'that which makes normal' and which can be a description of a process or a person. 'Normalising' is the nearest English replacement.

Foucault chose to open two of his books with the description of very arresting phenomena: the ship of fools in *Madness and Civilisation* (1971, pp. 3–37) and the public attempt to hang, draw and quarter the regicide, Damiens, in *Discipline and Punish* (1977, pp. 3–30). Both books are also accounts of the transformation of the treatment of mental aberration and role infraction respectively from one state to another. Each form of treatment was accepted as appropriate at its own point in history, but over time the treatments were in conflict. The illustrations selected for the French edition of *Discipline and Punish* illustrate this transformation in the regulation of the norm. Both are lithographs of 'Orthopaedics or the art of preventing and correcting deformity of the body in children'. In the centre of one is a thick perpendicular pole to which heavy ropes tie the severely curved trunk of a growing tree. The rest of the landscape is barren except for a small shrub on either side of the pole. In the centre of the other lithograph is seated a young motherly figure by the side of two colonnades with a billowing canopy above her head. In contrast to the other's barrenness, this is obviously a form of civilisation. In her hands, the young woman holds a measuring rod which is positioned directly above the heads of the two young children at her feet. The rod is inscribed with the Latin '*Haec est regula recti*'. 'Normal' is derived from the Latin '*norma*', the carpenter's ruler. The inscription may thus be translated as 'This is the rule of the ruled' or 'this is the measure of the measured'. '*Recti*' also connotes 'correctness'. Hence 'this is a measure of correctness' is also implied. The length of the ruler is established for social purposes and has no existence as such in any natural order. The two lithographs capture the transformation of the regulation of the norm precisely from visible, physical constraint to invisible, abstract rationalisation. The illustration of the norm as a measure of what is measured is omitted from the English edition.

The English translation of Foucault's final works, intended as a trilogy upon the history of sexuality, has suffered in a similar way. *La Volonté de Savoir* (The Will of Knowledge) is the title of the first volume in the

French edition. In the opening pages (1980b, pp. 3–13) Foucault makes it plain that his central concern is that of bio-power and how the processes of objectification and subjectification have operated at different points in history in different cultures to create their subjects. Thus, while changed forms of sexuality are the sites for his analysis, his ultimate goal is an understanding of the processes of objectification and subjectification. The title of the first French volume, *La Volonté de Savoir*, announces this aim clearly. In the English version, the title is omitted and the first volume is described as 'An Introduction'.

MARX, WEBER AND FOUCAULT

A compelling study of Weber and Marx is now 60 years old and has recently been published in an English translation (Lowith, 1993). Despite the very important differences between Marx and Weber, not least their opposed political attitudes, their sociological perspectives are held together by a convergent philosophical anthropology. Both were above all else preoccupied with the question of the cultural significance and consequences of Western capitalism.

Marx elaborated the problem of humanity in bourgeois capitalism through the idea of 'alienation' and Weber through that of 'rationalisation'. The central idea of both may be linked to Foucault's notion of 'discourse as a term for thought as a social process' (Merquior, 1985, p. 18). Foucault's own position may be seen in the modes of objectification and the creation of subjects.

Lowith summarises Weber's idea of rationalisation as follows: 'Weber asserts that the First World War constitutes a further advance in the process of general rationalisation, that is, in the rationally calculating, labour dividing, specialised-bureaucratic organisation of all human institutions of authority. The process extends over the way of life of army and state as much as of factories, scientific-technical schools and universities. Specialised examinations of all kinds increasingly become the precondition of a secure position as an official' (Lowith, 1993, p. 73). Weber first outlined his thesis on the growth of rationalisation in his *The Protestant Ethic and the Spirit of Capitalism* (1930). The mechanism which transformed the haphazard acquisition of wealth to its systematic accumulation was that which liberated humanity from the constraints imposed by an external deity to the compulsion of an internal mechanism.

> Since religious asceticism undertook to remodel the world and to work out its ideals in the world, material goods have gained an increasing and finally an inexorable power over the lives of men as at no previous period in history...victorious capitalism, since it rests on mechanical foundations, needs its support no longer ... the idea of duty in one's calling prowls about our lives like the ghost of dead religious beliefs. (Weber, 1930, pp. 181–2)

Rationalisation which lies at the heart of bourgeois capitalism has thus constructed an iron cage for human beings and 'the world has been rendered increasingly meaningless by the erosion of charisma, religion or enchantment' (Turner, 1993, p. 23).

Marx's ideas on human alienation are well documented and need little elaboration (cf., Bottomore and Rubel, 1963, pp. 175–85). In the Preface to the first German edition of *Capital*, Marx states his concern for philosophical anthropology: 'Inasmuch as I conceive the development of the economic structure of society to be a natural process, I should be the last to hold the individual responsible for conditions whose creature he himself is, socially considered, however much he may raise himself above them subjectively ... if I speak of individuals, it is only insofar as they are personifications of economic categories, representatives of special class relations and class interests' (1957, p. 864). Thus capitalism dehumanises mankind.

While Weber and Marx share a concern to theorise the condition of humanity in bourgeois capitalism, the conclusions of each are different. In Marxism, humanity is rescued from capitalism and is restored in the final transition to communism In this respect, 'Marx's historical materialism is a secularised version of the Christian teleology' (Turner, 1993, p. 15). Thus, for Marx, the opportunity for social transformation was to be seized ultimately by the revolutionary struggles of the working class. Weber, on the other hand, was ambiguous about any ultimate escape from 'the iron cage'. His thinking had gone beyond the Cartesian subject/object division and the dualism of mind and body. First, there was the realisation that reality cannot be separated from the knowing subject, because 'reality' is in some sense 'produced' by the paradigms which seek to understand it. Second, mind and body are not separate but human beings are 'embodied'. Weber was on the threshold of developing a more reflective and dialectical conception of philosophical anthropology in which there was a realisation that the knowledge of the world furnished by modern science is itself conditioned by the nature of the modern capitalist world and that realisation presented human beings with some autonomy.

It has been proposed that there are two Max Webers, so to speak. The first is the familiar figure revealed by the exposition and interpretation of increasing machine production, the inexorable power of material goods and the extension of bureaucratic regulation who is characterised as the 'liberal individual'. The other Weber was the fierce nationalist advocating strong political leadership to establish and to maintain Germany's power on the world's stage, who is characterised as the 'ardent nationalist' (Bottomore and Outhwaite, 1993, p. 38). Weber's notion of charisma offers a 'frail bridge between these seemingly antithetical intellectual orientations' (ibid., p. 39). Charisma based upon individual values can be a force behind change in society and culture but it can also be the basis for charismatic political domination. The recognition of the possibility of autonomy furnishes the possibility of the escape from the iron cage. A more central role for the concept of charisma has been noted by one commentator:

> charisma has a special place and function within Weber's work. In so far as Weber's analyses of history rotate around a general conception of a continuous process of rationalisation and its effects, the conception of charisma has provided the requisite means for thinking discontinuities, for identifying those moments of crisis when everyday routines are disrupted or destroyed. (Smart, 1983, pp. 129–30)

This brief exposition of Marx's and Weber's philosophical anthropology provides an understanding of the backdrop of ideas and organisation within which the question of the education of feeble-minded children arose. This was characterised by rationality both in terms of mode of thought, which is best characterised by science, and by the mode of social organisation, characterised by bureaucracy. For Weber and Marx, human beings were the producers and products of capitalism. The successful and powerful were most in tune with the demands and dispositions of capitalism. Officials in a bureaucracy were qualified and legitimated through rationality. Hence it could be expected that the tenets of science would inform their thinking and would be called upon to solve problems and resolve disputes. Again, for the successful and powerful the logic of capitalism has been internalised, the idea of 'duty in one's calling' becomes a substitute for external compulsion. There is a firm link with Foucault's thinking here. In his analysis of the transition of the penal code from public torture to normative judgment, he suggests the transition entails the transposition of the body–soul thesis and that now 'the soul is the prison of the body' (1977, p. 30).

Foucault's ideas regarding discourse or thought as a social practice of treatment in prisons, hospitals and schools, have much in common with Weber's and Marx's conceptualisation of philosophical anthropology. Foucault too is concerned to identify a transition or transformation from one manner of conceptualising social practice to another: from inclusion in society to exclusion in institutions of the mentally ill; from punishment as physical torture to internal reflection and inspection. Discourse is the realisation of concepts in social action. The concepts produce the social action and the action delineates the concepts. The action also confirms the concepts. Knowledge produces power but power also produces knowledge.

Marx's and Weber's transformations are on a grand scale, from conceptions of the total human condition in pre-Christian and Christian theology to those of so-called rational science. Although for some individuals, for the incarcerated for example, Foucault's transformational discourse may be total, for others it is partial and dependent upon that segment of life exposed to the discourse. It is also evident that in the absence of the continuous presence of physical repression or coercion, for discourse to be effective it must be pervasive and continuous. Discourse, however, itself becomes perilous when it encounters another conflicting discourse in the open, so to speak. The most open situation would appear to be an area such as the public inquiry whose *raison d'être* is precisely to make judgments between discourses. That there exist different discourses simultaneously is not problematic because social life, knowledge and practices are not uniform.

There is, however, an important difference between Foucault's form of theorising and that of Marx and Weber. For while to Weber rationalisation appears to take on the form of an all-embracing historical process, which is equally manifest in economic enterprises, the bureaucratic administration of the state and in a more general intellectualisation of the world, Foucault was much more sceptical both about the idea of a single all-encompassing process and of the possibility of a unitary science of truth. 'I think that the word *rationalisation* is dangerous. What we have to do is analyse specific rationalities rather than always invoking the progress of rationalisation in general' (Foucault, 1982, p. 210). His concept of episteme derives from this thinking:

> the episteme ... [is] the total set of relations that unite, at a given period, the discursive practices that give rise to epistemological figures, sciences and possibly formalised systems ... The episteme is not a form of knowledge ... or type of rationality which, crossing the boundaries of the most varied sciences, manifests the sovereign

unity of a subject, a spirit or a period, it is the totality of relations that can be discovered, for a given period, between the sciences when one analyses them at the level of discursive regularities. (Foucault, 1974, p. 191)

Further, the analysis of an episteme entails 'a questioning that accepts the fact of science only in order to ask the question what it is for that science to be a science ... not its right to be a science but the fact that it exists' (ibid., p. 192). Given that, for Foucault, there is no absolute form of rationality, the task is translated into the investigation of 'rationalities inscribed within different social practices, of determining how a particular regime of rationality simultaneously constitutes roles and procedures for doing things ... and produces "true" discourses which legitimate these activities by providing them with reasons and principles' (Smart, 1983, p. 122).

FOUCAULT'S CRITICS

Foucault's work is not without its critics (see Merquior, 1985, *passim*; Dews, 1989, pp. 64–71; Barker, 1993, *passim*). Some justification for reference to his ideas is therefore in order.

An anomaly runs through the criticisms of Foucault's work like a seismic seam. Foucault aimed to construct a history of the present which entailed a different form of critical analysis, an episteme, and a recognition that theory was based upon discourse in the sense that thought is a social process. His critics, however, while aware of these facts, proceed to construct their critiques on the assumption that there exists an accepted, established and proven form of analysis. This, however, was a position which Foucault was at pains to reject. This was well illustrated when Noam Chomsky and Foucault were brought together to debate the topic 'Human Nature: Justice versus Power' (Elders, 1974). It turned out to be a non-event because while Chomsky sought rationally to lay the grounds for human nature and justice, Foucault sought to establish the different forms which human nature and justice had taken in different forms of analysis at different times in the past (see ibid., pp. 136–70). It is also evident in Foucault's refusal to become involved in the Althusserian debate seeking to distinguish ideology and science (cf., Beechey and Donald, 1985, pp. xi–xviii). In an interview in 1977, Foucault made his position clear:

> The notion of ideology appears to me to be difficult to make use of [because] like it or not, it always stands in virtual opposition to something else which is supposed to count as truth. Now I believe that the problem does not consist in drawing the line between that in a discourse which falls under the category of scientificity or truth, and that which comes under some other category, but in seeing historically how effects of truth are produced within discourses which in themselves are neither true nor false. (in Gordon, 1980, p. 118)

Foucault's professional publications spanned a period of roughly 30 years and he died before retirement at the age of 58 in 1984. The criticism of his work can be described as dualistic and dialectical. On the one hand, the originality of Foucault's writings and thought in opening up new areas and vistas of study was fully recognised. On the other hand, the critics' prime claim to fame is precisely their critiques of Foucault's originality (Dews, 1979, 1984; Merquior, 1985; Barker, 1993). The critics are thus different in kind from the focus of their criticism.

Taking the writings which bear most pertinently upon the topic of present concern, those concerned with the studies of madness, power and penal and related institutions, the critics produce three main grounds for their reservations: the historical accuracy of Foucault's data; the sketchy basis of theory; and the teleological nature of the argument. Is there a defence against these accusations?

The first line of argument is that Foucault's propositions should be taken as heuristic devices rather than proven facts. As the basis for exploration of practices, the propositions may rest more comfortably with the intention of Foucauldian methodology.

The second argument is that the aim of the episteme is to break with existing, accepted patterns of thought, but must perforce operate within and with existing patterns. The episteme is precisely based upon discourse or thought as a social process. His critics, while fully aware of this aim, employ the tools of existing paradigms to criticise the novel.

The third defence is that all history constitutes a selection from the past. Hence, the dispute centres upon the basis for selection of items included. This, in turn, hinges upon the length or rather contraction of the time-span chosen. In a similar way, the proposition that changes appear synchronous is dependent upon the extent to which the analysis focuses upon the detail of diachronous developments. Foucault's awareness of discontinuities and caesurae are additional defences.

Finally, the accusation of the teleological basis of Foucault's argument may be sound but it may also be irrelevant. The trenchant critique of teleological argument is its basis in the proposition that functionalist theory is utopian (Dahrendorf, 1958). Such criticisms can hardly apply in this case, since Foucault is at pains to establish the precise location of ideas and practices in particular historical contexts. Also the strength of functional theory is the analysis of different social phenomena in relationship to each other. Thus Foucault can be argued to have clearly highlighted the interrelationships between power, the conceptions of madness and penal and other institutions.

FOUCAULT AND THE DISCOURSE OF THE EXAMINATION

For Foucault, discourse is thought as a social practice. Every exercise of discourse tends to support, reinforce and validate the discourse. Power produces knowledge, but knowledge also produces power.

> We should rather admit that power produces knowledge (and not simply by encouraging it because it serves power or by applying it because it is useful); that power and knowledge directly imply one another; that there is no power relation without the correlative constitution of a field of knowledge, nor any knowledge that does not presuppose and constitute at the same time power relations. (1977, p. 27)

Surveillance, watchful supervision, the 'gaze', lies at the centre of the modern penal system, whether that of disciplinary function, sentence or imprisonment. Likewise, it is at the centre of clinical diagnosis and subsequent treatment. Surveillance impacts upon all its subjects alike, unlike the penal system under personal domination which is capricious and in which individuals out of sight remain unaffected, escaping detection. In the workshop, school and army, 'the web of discipline aims at generalising the *homo docilis* required by rational, efficient, technical society: an obedient, hard-working, conscience-ridden, useful creature, pliable to all modern tactics of production and warfare' (Merquior, 1985, p. 94).

The school examination constitutes the paradigm of surveillance. 'The examination combines the techniques of an observing hierarchy and those of a normalising judgement' (Foucault, 1977, p. 184). Four conditions are necessary for discipline to obtain: an art of spatial distribution (as in the differentiation of the workshop); the control of activity proper (as in the daily timetable); exercise (as in control of type and length of activity); and, finally, tactics (as in an orderly combination with others). Discipline based upon surveillance demanded its agents and therefore it needed to delegate supervision. 'Hierarchic observation became a role, both at the factory (as required by the complication of the division of labour) and at the school (where pupils were chosen to act as heads of form), let alone in the armed forces' (Merquior, 1985, pp. 93–4). Surveillance thus produced a hierarchy of watchful officials.

Discipline in the normalising judgment, fills the space left empty by formal laws. Discipline specifies correct behaviours and punishes infractions.

> The workshop, the school, the army were subject to a whole micro-penalty of time (lateness, absences, interruptions of tasks), of activity (inattention, negligence, lack of zeal), of behaviour (impoliteness, disobedience), of speech (idle chatter, insolence), of the body (incorrect attitudes, irregular gestures, lack of cleanliness), of sexuality (impurity, indecency). (Foucault, 1977, p. 178)

That which does not observe the rule, that which does not measure up to it or that which departs from it, is subject to discipline. 'The whole indefinite domain of the non-conforming is punishable: the soldier commits an "offence" whenever he does not reach the required standard; a pupil's "offence" is not only a minor infraction but also an inability to carry out his tasks' (ibid., p. 179). The fundamental nature of discipline also changed from, for example, that which restrained soldiers from desertion and pillage to that which improved their efficiency.

The order specified by a law, programme or set of regulations is an abstract construct. However, the order can be defined by natural and observable processes, for example, the length of an apprenticeship, the time required to perform an exercise. Pupils must not be placed in a lesson which they are not capable of mastering because they would be exposed to the danger of being unable to learn anything. But regulations fix the duration of each stage in schooling. Pupils not successful within stages may be retained within a stage and not transferred to a higher form. Hence they are visible in the midst of pupils who know least. Disciplinary punishment aims to reduce gaps. It is essentially corrective and typically entails exercises which are further practice of the infringed norm. The norm is abstract but the exercise visible.

The examination, according to Foucault, is

> a normalising gaze, a surveillance that makes it possible to qualify, to classify and to punish. It establishes over individuals a visibility through which one differentiates them and judges them. That is why, in all the mechanisms of discipline, the examination is highly

33

ritualised. In it are combined the ceremony of power and the form of the experiment, the deployment of force and the establishment of truth. At the heart of the procedures of discipline, it manifests the subjection of those who are perceived as objects and the objectification of those who are subjected. (Foucault, 1977, pp. 184–5).

The examination does not operate through visible force but through invisible power which renders the subjects visible. The invisible power of examination is a mechanism which objectifies its subjects. 'The examination that places individuals in a field of surveillance also situates them in a network of writing; it engages them in a whole mass of documents that capture and fix them' (ibid., p. 189).

Documentation operates in two important dimensions. First, a corpus of knowledge permits the creation of a comparative system which measures overall phenomena and describes groups and their distribution within the population. Second, the file, which renders the individual as a describable and analysable object, exposes individual features, aptitudes, abilities and disabilities to a corpus of knowledge.

The discourse of examination, with its panoply of documents and files, transforms living human beings into cases. The purpose of writing itself is changed in the process. 'This turning of real lives into writing is no longer a procedure of heroisation; it functions as a procedure of objectification and subjection' (ibid., p. 192). In this way Foucault 'stresses the changed function in the transcription of human lives: the contrast, that is, between the chronicle, with its accent on the heroic and memorable, and the file, measuring up observance as deviation from the norm' (Merquior, 1985, p. 95).

CONCLUSIONS

This chapter has set out the background to the two main theoretical approaches adopted in the main body of the analysis. More attention has been paid to Foucault's work because it is more controversial and not without its critics. The next chapter outlines the social background and growth of Elementary schools.

3

Social, Economic and Administrative Background to the Establishment and Growth of Elementary Education

This chapter oulines the social and industrial background to Elementary education. The main features of the Elementary school system and its control are also presented. Data on the increase in pupil numbers under the School Boards are introduced. The evidence presented to the Cross Commission by teachers, Board members and Her Majesty's Inspectorate (HMI) is used to pull together the factors which point towards the identificaton of the dull pupil.

SOCIAL AND INDUSTRIAL BACKGROUND

The most pervasive and intractable legacy of the industrial revolutions in Britain was the creation of 'a workforce too largely composed of coolies, with the psychology and primitive culture to be expected of coolies' (Barnett, 1986, p. 187). Barnett's terminology appears apt: 'coolie' is a transliteration of the name of an aboriginal tribe of Gujerat, India, which quickly assumed the transferred meaning of a hired native labourer in India and China. Subsequently, the term was used pejoratively in South Africa. Hence Barnett's choice of 'coolie' brings together the connotations of social class and status. The mental disposition of the industrial workforce has been described by Tocqueville (1945, vol. II, pp. 168–71) and summarised for industrialising England by Hobsbawm (1969, pp. 85–9). Fierce competition and unbridled exploitation characterised the experience of the new industrial workforce. The rhythms of the land or self-employed crafts which in themselves may have been hard, were exchanged for the harsh mechanical discipline, pace and clamour of the mill (cf., Thompson, 1967, pp. 56–97; Hobsbawm, 1969, p. 85).

The locale of population shifted because water power, coal and iron existed in locations previously without population and culture. The villages of Manchester, Birmingham, Leeds, Huddersfield, Bradford,

Halifax and Middlesbrough 'proliferated into vast brick-built industrial camps; nothing but mean dwellings, drink-shops and "works"' (Barnett, 1986, p. 188). The population in the 'industrial camps' increased rapidly and exponentially. The housing was dense and shoddily built. Walls of houses were typically only half a brick deep, houses were built back to back, lacking ventilation or drainage. Double rows of ten houses would form courts with a privy at one end and a pump at the other. Moreover, such situations persisted: 'Two rooms, seven inmates ... dirty flock bedding in living-room placed on box and two chairs. Smell of room from dirt and bad air unbelievable ... There was no water supply in the house, the eight families having to share one tap ... with eight other families who are living in other houses. The grating under this water-tap is used for disposal of human excreta' (Rowntree, 1910, pp. 23, 153). And it persisted further: 'Even by the late 1930s ... the bulk of the industrial population were [*sic*] still living in the same grim "camps" first run up to house their great-grandparents' (Barnett, 1986, p. 197). Engels has chronicled vividly the transformation of British society in the course of the Industrial Revolution and the creation of the condition of the urban, industrial proletariat (1969, pp. 54–107).

The transformation of society and particularly 'the rupture of the pre-industrial rhythms of work', which produced 'a mechanised regularity of work which conflicts not only with tradition but with all the inclination of humanity as yet unconditioned into it' (Hobsbawm, 1969, p. 86), may indeed have rendered the industrial worker an estranged alien in a different social world. While alienation may produce highly collectivist values which cement a class in resistance to impositions from above and intolerance of infractions by their peers, it may nevertheless also generate resistance to the ideas and mechanisms which may be a source of improvement of the working class's social condition. Thus, while strong family bonds and sentiments of community which afford individual strength and support may be developed, an attitude of indifference toward matters considered beyond individual control may also be engendered. A conception of fatalism may undermine and prevent a realisation of social life capable of improvement through individual striving and planning (cf., Stedman Jones, 1983, p. 235). Moreover, if the mechanisms of improvement, such as a knowledge of the natural world and the skills of reading and writing, are identified as characteristics of the ruling group, then there is further reason why such skills and knowledge should not be pursued. Alongside the housing, such sentiments are regarded as having persisted (see Hoggart, 1958, pp. 53–78).

British coolies' social and working lives were regarded as being at the mercy of a master who was a practical man and who believed that the profitability of his business depended upon low wages and long hours. Coolies' and masters' lifestyles were visibly distinct and geographically separated. Manchester more than quadrupled its population of 70,000 in the first half of the nineteenth century and continued to grow. The paradox which was Manchester's essence at this time has been summarised by a contemporary writer:

> From this foul drain the greatest stream of human industry flows out to fertilise the whole world. From this filthy sewer pure gold flows. Here humanity attains its most complete development and its most brutish, here civilisation works its miracles and civilised man is turned almost into a savage. (Tocqueville, 1960, pp. 107–8)

Manchester was also the inspiration for Engels's *The Condition of the Working Class in England*, which was first published in English in 1892.

THE NATURE OF ELEMENTARY SCHOOLING

The 1867 Reform Bill gave the vote to householders who paid rates. The artisans of the big industrial towns who had not qualified as 'ten-pound householders' under the 1832 Reform Act, were thus enfranchised. While the franchise still remained relatively restricted, nevertheless the risk entailed in harbouring a population which was not educated for its new responsibility became evident to politicians.

A Royal Commission under the chairmanship of the Duke of Newcastle was appointed in 1858 'to enquire into the Present State of Popular Education in England, and to consider and report what measures, if any, are required for the Extension of sound and cheap Elementary Instruction to all Classes of the People' (1861, p. ii). One of the chief weaknesses of the Elementary school system identified by the Commission was the low average level and irregular nature of school attendance. The Commissioners estimated that in 1858 almost 39 per cent of children of school age attended school for less than one year.

Robert Lowe was Vice-President of the Education Department at the time. The Vice-President had a seat in the Commons and managerial responsibility for the day-to-day decisions made in the Department. The President had a seat in the Lords and spoke in the Cabinet concerning policy. Lowe decided that the problem of attendance should be tackled by market forces. Thus grants to schools were to be made dependent on the attendance of pupils under a certificated teacher and subject to the results of an examination of each child in the 'three Rs' (reading, writing, arithmetic) by an inspector. Among other measures the teachers' pension scheme, grants for apparatus and pupil teachers' stipends were withdrawn. Grants to training colleges were also reduced. These measures were embedded in the 'Revised Code' of 1862. The Code was a document issued by the Education Department and had statutory force. In 1860, Lowe had codified the various minutes which were in force and hence the 1862 version was a 'Revised Code'. Lowe's proposals encountered resistance in the Commons and in reply to his critics he justified the changes in the system as follows: 'If it is not cheap, it shall be efficient; if it is not efficient, it shall be cheap' (Parliamentary Debates (PD), Vol. CLXV, 1862, p. 229). The system of 'payment by results' endured with modification for more than 30 formative years in the Elementary school system and was finally removed by the Code of 1897.

What was the impact of the Revised Code upon schools, pupils and teachers? The main source of evidence is found in the inspectors' reports issued in the ensuing years. The inspectors appeared divided in terms of praise or condemnation of the system. Amidst this ambivalence, '[o]ne point seems clear, namely, the officials of the Education Department strove hard to emphasise its virtues and to minimise its defects' (Smith, 1931, p. 262). Indeed, Lowe resigned from the Vice-Presidency in 1864 after there had been outspoken protests that the Department had edited and 'mutilated' inspectors' reports (Sutherland, 1973, p. 21; Sturt, 1967, pp. 257–8).

The main features of the Revised Code have been recorded in detail (Smith, 1931, pp. 249–312; Barnard, 1947, pp. 107–19; Simon, 1965, pp. 112–20; Sturt, 1967, pp. 260–89; Sylvester, 1974, pp. 58–116). These features may be summarised in terms of curriculum, teaching and pupil grouping. The curriculum initially tended to concentrate narrowly upon the three Rs, and attention was focused upon the first three standards or classes because that was where payment for success could be most readily secured. The preferred teaching method was mechanical and uniform, consisting of practices such as group reading aloud, 'barking at print', and chorusing of poetry and tables. '[T]eaching degenerated into a dull mechanical grind' (Smith, 1931, p. 268). Indeed, Patrick Cumin, Secretary to the Education Department, in his evidence to the Royal Commission appointed to inquire into the working of the Elementary Education Acts in 1886, declared his familiarity with mechanical teaching methods:

The best illustration of what is called mechanical teaching, and the result, was given in a celebrated report by Mr Brookfield (an inspector) .... That is an illustration of what he meant and what other persons meant by reading without really knowing what they were talking about? [Chairman] 'If I remember it is the report which speaks of a child saying a catechism "baying" the Queen?' Yes. It is the sort of fault which children reading aloud together in class without reading individually, are sure to fall into. (RCEEA, 1886, p. 7)

The Royal Commission also includes specimens of school timetables and summaries of timetables approved by HMI (RCEEA, 1886, pp. 540–3). The first point to stand out is that there is very little variation in the subjects and their weighting between classes. Reading and writing together consume almost one third of the allocated time of 23 hours per week. Reading itself is divided into 'reading' and 'reading on blackboard'. Arithmetic, which includes mental arithmetic is the next largest activity, but close on its heels is Religious Instruction, which consisted of the learning and repetition of texts from the Old and New Testaments.

The withdrawal of pupil-teachers' stipends brought about a considerable fall in their number. From figures in the Education Department's Minutes it has been calculated that there were roughly 41 pupils for every teacher in 1870 (Smith, 1931, p. 270). And that calculation includes certificated, assistant and pupil teachers. The London School Board also set the pattern for the schools' main architectural features. Previously schools had consisted of one large hall together with one or two small rooms. London adopted the Prussian practice which had a separate classroom for each teacher and class. The rooms were designed to accommodate 80 pupils (cf., Wardle, 1976, p. 71; Armytage, 1964, p. 146). Additionally, the status of teaching tended to decline. The Revised Code reduced teachers' average salary. Inspectors reported that both teachers and pupil-teachers were less zealous in their work. Pupil-teachers became more difficult to recruit and consequently admission standards were reduced. The system appeared mechanical and inflexible while teachers were dispirited and harassed to achieve payment through pupils' attainment of standards. As a result, '[t]he child was literally sacrificed to a system' (Smith, 1931, p. 269).

ORIGINATING FACTORS FOR SPECIAL SCHOOLS AND CLASSES

The conjunction of a number of factors gave rise to special schools and classes at a particular point in history. These factors were: the extension of education policy to include the whole of the relevant age cohort; the preferred school curriculum; the nature of the teaching profession; and the urban environment.

Increase in the School Population

Table 3.1 is derived from the First Report of the Royal Commission on the working of the Education Acts.

TABLE 3.1
PUPILS IN ELEMENTARY SCHOOLS, 1860–85

Year	Number of scholars on registers	Average number of scholars in attendance	Average attendance (%)	Number of schools
1860	957,936	712,193	74.35	5,141
1870	1,693,059	1,152,389	68.07	8,281
1880	3,895,824	2,750,916	70.61	17,614
1885	4,465,818	3,406,076	76.27	19,063

Source: RCEEA (1886, p. 518).

It may be observed that the numbers of scholars on registers increased almost by a factor of five between 1860 and 1885. In addition, the number of pupils in Elementary schools more than doubled from 1870–80. Thus school attendance increased rapidly between the permissive Act of 1870 and the one of 1880 which made attendance compulsory. The effect of this latter, however, may be seen in the increase of attendance between 1880 and 1885 which is of the order of more than ten per cent. Allied to this factor is that of the increase of the average level of attendance by more than six per cent between these two same dates. An additional factor was the increasing number of older pupils in school. This was brought about by the requirement for attendance and the regulations proscribing the employment of children under ten years of age. There were therefore not simply more pupils in attendance but in regular attendance. The Secretary of the Education Department, giving evidence to the Committee, declared that the nature of the population of pupils in Elementary schools had changed considerably between 1860 and 1885: 'in the year 1860 the class of children in those schools was a very much more regular class of children than exists now ... In the year 1860 ... the inspected classes had not reached the really poor class, whereas in the year 1885 they have reached them' (RCEEA, 1886, p. 7). He made the same point in a different way: 'to the classes then [1860] being superior to what they are now, the real fact of the case is that whilst there were not so many of the better classes there were far fewer of the lowest classes' (ibid.). The chairman concurred: 'Is that not tantamount to what you have said, that the ragged children and the lowest classes [were] out of the schools?' Thus the increase in attendance between 1880 and 1885 may be attributable to the increase in the presence of children from 'the really poor class' and 'the lowest class'.

To concentrate attention upon the average attendance rate, however, overlooks the fact that there was a disparity between urban and rural attendance rates. By the end of 1871, the Education Department had already sanctioned more than 100 sets of bye-laws for compulsory school attendance. The bulk exempted scholars who were more than 10 years of age and who had passed Standard V and half-time exemption for those of a similar age who had reached the standard below. While London (cf., Rubinstein, 1969, pp. 75–89) gave a lead to other School Boards, 'compulsion spread more rapidly in towns than in rural districts. By 1873, 40 per cent of the whole population were under bye-laws and by 1876, 50 per cent. In the boroughs, the figure in the latter year was 84 per cent, a proof of the slowness of the rural school boards to apply compulsion' (Smith, 1931, p. 296). Thus the presence of children of 'the really poor' and 'the lowest class' was most marked in schools in urban areas. Here, the attendant difficulties presented themselves to schools and teachers earlier and in larger numbers.

Teaching Method

The main focus of the curriculum, the preferred teaching method and the size of classes have already been mentioned. In themselves, these factors appear sufficient to create learning difficulties for pupils because '[a] system which exalts mechanical tests must of necessity be ill-suited to all the types of children and all the varying circumstances that the school caters for' (Smith, 1931, p. 269). Another factor may be the nature of the teaching force. Table 3.2 is derived from a part of the evidence which the Secretary to the Education Department presented to the Commission in 1886.

The Nature of the Teaching Force

TABLE 3.2
THE TEACHING FORCE, 1860–85

Year	Number of			Total
	Certificated teachers	Assistant teachers	Pupil-teachers	
1860	6,393	249	13,141	19,783
1870	12,676	1,210	14,612	27,498
1880	31,422	7,652	33,733	72,807
1885	40,706	16,618	25,750	83,074

Source: RCEEA (1886, p. 520).

Table 3.2 should be treated with some caution, however, as teachers who were unqualified are omitted.

Previously it has been demonstrated that the number of pupils increased roughly by a factor of five between 1860 and 1885. Over that same period, however, the total number of teachers increased by slightly more than a factor of four. Hence the number of pupils were an increased pressure upon teachers. The nature of the teaching force had changed radically during this period. Certificated teachers were recognised as qualified having followed a period of successful and efficient training. Assistant teachers were adults who taught classes under the direction and supervision of the headteacher in the school (cf., Wardle, 1976, pp. 64–8; Hurt, 1972, pp. 110–46). In 1860, there were more than twice the number of pupil-teachers to certificated teachers and assistant teachers were almost insignificant proportionately. It may be inferred that the bulk of the teaching was undertaken by pupil-teachers. That situation had changed by 1870 when the combined numbers of certificated and assistant teachers were roughly equal to those of pupil-teachers, and it may be inferred that teaching responsibilities were shared between pupil-teachers and others. By 1880, however, the combined numbers of certificated and assistant teachers exceeded those of pupil-teachers by roughly 15 per cent. That trend appeared confirmed in 1885 when certificated and assistant teachers exceeded the numbers of pupil-teachers by more than half. Thus it seemed that the bulk of the teaching was undertaken by certificated or assistant teachers. However, the figures may point to a different conclusion. In order to earn its grant, a school had to be in the charge of a certificated teacher. There was, however, no regulation of teachers, the training colleges were unable to supply trained teachers to match demand and teachers could obtain certificates by alternative means. Hence, the proportion of pupil teachers and assistant teachers exceeded that of certificated teachers throughout the period. From a proportion of 2:1 in 1860, it fell to 5:4 in 1870 but rose to 4:3 in 1880 and settled at roughly equal in 1885. Certificated teachers were persistently in a minority.

The Practice of Inspection

Further evidence submitted to the Commission by the Secretary of the Education Department in 1887 revealed that the trend for inspectorial staff had been different.

TABLE 3.3
INSPECTORIAL STAFF, 1871–85

Year	Inspectors	Sub-inspectors	Inspectors' assistants	Total
1871	87	-	86	173
1875	115	-	81	196
1880	141	-	115	256
1885	121	29	162	312

Source: RCEEA (1887, p. 710).

The steady increase in the total number of personnel involved in inspection duties is clearly evident in Table 3.3. However, there is also an element of elaboration or differentiation which emerges in the hierarchy of personnel. Thus, while the number of inspectors' assistants roughly doubles over the period, the position of sub-inspector is only established in 1882. By 1885 the status differential between inspectors and sub-inspectors emerges. It is notable that the proportion of inspectorial staff and assistants is roughly equal in 1871 as it is with the larger numbers in 1885. However, at the latter date, the number of assistants equates roughly to a hierarchy of personnel with internal status differentials.

The Codes drawn up between 1870 and 1885 were the creation of a small number of men in the Education Department (cf., Sutherland, 1972, pp. 263–85). The intention of the Codes was seen as increasing the demands made upon schools and teachers and at the same time closing all the loopholes for evasion during inspection. 'The three features of the Code [of 1878], the percentage grant, the merit grant and the regulation that all children who had been on the register for twenty-two weeks must be presented, formed a most efficient engine of tyranny' (Sturt, 1967, p. 347). In addition, there was the pressure upon the teacher of the expectation that pupils would pass the examination in each Standard and advance up the Standards. This, in turn, led to the creation of a Standard '0', which accommodated pupils judged unable to tackle Standard I.

The internal organisation of the Education Department was such that inspectorial staff held, *de facto*, virtually absolute power over the award of a school's grant. From 1870, with the abolition of denominational inspections, clergymen were no longer appointed to the Inspectorate. Many, however, had been appointed before that date and had attained positions of considerable seniority during the period which felt the impact of the 1870 and 1880 Acts. As clergymen, they often enjoyed stipends in addition to their official salaries. They tended to reside in the capital which they seldom left. Their shared interests and lifestyles made them a status group in Weber's terms. The group next in rank, district inspectors, did live in their respective districts. On occasion they made short visits to schools. Beneath them were the newly appointed members and sub-inspectors. These latter were appointed from the ranks of certificated teachers and were required to undertake the tasks of checking results and returns and marking papers.

That inspections were brief and arbitrary events was openly acknowledged. The Secretary to the Education Department in his evidence to the Commission (RCEEA, 1886, p. 36) reported that the Inspectorate had been given written instructions that 'the general principle that all hurry or undue haste on the day of examination is incompatible with the proper discharge of your main duty'. He went on to record complaints that children had been examined at irregular times and sometimes very late in the day, that children had been retained during their dinner hour or when ill, and 'about embarrassing young scholars by want of clearness in diction and also about the importance of a short interval for recreation' (ibid.). This Secretary became notorious for his own unreliability (cf., Kekewich, 1920), but nevertheless reports the failings of the inspection process in this instance.

Inspectors increased teachers' worries and suspicions by their tactic of divising trick questions intended to reveal pupils' real understanding and by their habit of concealment of results or the withholding of credit upon what appeared to be arbitrary grounds. Without doubt, the system subjected teachers to pressure and there was, indeed, an outcry of 'overpressure'. In 1884, the National Union of Elementary Teachers published a pamphlet which contained harrowing details of young certificated teachers who, although judged successful, had broken down and died. Likewise, it was said that young children had collapsed under the strains of inspection. In the same year, 'One ingenious statistician calculated that the death rate among teachers was three times that of the armed forces and six times that of prisoners in gaol' (Sturt, 1967, p. 355).

The London School Board acknowledged these problems and in 1883 moved to provide some protection for their employees by introducing fixed salaries for teachers. From that point on, any variations in schools' grants were to be accommodated by variation of the rates. The other large urban Boards followed suit shortly afterwards. The Boards also appointed their own local inspectors to try to ensure that the work was done as well as local conditions permitted. Although local inspectors in part duplicated the work of Her Majesty's Inspectorate, they also encouraged and advised local teachers. Thus, paradoxically, the attempt to impose from the centre a set of regulations uniformly on all schools, in fact encouraged a recognition by local Boards of their own differences and unique circumstances and led to an endeavour by them to develop policies and personnel to respond to those circumstances.

The Urban Environment

The urban environment within which schools were situated has received some attention earlier. To explore the impact of the urban environment in any detail is beyond the scope of this book. It may, indeed, be sufficient simply to acknowledge that teachers recognised that features of pupils' learning difficulties could be attributed to the urban environment. The evidence presented by the headmistress of a Voluntary Church of England school, situated in Woolwich, to the Departmental Committee (of the Education Department) on Defective and Epileptic Children (DCDEC), in 1898 illustrates very clearly the nature of urban teaching and Elementary schooling. A part of the Committee's brief was to report upon which children within the feeble-minded group might properly be taught in ordinary schools and which should be taught in special schools. The headmistress's evidence stood out as a tiny island which separated, on the one hand, voluminous evidence presented by medical practitioners concerning the demarcations of feeble-mindedness and, on the other, lengthy detail of the London Board's policies and practices in its special schools and classes.

The headmistress opened her evidence by stating: 'I have 230 [pupils] on the books ... A certificated assistant, two teachers under Article 68 and three pupil-teachers' (DCDEC, 1898, vol. II, p. 55). The lowest class, which consisted of 51 pupils, she went on, was taught by 'a first year pupil- teacher' who was, she thought, 15 years old. She concluded that this was a satisfactory arrangement because '[s]he is the best teacher I have, with the exception of the certificated assistant'. In further questioning it emerged that the headmistress superintended the teaching of the lowest class herself and shared the teaching of the Standard II class with another teacher. The pupil-teacher carried out the headmistress's instructions in her absence with the other class. The headmistress regarded herself as responsible for both classes.

The Standard I class of 51 pupils contained four pupils whom the headmistress assessed as feeble-minded. A fifth had very recently left the class having reached the age of 14. Two of the pupils aged between 12 and 13 had learning difficulties compounded by physical disabilities or neglect. Two 10-year-olds, on the other hand, were capable of undertaking practical activities such as needlework and knitting while one often undertook errands for her mother who was a laundress. Both, however, were 'generally naughty girls'. Examples of misbehaviour were mutilation of school property, poking other children, and tearing their own clothes. One of the four displayed behaviour which in modern parlance would be described as 'dyslexic'. Thus, 'she does everything backward ... Does she begin to write at the wrong end of the page? No, she will begin at the right end but forms the letters backwards. "On" for "no"? Yes' (ibid., p. 56).

In the course of presenting her evidence through question and answer, the headmistress demonstrated implicitly that her decisions were informed by a sophisticated understanding of children and learning. First, she believed that all four of these children were capable of improvement and, indeed, had improved '[c]hiefly through their own exertions' (ibid., p. 55). The prime factor for their slow rate of progress was the fact that they were members of a class of 51 pupils under the shared direction of herself and the pupil-teacher. Second, in the previous term, she had experimented by making the four pupils the sole responsibility of a paid pupil-monitor who was shortly to become a pupil-teacher. However, the experiment was assessed as a failure because the pupils had been able to learn very little from each other and because the pupil-monitor had found her responsibilities too demanding and irksome. Third, the presence of the four had a positive effect upon the rest of the class members in terms of their behaviour and attitude: 'Do the other children behave nicely to them? Yes, I do not think there has been one instance in which I have found the pupils unkind to them. They have a humanising influence, then, upon the class? Yes' (ibid., p. 56). Fourth, the headmistress attributed the four pupils' conditions to factors associated with their family circumstances and the urban environment: 'Supposing that your school were in a rural district entirely ... you would consider they might do fairly well, as they do with you? Yes' (ibid.). Thus a rural environment was considered able to compensate for the factors associated with the urban environment provided that the children received family support. 'Supposing the children were the same but that their home surroundings were fairly good, would you think then that they would do better [boarding] in an institution? No, then, I think, they would be better among children more as they are now' (ibid.). But when 'the home surroundings are not what they should be with some of our children ... they would get on better in an institution where they would live' (ibid.).

There was also judged to be a nice balance between the beneficial effects of removal from a bad home circumstance and the harmful effects of being institutionalised with other feeble-minded pupils. 'But do you not think the association with other children of the same kind or feeble-minded children would not neutralise the benefit [of removal from the family] that they might get? I think not, if they were under instruction' (ibid.). Finally, the headmistress's philosophical stance is straightforward. 'If you had a teacher who could give her whole time to these four children, should you like to keep them in your school then? Yes' (ibid.). To this teacher, the prime factors were the nature of the family background, the urban location, the size of pupils' classes and the quality of teaching.

The preceding, then, has been a summary review of the factors which led to the formation of special schools and classes. These factors were firmly embedded in the nature of Elementary education at the time.

GOALS OF THE CODE

Robert Lowe was by training an economist. His intentions for Elementary education were made abundantly clear in the remark which he made in the Commons in defence of the Revised Code: 'If it is not cheap, it shall be efficient: if it is not efficient, it shall be cheap' (PD, vol. CLXV, 1862, p. 229). His general philosophical stance regarding state education is evident in a remark to the Commons on 15 July 1867 concerning the passing of the Reform Bill. He declared that 'I believe it will be absolutely necessary that you should prevail on our future masters to learn their letters' (Lowe, 1867, quoted in Reeder, 1980). This was popularised as 'We must educate our masters'. Later that same year, in an address on Primary and Classical Education delivered to the Philosophical Institution of Edinburgh, he elaborated on the foundation for his thinking about education.

> The time has gone past evidently when the higher classes can hope by any direct influence, either of property or coercion of any kind, to direct the course of public affairs. Power has passed out of their hands and what they do must be done by the influence of superior education and superior cultivation: by the influence of mind over mind ... The lower classes ought to be educated to discharge the duties cast upon them. They should also be educated that they may appreciate and defer to a higher cultivation when they meet it; and the higher classes ought to be educated in a very different manner in order that they may exhibit to the lower classes that higher education to which, if it were shown to them, they would bow down and defer. (Lowe, 1867, quoted in Reeder, 1980, pp. 102–3)

These remarks seem to fit perfectly into Bourdieu's model of social reproduction outlined earlier. The prime intention of such reproduction is not simply to replicate precisely any social, economic or political inequalities through generations, but rather to reproduce a set of relative advantages and disadvantages which underpin a set of class relationships. Thus, when a whole generation of children is to be offered education and thereby the opportunities which may arise through education, a certain segment of the young is to be offered a form of education which is manifestly regarded as superior. As the basis of social control changes from property and wealth to a more open democracy, then the mechanism for the social reproduction of advantage and disadvantage shifts towards the realm of ideas, argument, debate and proof.

The terminology 'elementary' signals the firm boundary for part of the system. The more general support from administration, inspectors and officials for the policies and practices embodied in the system of Elementary education, may be derived precisely from the recognition on their part that the system was restricted. Thus, in Weberian terms, the consequences which flowed from Elementary education appeared unlikely to produce radical changes in social-class position and was supported by higher-status groups. In fact, Lowe's intentions could be interpreted as a vehicle for the preservation of existing social status. It has been observed that 'Lowe is quite clear that political reasons must dictate educational change, and equally clear about the end political and educational reform is to serve' (Simon, 1960, p. 356). Lowe advocated a higher form of education for the higher classes and that the lower classes should be educated to appreciate this higher cultivation in these classes when they encountered it. In a sense, the system of Elementary education may be regarded as a mechanism 'to stabilise class society' (ibid., p. 354).

ADMINISTRATION OF ELEMENTARY EDUCATION

Lord President and Vice-President

A Committee of the Privy Council was technically responsible for the work of the Education Department. The Committee's major commission was to oversee the spending of any sum of money voted by Parliament for the promotion of public education. Membership of the Committee varied but was impressive on paper, including the Lord President of the Council, the Lord Privy Seal, the Home Secretary and the Chancellor of the Exchequer. The Committee's responsibilities were extensive and included consideration of draft legislation, supervision of the annual Code of Regulations which related to schools' grants and the overseeing of other expenditure. However, formal meetings of the Committee were rare and there exist no records of them (Parliamentary Papers (PP), 1884, xiii, pp. 2, 43).

The Lord President and Vice-President of the Education Department were both politicians. The Vice-Presidency had been created in 1856 with the intention that the incumbent should have a seat in the Commons and be the Minister responsible for all matters concerned with education so far as the government was concerned (RCEEA, 1888, p. 10). However, the Lord President was invariably a peer and spoke for education in the Government.

The division of labour was such that the Vice-President was expected to take responsibility for the general working of the Education Department while the Lord President was consulted should new issues and/or principles arise (PP, 1884, xiii, pp. 93, 112). The Lord President exercised the powers of patronage and promotion. He usually consulted the Vice-President concerning promotion but not new appointments. He also exercised responsibility for disciplining officials in the Department.

Permanent Officials

Beneath the political heads of the Education Department there were two classes of officials divided horizontally: the Examiners, from whose members the Permanent Secretary and Assistant Secretary were selected, and the Executive and Clerical Officers of different grades who were described as 'Clerks'. Occasionally, the politicians introduced their own private secretaries. An effect of the 1870 Act was almost to double the number of officials to a total of 24. This included the Permanent Secretary, a third additional Assistant Secretary and the reorganisation of Examiners into a hierarchy of six Senior Examiners and 14 Junior Examiners.

The Lord President appointed Examiners by selection from a list prepared by his secretary of those who had put themselves forward and were considered suitable. Because of the nature of the work, Examiners were expected to display qualities of judgment and attainment such as were not acquired simply by experience of public service. Although appointments were open to an accusation of patronage, R. R. W. Lingen, who was Permanent Secretary from 1849 to 1869, successfully advised successive Lord Presidents to appoint candidates qualified as graduates. Examiners were thus frequently graduates from Oxbridge with very high academic attainments. Such qualities may have been a public defence against the private exercise of patronage.

The Examiners thus constituted a status group with a distinctive life-style and a distinctive preference for literary and artistic conventions. Their status honour consisted in the reproduction and elaboration of the values which underpinned their own distinctive educational careers and life-styles. The creation and formulation of educational policy was, with notable exceptions, the least of their concerns. Their work in the Education Department was a device for the fulfilment of their own purposes. Their impact upon schools, although important in terms of the construction of schools' grant agendas, was insignificant in terms of the effects upon policy. When a Code Committee was established in 1881 to consider modification to the Code's principles, it consisted of the Permanent Secretary, two Assistant Secretaries and seven Senior Inspectors. Although Examiners, through their experience of the resolution of difficult cases, had a potential contribution to make, a different sort of practical experience was preferred for the Code Committee.

At the bottom of the Department's hierarchy were the Clerks. The work of the established Clerks was supplemented by the practice of hiring, on a temporary weekly basis, writers from a stationers' firm. The 1870 Act had little effect on the numbers of established Clerks which remained at roughly 50. However, the number of writers hired was increased by nearly 100 by 1874.

As far as the Education Department is concerned, the chief players regarding policy appear to be the Lord President, the Vice-President and the Permanent Secretary. However, a Senior Examiner in the Department was a member of the Department's Committee on Defective and Epileptic Children (1898) and presented evidence to the Committee on the administration of the Blind and Deaf Children Act (ibid., pp. 186–9). His evidence consisted for the most part in the presentation of figures regarding the number of pupils, the comparative size of schools' grants and teachers' salaries. There was no comment upon the optimum mode of education for the feeble-minded.

The Permanent Secretary's presentation of evidence to the Royal Commission to inquire into the working of the Elementary Education Acts in England and Wales (RCEEA, 1886, 1887, 1888) was extensive. It took the form of oral examination and the submission of statistical analyses of most aspects of Elementary education. The subjects covered in the Commission's three reports included that of 'dull and deficient pupils'. The Permanent Secretary had nothing to report on that subject.

The Inspectorate

Unlike the Examiners, whose knowledge of Elementary schools came second-hand through reports, inspectors had direct contact with the schools. Their knowledge of the schools and the actual working of the regulations in the Codes meant that they had potentially useful information which could influence policy. However, because they tended to work alone in their allotted districts, they were not in a position to develop a spirit of camaraderie or to sharpen their wits through mutual exchanges as were the Examiners. Inspectors, like Examiners, were expected, however, to display personal qualities of judgment which could not simply be acquired through work in the public service.

The numerical strength of the Inspectorate has already been presented (see Table 3.3, p. 43). The Inspectorate was divided horizontally into inspectors and inspectors' assistants. Each assistant reported directly to the inspector for whom he worked and each inspector had his own district. The hierarchical order within each district reflected that at the centre: the chief inspector, while having his own schools to inspect, planned and supervised the inspection of the whole division, which was undertaken through district inspectors each with a retinue of sub-inspectors and assistants. On the basis of reports submitted by his staff, the chief inspector wrote a general report for publication every other year.

The early development of Elementary education by the government took place through the support and encouragement of voluntary endeavour. Because the Church had been responsible for the development of the vast majority of Voluntary schools, it was able to insist that most of the inspectors be Anglican priests. The recruitment of clergymen ceased in 1870, with the attempt to create a national system of Elementary education and with the removal of the requirement that religious instruction form part of the inspection. However, in 1871, 70 per cent of the inspectors were clergymen as were seven of the ten senior inspectors. A similar proportion were chief inspectors in 1884. Several held livings in conjunction with inspectorships and, if not, there was an expectation of a comfortable living on retirement (Sutherland, 1973, pp. 56–8). This situation was also reflected in the staff of public schools and Oxbridge. Laicisation thus became entangled with modernisation and bureaucratisation of the state form.

'[T]he published Inspectors' reports were seldom stimulating or striking ... Neither conferences nor reports were used by Inspectors ... as platforms for their views on policy' (Sutherland, 1973, p. 66). A witness to the Royal Commission summarised the nature of the inspectors' work:

> [The state] employs a number of officers called inspectors, whose sole business it is to visit the schools, to examine and observe them, and to report on their work; but the primary purpose of this arrangement is not to impose upon the schools of the country any theory or ideal of instruction desired by the state, or even to improve the efficiency of the schools themselves, but simply to see whether the conditions are fulfilled upon which a grant of public money is to be made, and to determine the sum which the managers of the school are entitled to claim. (RCEEA, 1887, pp. 595–6)

Other witnesses underscored the point that inspectors were concerned with the examination of schools and not their development (ibid., pp. 3–4, 17, 291). Indeed, the explosion of the number of pupils in the schools, and the increasing complexity of the Codes, perhaps dictated that their work should be so restricted.

Inspectors' Comments upon Dull and Deficient Children

What contributions did members of the Inspectorate make to the deliberations of the Royal Commission on the Elementary Education Acts on the subject of 'dull and deficient' children? The opinions of two chief inspectors, both also clergymen, and a former chief inspector of schools form part of the evidence in the Royal Commission's first report (RCEEA, 1886). The starting point of the Commission's thinking was perhaps encapsulated in a member's question to one of the chief inspectors: 'Did not the Report of the Duke of Newcastle's Commission practically show that the cleverer children were well taught, but that the medium and dull children were very largely neglected?' (RCEEA, 1886, p. 145). The witness agreed. The connotations of the term 'dull children' were not explicated and appear to be taken for granted. The focus of the Commission's concerns centred upon whether the progress of dull children was impeded by teachers' attention to the clever or whether the attainment of clever children was curtailed by teachers' concentration upon dull pupils. There was also the question of 'over-pressure' upon pupils, since the schools' grant was most readily realised by concentration upon the first three Standards.

One chief inspector observed a consequence of the 1880 Act and the fact that children from all social groups were now present in schools: 'Is there much *Esprit de Corps* in the schools? ... I think there is a good deal of *Esprit de Corps* in some schools. Children of a certain social class will have none amongst them who do not belong to that class, and in some cases get rid of very poor children' (RCEEA, 1886, p. 113). The inspector did not explain how the ostracism of 'very poor children' occurred. However, it is clear evidence for the existence of different status groups and, quite possibly, a mechanism whereby relative social advantages and disadvantages were reproduced.

Regarding the effect of the presence of clever children upon the dull, the opinions expressed were both unequivocal and pessimistic. 'I think it is only natural that there should be a tendency to pass [the dull] by as being hopeless under the strain of a very special examination. But I do not see how to provide against this temptation' (ibid.). A member of the Commission pressed the point further by observing that there were scholarships to be won which encouraged clever children to pass on to advanced schools, and went on to say: 'but the difficulty is to secure encouragement for those who are slow at learning .... Have you any plan to suggest to us by which the education of that class of children would be improved?' 'I have not' was the inspector's reply (ibid.). Thus the inspector seemed aware that an inevitable consequence of the system was the advance of some children at the cost of others. The social reproduction of sets of advantages and disadvantages was built into the system. That teachers would 'naturally' regard some children as 'hopeless' was taken for granted. In this way status groups are reproduced.

By contrast, another inspector analysed the situation from the class perspective of the market-place and perceived how a feature of the system may be to the benefit of all children. That feature lay at the heart of the system and was the securing of the annual grant itself: 'Is there any tendency for the present system to neglect a clever for a dull child?' 'I think both may be equally well taught. The merit grant encourages the cultivation of the intelligence and the object of the percentage of passes grant is ... that a dull child shall have proper attention paid to him and be brought up to a reasonable standard' (RCEEA, 1886, p. 174). Moreover, this inspector took a much more sanguine view of the effects of the system and located the source of a major difficulty in the progress of dull children outside the system itself. A member of the Commission asked: 'What is the effect of the present system upon a dull scholar?' (ibid.). To which the inspector replied: 'If a dull scholar is regular in attendance, he can easily go from Standard to Standard each year' (ibid.). However, absenteeism was the indirect source of 'over-pressure'. The inspector continued: 'I know of no cases where over-pressure should exist, except the one I have mentioned, where a dull child who has been irregular in his attendance is over-pressed towards the close of the year in order to pass the same examination as the others.'

The reasons for irregular attendance are various: ill health, a social convention or financial necessity of gainful employment. It would be surprising, however, if the link between poor school performance, ill health, unemployed parents or parents in low-paid work did not operate then as powerfully as it has been demonstrated to do more recently (Wedge and Prosser, 1973). In addition, the concept of the cycle of disadvantage embraces explanations of how status groups are renewed, both at the highest and the lowest social levels (Spinley, 1953; Rutter and Madge, 1976). The renewal of a social hierarchy is implicit in such a theory. It also points towards the social reproduction of sets of advantages and disadvantages (Holman, 1978, pp. 105–238).

The evidence of another chief inspector, Rev. D. J. Stewart, argued that the system failed the clever and the dull child alike. 'Do you think that the present system is favourable or unfavourable to the clever boys? Naturally it is unfavourable to both clever and ordinary boys' (RCEEA, 1886, p. 204). The inspector agreed to the question: 'Then you describe what we want as being thorough education, whereas we have only mechanical education?' (ibid., p. 214). The reason for this, he suggested, was that 'Our system is more irksome than a system under which [teachers'] powers, their invention and their resources of all kinds would be more called forth' (ibid., p. 204). The consequences are serious because 'it leads to pupils not being taught in the best way in which they might be taught ... the present system leads to children not being taught as much or as well as they might be ... the middling children and the dull children also lose by not being better and more skilfully taught as much as the quick ones' (ibid., pp. 204, 213).

The witness declared a preference for the continental system which gave scope for teachers' initiative and imagination in the planning and conduct of lessons. While these remarks support the view that the system itself was at the time the source of difficulties for dull children, his stance regarding 'thorough education' or the potential inherent within education appears to be neutral in so far as it is regarded as potentially beneficial to different status groups. For this reason these remarks may be located within the democratisation of education thesis which assumes that technical improvements in education will have equal impact on disparate groups. Thus, like Durkheim's analyses of education, the possibility is ignored that the renewal of social hierarchies may be realised through education and that the education system is a source of unequal distribution of sets of social advantages and disadvantages.

LOCAL AUTHORITIES

There were three kinds of authority at the level of local government concerned with schools: School Attendance Committees, the Management Committees of Voluntary schools and the School Boards which were created by Forster's Act of 1870.

The attendance bye-laws circumscribed the powers of the Attendance Committee. Hence it could not be regarded as concerned with school policy in any wide sense. The establishment of School Boards was a recognition that existing Voluntary schools were unable to provide Elementary education which embraced the whole nation's children. The School Boards were intended to supplement the provision of school places by the Voluntary schools. The 1870 Act divided the whole country into 'school districts' which were coterminous with either the borough or the civil parish. The School Boards could be brought into being either by the request of a majority of a local council and/or ratepayers, or by the imposition of the Education Department where the provision of school accommodation was found to be insufficient. School Boards varied in size from five to 15 members in accordance with the size of the district population. Board members were elected triennally and were empowered to make and enforce bye-laws which compelled the attendance of children between the ages of 5 and 13 in their districts to attend a public Elementary school or a Voluntary school. Boards established by the Education Department because of a deficiency in school accommodation were obliged to put such bye-laws in place. Boards were empowered to issue a precept to the local rating authority for the sums of money needed to run their schools. Thus the rates could be drawn upon to pay the Board's attendance and administrative officers, to build, hire or otherwise acquire and furnish school buildings, to pay teachers and, once the schools were operational, to supplement the income earned from the annual grant and fees.

School Boards managed directly or indirectly through their appointed deputies, the schools which they built, rented or hired. They were able to fix the rate of the weekly fees, and could remit them in part or in whole in appropriate cases. They oversaw the appointment of teachers. The Boards had control of the conduct and curriculum of schools in so far as they were able to pursue any preferred policies provided that the principal part of the instruction was deemed Elementary and thereby grant-earning under the Code of Elementary Education. In addition, Boards could choose between undenominational religious teaching according to their own syllabus or no religious teaching at all. School Boards in this way had considerable powers and discretions. However, they were not autonomous. For example, any bye-laws requiring compulsory attendance had to meet the approval of the Education Department before they were submitted to the Queen in Council. The Education Department was the final arbiter, through its appointed arbitrator, of the degree of deficiency of school accommodation in a district. A school which was judged to have been built unnecessarily could be refused consideration for the annual grant. The Department was needed to approve the scale of fees which was set by a Board and to sanction proposed remissions or exemptions. In particular, the Department exercised considerable control over the conduct of the curriculum through the mechanisms of the Code, Her Majesty's Inspectors and the annual grant.

The London School Board did not arise spontaneously but was a part of the 1870 Act. For several decades, the deficiency in school accommodation in the capital had been clearly recognised and considered scandalous (Spalding, 1900, pp. 3–5; Marsden, 1977, pp. 49–73; Rubinstein, 1969, pp. 19–27). The London School Board had 49 members who were elected triennially by the ratepayers arranged in 11 divisions. There were slight variations in the numbers to be elected from different divisions and the total number of members was increased to 55 in 1882.

The management committees of Voluntary schools had technically more freedom from the oversight of the Education Department than the School Boards. Their income came from subscriptions, fees and the annual grant. While, like School Boards, their expenditure had to be justified to the Exchequer and the Audit Office, they were not overseen by the Poor Law auditor and were not required to submit their table of fees to the Education Department. Voluntary schools also enjoyed a cohesive strength through their affiliation to the educational organisations of the various denominations. Thus Anglican schools' managers were able to link themselves to the National Society and Roman Catholic schools had their Catholic Poor School Committee. However, they were subject to the Education Department's control in so far as it was necessary for them to satisfy the requirements of the Code in order to earn the annual grant. They had also to operate a conscience clause with regard to the timetable whereby the part of each day to be spent in religious instruction was clearly specified so that parents could withdraw their children should they disapprove.

In terms of the pursuit of initiatives in education, it can be argued that the Board schools had the advantage over the Voluntary schools. In the first place, School Boards were created precisely because of the deficiency and shortcomings in the Voluntary schools' provisions. In the second place, Voluntary schools' paramount concern was religious affiliation and religious instruction. School Board members, on the other hand, were primarily concerned with the education of pupils. Moreover, they had the means to pursue their aims through a precept to the local rating authority. The growth of their influence may be assessed from the number of pupils who increasingly came into their domain.

TABLE 3.4

GROWTH IN NUMBER OF CHILDREN IN AVERAGE ATTENDANCE AT BOARD AND VOLUNTARY SCHOOLS, 1870–85

Year	Board	Voluntary
1870	–	1,152,389
1875	227,285	1,609,895
1880	769,252	1,981,664
1885	1,187,455	2,183,870

Source: PP (1897, xxv, p. 49).

In 1875, the roughly one-quarter of a million pupils in Board schools were about one-eighth the number of those in Voluntary schools. The quarter of a million constitutes a phenomenon of organisation and planning in its own right. That number tripled, however, between 1875 and 1880. By

1885, about half the places in Elementary schools were occupied by pupils in Board schools.

DULL AND DEFICIENT CHILDREN IN SCHOOLS

A total of 153 people presented oral evidence which formed the basis of the Cross Commission's three reports on Elementary education. Slightly less than half of these witnesses (70) commented upon 'over-pressure in the school system'. Roughly a quarter of these mentioned 'over-pressure' in relation to 'dull', 'deficient', or 'delicate' children. However, opinions were divided. The chairman of one urban Board believed '[t]here is much over-pressure both with dull children and with quick' (RCEEA, 1887, p. 774), while the chairman of another maintained that 'the dull are pressed to produce certain results' (ibid., p. 307). An urban Board schoolteacher claimed that '[c]lever children are neglected and teachers look after dullards' (ibid., p. 447), while a sub-inspector in London maintained that 'over-pressure is very rare but very bright children will over-press themselves' (RCEEA, 1888, p. 491). The headmasters of three schools, as well as an inspector, linked over-pressure with irregular attendance and dullness: 'There is over-pressure on the dull and irregular who must be kept in after school' (RCEEA, 1887, p. 142). Two headmistresses perceived a connection between the child's domestic and nutritional conditions. For example, 'The wretched homes and want of food make it very necessary not to press the child's brain unduly' (ibid., p. 67). Finally, another headmistress claimed that she '[o]bviates over-pressure on the dull children by interesting them' (ibid., p. 163). It is evident that the relationship between over-pressure and a child's dullness was conceived of and explained in many different ways; and dullness itself was not necessarily regarded as the source of over-pressure.

The Rev. Dr Crosskey was chairman of the School Management Committee of the Birmingham School Board and presented evidence to the Commission on four occasions. A small part of his evidence concerns dull children. It also illustrated how School Boards set about their work: 'I have not been engaged in practical teaching myself, but as chairman of the School Management Committee I am constantly through the schools; we have no managers; we see reports from our own inspectors on every school and I am perfectly familiar with the working of them' (RCEEA, 1887, p. 596). Dr Crosskey's first appearance before the Commission was intended to rebut an accusation contained in an HMI report on the Board's schools that 'the excessive competition among teachers, especially under the Board, renders the temptation almost irresistible to place the interests of the individual child somewhat in the background relatively to the swelling of the grant and to regard him as a grant-earning and a reputation-earning machine' (ibid.). The inspector's catalogue of criticisms of schools' practices is redolent of recent analysis of the consequences of the 1988 Education Reform Act (Copeland, 1991). In addition to criticism of teaching-to-the-test, the catalogue included: 'the tendency to abuse the provisions of the ... exception clauses of the Code; the irregular getting rid of children unlikely to do credit to the school; forcing children to take more subjects than they can properly master and ... the detention of dull children long after the proper school hours' (ibid.). Children's morning and afternoon recreation was also curtailed. The chairman of the Management Committee conceded that the school day had been lengthened for pupils with learning difficulties: 'A year ago a good many complaints were made with respect to detaining dull children; they were examined into, and the practice was practically stopped' (ibid.).

Again, the import of this evidence is ambivalent. On the one hand, it may be interpreted from the democratisation of education perspective or from the Weberian class-basis as an attempt to enlarge the market-place share of education for all, on the assumption that the consequences of education are even handed. On the other hand, it may be evidence for the social reproduction of sets of advantages and disadvantages whereby the disadvantaged are clearly identified. Thus by the teachers' decision to work in a particular way which continually reinforces in pupils the things they are unable to achieve, pupils are confirmed in their lowly status, in the eyes of more successful pupils if not in their own. Moreover, that process is reified through the practice of detaining dull pupils after school, which identifies and labels them for the rest to see.

The evidence presented by the headmaster of a Board school in Dudley was intended as a commentary upon the efficiency of the school system but is also a clear indication of the attitude adopted towards pupils who were regarded as dull. He considered 'that [a] terrible waste of time is involved to three fourths of the school in waiting for the dullards' (RCEEA, 1887, p. 86). Previously he had declared 'that [the present system] makes no provision for the cultivation of the special faculty of a clever child; that it is cruelly unjust and injurious to the dull and semi-imbecile children; and that it deadens the faculties of teachers and scholars' (ibid., p. 85).

If the system of schools was itself rooted in financial considerations, then to at least one headmaster of a Voluntary Church school in London the solution to the problem of dull children in the school was to raise money from them. 'You had for some years a rule in your school that a shilling should be charged for backward children?' 'Yes', he replied (ibid., p. 39). His additional explanation was brutally frank:

> When the age classes were first threatened to be introduced, the managers considered that it would be a dead loss to take children who could not come up to the standard which, according to their age, they should come up to; and, therefore, that rule was passed that they should be charged a shilling a week under the circumstances. (ibid.)

The curriculum in the 1871 Code included the elementary or obligatory subjects – the three Rs and 'specific' subjects, for example, the natural sciences, political economy and languages, which were grant-earning for schools but limited to pupils examined in Standards IV, V and VI. The 1876 Education Act introduced a third category, namely 'class' subjects: 'These consisted of grammar, history and plain needlework which, unlike the other two categories, were based not upon the proficiency of individual pupils, but on that of the class as a whole' (Gordon and Lawton, 1978, p. 15; cf., Armytage, 1964, p. 150). This new requirement had clearly placed a burden upon schools for which they felt obliged to charge, and which put them in breach of the 1870 Act's stipulation that although Boards could prescribe weekly fees they should not be more than nine pence (cf., Lawson and Silver, 1973, p. 317). In reply to a further question, the headmaster indicated that at one point 12 pupils, roughly an eighth of the total, were paying the shilling. These children were also a focal point of the teachers' work-load and he went to state: 'The dull children and those in any way deficient receive more than their fair share of attention. If any master's memoranda were examined it would be found that the names of the dull and those likely to fail at the examination were much more frequently recorded than those of the clever' (ibid., p. 36).

The headmaster believed there was over-pressure in the school system. When asked: 'Do you find over-pressure among the teachers in your school?', he replied: 'We have had several breakdowns in health' (ibid., p. 41). Moreover, this over-pressure affected the children too and particularly those with learning difficulties. The headmaster declared: 'I say distinctly that [the working of the system] introduces a very large amount of unnecessary worry and anxiety; and that tells upon health ... I say the same with regard to children, most decidedly the dull children, the children of slower parts' (ibid.). Again, there is an indication that the shilling levy is a process which identifies and confirms a status group and through the pressure built into the system the sets of social advantages and disadvantages are reproduced.

In the judgment of the headmasters of urban schools who gave evidence to the Commission, the incidence of children with learning difficulties ranged from one in four to one in eight. In contrast, the headmaster of a Voluntary school in a country district gave evidence to the effect that all the hundred or so pupils in his school were backward. When asked by the Commission's chairman whether he had anything to say in regard to the standards of secular education, he replied: 'Yes, my idea is that so far as rural children are concerned, the inspectors as a rule do not make sufficient allowance for the dullness of the children' (RCEEA, 1887, p. 71).

He then proceeded to identify one of the mechanisms whereby sets of social advantages and disadvantages were transmitted from generation to generation through the vehicle of the education system. The chairman remarked that many teachers had complained to him about the difficulty they found in getting children to read fluently and intelligently. The headmaster replied that there were two reasons for this state of affairs. The first was social in origin and the second arose from the education system. He declared that, for the reading difficulty, 'There is one reason, and it is a reason that is often forgotten, and that is that there are still in our rural villages a great many parents who themselves cannot read and the children do not read at all at home' (ibid.). Hence rural children lacked the encouragement of role models and, equally important, additional practice to gain fluency. Thus the seemingly neutral or, in Bourdieu's term, 'disinterested' educational system is, in fact, based upon the social conventions of particular status groups.

The educational reason for poor readers given by the headmaster was the Code's insistence upon a narrow range of books for reading. In reply to the chairman's statement that 'I believe you think the present system of confining reading to three books is objectionable', the headmaster said: 'Yes, I think it is an utter mistake ... The great object I take to be this, that children should acquire a love for reading and they do not acquire it now because they are simply ground in these three books' (ibid.). Hence the priority of the Code's demands inhibited the adoption of teaching and learning strategies which would benefit all children and particularly those with learning difficulties.

The potential for the transmission of social capital from one generation to another is perhaps most clearly identified in this rural context. The seemingly rational insistence upon a particular format for reading for all children carries with it the same sort of consequences as the system of intelligence testing. In this latter context, 'While we shall always be faced with substantial differences in learning ability among all children, we have to face the really hard fact that we are now meeting this problem in a particular way which serves in the end to magnify the differences and then pass them off as a natural order' (Williams, 1965, p. 168). The content of the Code and the consequences of the Code represent a particular selection, a particular set of emphases and omissions from a larger culture, the choice of which was made by particular status groups. The consequences were to confirm the status groups in their relative positions and to facilitate the transmission of a social hierarchy from one generation to the next. Thus what to many seemed a neutral and objective vehicle of Elementary education was a mechanism that both created and confirmed the social differences between groups.

To approach these events from a different perspective, however, may point to a different conclusion. In 1870 there were slightly more than one million pupils in average attendance in Voluntary schools. In 1880 that figure had more than doubled to roughly two-and-a-half million in Voluntary and Board schools. By 1885 there were slightly more than three million pupils in Elementary schools. In a period of 15 years the system's capacity had expanded threefold. Given the nature of the Code and the rapidity of the system's expansion, then the proper question may be why were there not more casualties than in fact was the case. Quantification of dull and deficient pupils is difficult and, as has been demonstrated, ranges from the whole rural school population to one in four and one in eight in urban areas.

Mrs E. M. Burgwin, at that time headmistress of a Board school in central London but subsequently the London Board's first superintendent in charge of the organisation of its special schools, gave evidence to the Commission. In 1887, Mrs Burgwin had 21 years' experience as a teacher in different central London schools. The first six years were as a pupil-teacher and the last 13 as headmistress of her present school. Early in her evidence she made the point that she thought there was evidence of over-pressure in her school. However, subsequent evidence revealed her ambivalence concerning its source. In the first place she declared: 'I attribute the over-pressure [in the school] to the system of payment by results ... I do know that many of the children are over-pressed with the work. I had a child standing before me only yesterday morning; she stood for a little while and I noticed she was shaking her head; she seemed unable to grasp anything' (RCEEA, 1888, p. 115). When pressed by the chairman whether she was able to identify particular children at risk of over-pressure, she replied: 'I think generally the backward; it is the backward, underfed, poor and neglected children' (ibid., p. 117). It is perhaps noteworthy that these are the same factors identified by the London headmistress mentioned earlier who gave evidence to the Departmental Committee on Defective and Epileptic Children.

When the school opened in 1874, Mrs Burgwin had initiated a system of penny dinners for pupils in her school. But this had attracted a better class of children and there were hundreds who could not even afford a penny. Wherefore, 'from 1874 I have provided dinners for them quite free, free entirely; 140 went today for the free dinner' (ibid.). She also attempted to pursue a suggestion by an HMI that a school bath be installed and an oven to fumigate children's clothes. The London Board rejected both on the grounds of cost (Horn, 1990, pp. 49–50). In fact, at a later point in her evidence, she changed her reason for the existence of over-pressure from payment by results to the child's domestic and nutritional circumstances. When asked: 'Do you attribute the over-pressure mainly to the wretched homes and the insufficient food of the children?' she replied, 'I think that largely contributed to the over-pressure' (ibid., p. 118). The chairman pressed the point further: 'Do you think that if you had a school in a good part of London with well-to-do parents and well-fed children you could educate those children so as to make the school thoroughly happy to the children?' Mrs Burgwin replied, 'Yes, I think so, with very few exceptions' (ibid.).

Mrs Burgwin's evidence is also interesting for another reason. The evidence given to the Commission by HM Inspectors and headmasters employed terminology such as 'dull', 'dullness', 'dullard', 'deficient', 'semi-imbecile', 'children with slower parts'. This terminology may be interpreted as an attempt to categorise children in accordance with some characteristics they were considered to possess. They all fit readily into a model of attainment in education which is based upon personal deficiency. The paradox appears that while witnesses were able to understand the operation of the Code as a system of education, the children's response to the system was perceived in terms of their imputed personal characteristics. Thus the impact of the Code, whose origins were cultural and social, was explained and understood by both operators and recipients in personal terms. In this way, ideology transmuted the social into the personal.

Mrs Burgwin, however, was slightly different. The terminology in her evidence is that of 'backward'. The essence of the idea of 'backward' is primarily mobile and relative, unlike 'dull' and 'deficient' which is absolute and static. In 1978 the Warnock Report sought to transform thinking about learning difficulties by concentrating upon what the child may need in educational terms to flourish. It was an attempt to move from the prevailing medical model of personal deficiency. Warnock's success was evident in one of the definitions of a child with special educational needs, given in Section 1 of the 1981 Act, as having 'significantly greater difficulty in learning than the majority of children of his age'. The ideas of 'greater difficulty' and 'majority of children' imply that educational needs must be seen as relative and changing as circumstances change. Did Mrs Burgwin's thinking anticipate that of Warnock and the 1981 Act? The residual problem is that of 'significant'. At what point is the line to be drawn to identify a difficulty? It is a task which is made more difficult by the idea of a continuum of need. However, following the three reports on the Elementary Education Act in 1886, 1887 and 1888 respectively, the next task that emerged was to establish a definition of 'defective' which would distinguish the educable from the non-educable and provide a rationale for the sort of treatment different categories within the two groups should receive.

CONCLUSIONS

The extension of compulsory education to the whole age cohort, the nature of the school curriculum and of the teaching profession within a system policed by payment by results, created the context for the producton of the dull pupil, particularly in the urban context. The overseeing of the system was in the hands of HMI who, in turn, were answerable to Education Department officials. The whole was the responsibility of senior politicians. HMI evidence presented to RCEEA pointed towards the Elementary system producing dull and deficient pupils. Members of School Boards and the teachers themselves concurred with this view in their evidence. A second Commission had been set up to consider the education of pupils with disabilities in Elementary schools. The Commission's deliberations and recommendations are taken as the next area for analysis because here the categorisation of the dull pupil is more detailed and explicit.

4

The Egerton Commission: Proposals for the Education of Mentally Deficient Children

Following on from the identification of dull and backward pupils in Elementary schools by teachers and inspectors in the preceding chapter, this Chapter examines the Egerton Commission's recommendations for the education of the blind, the deaf and the feeble-minded. It then explores at some length the contrast in the evidence presented to the Commission by two leading exponents in the field of the science of the mind.

EDUCATION OF THE BLIND, THE DEAF AND THE AMPERSAND: THE EGERTON COMMISSION'S TERMS OF REFERENCE

When the Conservatives were returned to power in 1885, a Royal Commission was appointed to examine the working of the Elementary Education Acts. The Bishop of London was originally selected as chairman but, following protests against denominational bias to the Conservative Vice-President at the Education Department, he was replaced by Sir Richard Cross, later Lord Cross (Armytage, 1964, p. 155). Curiously, the chairman of another Royal Commission was shortly to be replaced. In the summer of 1885, a Conference of the Headmasters of Institutions for the Education of the Deaf and Dumb, after years of debate which had divided their ranks (Cole, 1989, pp. 13–20), finally agreed that the government should be lobbied for state aid for the education of the deaf. The Conference also agreed that Lord Egerton of Tatton, chairman of the Manchester School for the Deaf, should press their case with the government.

In the meantime, however, a Royal Commission had been appointed under the chairmanship of the Duke of Westminster, to inquire into the condition and education of the blind. This was a result of a Conference on the education of the blind in 1883 which was followed in 1884 by a meeting at Grosvenor House, convened by the Duke of Westminster. The Commission was perhaps approved because there was less schism in the ranks of the bodies concerned for the education of the blind. The Commission also met with the approval of the educators of the deaf, who believed they had little in common either theoretically or practically with the educators of the blind (Ritchie, 1930, p. 95).

Events turned out differently. Following Lord Egerton's deputation early in 1886, the terms of reference of the Royal Commission on the education of the blind were changed and enlarged. The terms of reference originally approved by Her Majesty had been 'to investigate and report upon the condition of the blind in the United Kingdom, the various systems of education of the blind, elementary, technical and professional, at home and abroad, and the existing institutions for that purpose, the employments open to, and suitable for the blind and the means by which education may be extended so as to increase the number of blind persons qualified for such employments' (RCBDD, 1889, p. xi). The terms of reference now 'were extended by the inclusion of the deaf and dumb and *of such other cases as from special circumstances would seem to require exceptional methods of education'* (ibid., italics added). Lord Egerton was appointed chairman in the place of the Duke of Westminster, who resigned from the Commission.

There had been lobbies on behalf of the education of both the blind and the deaf, and perhaps it was a pragmatic decision to synthesize the pursuit of their inquiries, even though at least one who worked on behalf of the deaf regarded the extension of the Commission's terms of reference as 'unfortunate in that it gave State recognition to the vicious bracketing of blind with deaf' (Ritchie, 1930, p. 95). The inclusion of the category *'and such other cases as from special circumstances would seem to require exceptional methods of education'*, appeared as a novel and surprising element. There had been no lobby on their behalf, although in 1877 The Charity Organisation Society had produced a report entitled, 'Education and Care of Idiots, Imbeciles and Harmless Lunatics' (COS, 1877). The publication of the report and its title is discursive in Foucauldian terms, being an example of the objectification of the subject. The new category may have been prompted by a desire to include all special cases in the inquiry so that it would be a thorough-going exercise. However, the reality was the bold title page of the report which announced the 'Report of the Royal Commission on the Blind, the Deaf and Dumb', the other special cases being represented by an ampersand. The effect of this has been such that one commentator throughout refers to the 'Royal Commission on the Blind and Deaf' (Pritchard, 1963). The Warnock Report itself, in its section on the historical background of special educational needs, identifies the Commission by this title (DES, 1978, p. 12).

STRUCTURE OF THE REPORT

Patrick Cumin, the then Secretary to the Education Department, presented evidence to the Commission. In his opening remarks, he declared: 'We consider the word "children" includes all children and therefore includes the deaf and dumb and the blind' (RCBDD, 1889, p. 719). In his lengthy submission he made no mention of children with learning difficulties for other reasons, nor was he asked to by any of the Commission members.

The main body of the report, excluding the commentary upon Scotland, Ireland and Reservations, was contained in 107 pages. The commentary upon the blind, the deaf and dumb ran to 92 pages. The additional element subsumed under the ampersand ran to 15 pages and constituted less than one-seventh of the total report.

The Commission held 116 meetings in London, to which '[w]e have summoned such persons as we judged likely to be able to give information … on the subjects of our enquiry' (RCBDD, 1889, p. xii). The Commission summoned exactly 150 witnesses. The evidence of seven witnesses alone is referred to in the 'ampersand' section. The Commission undertook a postal survey of blind persons in the United Kingdom and 'visited the principal schools and establishments for the blind and deaf and dumb in the United Kingdom and have, by personal inspection made ourselves acquainted with the systems of education, elementary, technical and professional, pursued in the leading establishments for the blind and deaf and dumb, not only in the United Kingdom but also in Paris, Germany, Switzerland and Italy' (ibid.). On the other hand, and regarding the ampersand clause, 'We have inspected the six principal institutions in the United Kingdom where the imbeciles and idiots who are capable of receiving some elementary education are trained, and so far as relates to the subject matter of our enquiry, we have examined witnesses thereon' (ibid.).

Thus the Commission consciously interpreted the terms of reference concerning *'such other cases as from special circumstances would seem to require exceptional methods of education'* as referring to 'the educable class of imbeciles'. The term 'imbecile' remained unexplicated. Also from the outset, the Commission took the position that such children would receive their education elsewhere than public Elementary schools: 'We now approach a class which comes under our terms of reference as requiring from special circumstances exceptional methods of education and which are practically excluded from the operation of the Education Acts' (ibid., p. 92). The Commission does not identify the practice which so excludes these children but continues, 'Our enquiries regarding the imbeciles and idiots have been directed towards ascertaining how many of them are capable of education and are able to benefit by training, and if so, whether it can best be carried out in some special institution distinct from an ordinary lunatic asylum' (ibid.). From the start, then, the Commission took the view that the task related to children who were somehow excluded from attendance at Elementary schools but who needed some institution other than the existing lunatic asylum.

From the outset, however, the Commission was aware that it was concerned with phenomena which were as much social as they were personal. Poverty, in particular, was both a causal and a consequent factor.

> Indigence is found to exist in the great majority of the cases of persons so afflicted, the greater part of the population from which such cases proceed being so little removed from want that such a calamity is sufficient in itself to produce indigence. It cannot be said that the group spoken of are, as a rule, impoverished by any fault of their own. (ibid., p. xii)

Pointing out that 'the education of the classes referred to is more expensive than of ordinary children', the Commission did not think it would 'be viewed as offering any reward to vice, folly or improvidence' (ibid., p. xiii). After all, this class consisted of 'paupers' not 'criminal paupers'. For all that, however, the prime purpose of this group's education was social and political rather than personal: 'The blind, deaf and dumb, and the educable class of imbeciles form a distinct group, which, if left uneducated, become not only a burden to themselves but a weighty burden to the State. It is in the interest of the State to educate them so as to dry up as far as possible the minor streams which ultimately swell the great torrent of pauperism' (ibid., p. xiii).

This outlook accorded with the view that 'the predominant reaction to the rediscovery of poverty in the early 1880s was not so much guilt as fear. The discovery of a huge and swelling residuum [of the poor] and the growing uncertainty about the mood of the respectable working class portended the threat of revolution' (Stedman Jones, 1971, p. 290). In turn, this sparked an extensive public debate in the press and quarterly journals (cf., ibid, p. 290, n. 28). The Charity Organisation Society, which had attempted to moralise the poor through systematic charitable relief in urban areas, began to be marginalised and its policies of 'charity for the thrifty, the modified workhouse test for the improvident and the workhouse for the vicious' (ibid., p. 303) were replaced. There was a realisation that a more coercive and interventionist policy towards the residuum was required and that Poor Law authorities lacked the powers of compulsory detention. By chance, the winter of 1885–86 was exeptionally severe for several months and was accompanied by civil unrest among London's poor and homeless. This appeared to crystallise policy towards the poor. It was also, of course, the time of the inauguration of the two Royal Commissions.

RECOMMENDATIONS FOR THE EDUCATION OF THE BLIND

The Commission's decision that it was dealing with the education of special cases which lay beyond the scope of Elementary schools is a crucial one. It points inexorably to the establishment of special institutions where pupils are segregated from their peers. Segregation seemingly was a mixed strategy, to aid the segregated in some way but also to restrict the social contagion of pauperism. This segregation contrasted with recommendations for the education of the blind. Children living in rural areas should attend their local village school and, if the teachers took the trouble to learn Braille, then the blind could learn alongside the sighted. In towns, there should be a peripatetic teacher of the different embossed types so that the blind could have similar access to schools as the sighted (RCBDD, 1889, p. 38).

RECOMMENDATIONS FOR THE EDUCATION OF THE DEAF

Opinions regarding the optimum method of teaching the deaf were divided. On the one hand, those who supported the sign and manual system maintained that it was the natural way for the deaf to express themselves. Thus the deaf may communicate with their fellow deaf. On the other hand, the oralists emphasised that the most important element was for the deaf to be able to communicate with the hearing world. Hence they attempted to make the deaf conversant with their own oral language which surrounded them. The schism between the two groups was deep and enduring. The Commission took evidence from both camps but felt unable to make a judgment between them and regarded it as unwise for the state to insist on one method. However, because the techniques of signing and oralism were mutually conflicting, it was recommended that each should be taught in separate schools or classes (ibid., p. 77). Thus the education of some of the Commission's classes of children was actively considered possible, and even desirable, alongside other ordinary children. The 'ampersand' group were excluded, however.

SOME IMPLICATIONS OF THE RECOMMENDATIONS

How are these different recommendations to be interpreted in terms of the model of social reproduction or otherwise? The recommendation for the education of blind children alongside their peers in ordinary schools appears to be an attempt to breach the social reproduction of sets of disadvantages and, through a technical mechanism such as Braille, to widen access to education. The suggestions for the deaf and dumb are a conflicting compromise. On the one hand, support for the signing and manual system of communication implies the social reproduction of sets of disadvantages, primarily because social and cultural intercourse would be restricted to a particular subset of the total population. In a similar vein, the suggestion that children involved in signing should be separated from those involved with oralism is similarly restrictive. On the other hand, the principle of oralism, which seeks to present the deaf with a means of access to the larger culture of which they are a part, appears to be an attempt to remove a set of disadvantages in social reproduction. The identification of educable idiots and imbeciles and the recommendation that they be educated in separate, specialist institutions is ambiguous. In the first place, it could be argued that by this mechanism these children would have experiences and opportunities which otherwise would be denied to them. The mould of disadvantage in social reproduction may be cracked if not actually sundered. In contradiction to this, however, is the argument that such identification and segregation forecloses the debate about the extent of such children's access to the culture of the larger society. In other words, the processes of identification and segregation put a fence around the potential for social interaction and a ceiling upon expectations of development. In this way, the social reproduction of sets of disadvantages seems an inevitable consequence. The Commission in its reference to poverty suggests that the deaf, the blind and the 'ampersand' group share the same class position by virtue of their relationship to the market-place and their skills. Their confinement and segregation through the mechanism of education, however, is likely to transform them into a status group with particular social conventions and values.

THE OUTCOME OF THE INQUIRY

The membership of the Cross Commission was announced on 15 January 1886 (RCEEA, 1886, pp. 3–4) and the reconstruction of the Commission on the Blind on 20 January 1886 (RCBDD, 1889, p. ii). Perhaps the very proximity of the establishment of the two Commissions is itself the reason for the extension to include other exceptional cases. For with the inclusion of the deaf and dumb, and with the addition of the 'ampersand' group, that would complete the picture, so to speak. The appointments to each Commission may also have been fluid because it is reported that Egerton was considered at one stage as chairman of the Elementary education inquiry (Sutherland, 1984, p. 9).

There is no logical or rational reason why the Egerton Commission should take up the position that a particular class of children should only be considered educable outside the system of Elementary education. The reason could, indeed, be entirely pragmatic. The Cross Commission completed its work with the presentation of its final report in 1888. In the event, there were two 'final' reports: a majority and a minority one. There was no difference between them on these matters. It was not until November 1888 that the Egerton Commission examined the first witness on the education of idiots and imbeciles. Perhaps Egerton took the pragmatic view that Cross had dealt with the issue from the point of view of public Elementary education. Hence the Commission looked for its chief witnesses beyond mainstream education to a specialist field of medical education.

The Egerton Commission's report was published late in 1889. On the basis of its recommendations, a permissive Bill for the Education of the Blind and Deaf was initially drawn up. George Kekewich, Secretary to the Education Department, proposed that school authorities should be obliged to make provision and the blind and deaf compelled to attend. In the meantime, the Education of Blind and Deaf (Mute) Children (Scotland) Bill was introduced and became law in August 1890. Although the parallel English Bill was introduced in that same session, because of disputes concerning finance, pressure by lobby groups for compulsory education to the age of 16 and a dissolution of Parliament, the Elementary Education (Blind and Deaf Children) Act did not receive assent until September 1893. By this means, blind children were to receive education from the age of 5 to 16 years and the deaf from 7 to 16 years. School authorities were obliged either to establish a school of their own for these pupils or to contribute to one elsewhere. In this way, the two groups of children which took up the lion's share of the Commission's inquiry achieved their outcomes. But what of the 'ampersand' group? In February 1897, eight years after the Egerton Report, a Departmental Committee on Defective and Epileptic Children began its deliberations (DCDEC, 1898). There was a link in players between the Egerton Commission and the Departmental Committee.

71

LINK BETWEEN THE EGERTON COMMISSION AND THE DEPARTMENTAL COMMITTEE

The link centred upon Dr G. E. Shuttleworth, Medical Superintendent of the Royal Albert Asylum, Lancaster, 1870–93, who formed a nexus between leading medical opinion, the Education Department and the London School Board. Shuttleworth was called to present expert evidence to the Egerton Commission. Major-General F. J. Moberly also presented evidence to the Commission as a member of the London School Board. In 1897, Shuttleworth was appointed a full member of the Education Departmental Committee on Defective and Epileptic Children. He also was the first witness called to present evidence to the Committee as a medical superintendent (DCDEC, 1898, vol. II, pp. 1–6). Moberly in turn gave evidence to the Committee in his capacity as vice-chairman of the London School Board and chairman of its sub-committee for defective pupils. In 1899, Shuttleworth was appointed Medical Examiner of Defective Children to the London School Board.

THE EDUCATION OF IDIOTS AND IMBECILES

There were 15 pages in the Egerton Report under the heading 'Idiots and Imbeciles'. However, in the final three pages a new classification was introduced, that of the 'feeble-minded'. Commentators such as Pritchard (1963, pp. 95–114) and Cole (1989, pp. 13–29) usually discuss the different sections sequentially. Thus there is discussion of the education of the blind, the deaf and the mentally defective. Each in this way appears coherent. As has already been pointed out, while the recommendations for the education of blind children may be coherent, those for deaf children certainly are not. In a similar way, the discussion of the education of idiots and imbeciles is not a seamless whole but a patchwork quilt of conflicting colours.

The 15 pages of this section of the report contain just over 90 references to witnesses' evidence. There was a total of seven witnesses. Two were Secretaries to Commissioners in Lunacy in England and Scotland. Two were responsible for asylums for idiots and imbeciles. One was a paediatrician and another a member of the London School Board. Dr G. E. Shuttleworth, Medical Superintendent of the Royal Albert Asylum for Idiots and Imbeciles, figures as a colossus in the bulk of the report concerning idiots and imbeciles. Exactly a half of the references are to his evidence. The concluding three pages on the feeble-minded draws upon the evidence of Dr Francis Warner, Professor of Anatomy and Physiology and consultant paediatrician to a number of London hospitals, and Major-General F. J. Moberly, of the London School Board.

RELATIVISTIC DEFINITION OF MENTAL DEFICIENCY

No definition of 'feeble-minded' is attempted. The Commission simply gives the reason for this part of its deliberations as 'The Royal Commission on the Elementary Education Acts ... suggested that the case of the feeble-minded children would come more appropriately within our terms of reference' (RCBDD, 1889, p. 104). There are definitions of idiots and imbeciles which are linked to the idea of lunacy. Lunacy, in turn, is defined in the Lunacy Acts (ibid., pp. 92–3). Towards the end of the sixteenth century John Locke made an important distinction between the madman and the idiot: 'In short, herein seems to lie the difference between idiots and madmen, that madmen put wrong ideas together and reason from them but idiots make very few or no propositions and reason scarce at all' (1965, p. 128). The important inferences from this are that if madmen had not lost their faculty of reasoning they may be amenable to treatment, training or education, but idiots may have insufficient faculty to reason at all. In turn, this leads to different possibilities for remedial action. On the one hand, one may concentrate upon the individual to ascertain the degree of mental ability or to establish a link between those who are likely to benefit from training and those who are not. On the other hand, one may concentrate upon the factors or circumstances which are thought to produce madness or idiocy. Stated another way, one may concentrate upon the personal and internal or the social and the external.

The Commission's report endorsed Shuttleworth's relativistic definition of the terms (RCBDD, 1889, p. 95): 'Idiocy means a lower degradation of intellect, a greater deficiency of intellect, and imbecility means a lesser degree of such deficiency' (ibid., p. 705). The report also accepted and reproduced a Lunacy Commissioner's aetiology for the condition:

> Mental unsoundness or mental defect, which dates from intra-uterine life or from an early period of extra-uterine life, that is, from infancy or childhood, is called idiocy or imbecility. The causes of the condition differ greatly, both when its origin is in foetal life and when it dates from childhood ... It does not represent the loss of

something which existed, but it always begins in an immature or undeveloped organ. (ibid., pp. 95, 670)

Thus the attention for diagnosis was upon the personal, mental and physical properties of the child. It was acknowledged that there was no clear line separating idiots from imbeciles but that 'idiocy is a deeper defect than imbecility. This view meets all requirements, whether for scientific purposes, or for purposes of medical treatment, or for practical purposes connected with care, management and education' (ibid., p. 670).

THE AETIOLOGY OF DEFICIENCY

Drawing from the case histories of more than a thousand from his asylum, Shuttleworth estimated that two-thirds of the cases were congenital and one-third non-congenital. The detail of his argument is available from his report for 1889 as Medical Superintendent of the Royal Albert which has been recently reproduced (Alston, 1992, pp. 30–1). The estimate was important because the congenital were regarded as considerably more capable of improvement than the non-congenital.

> The congenital class are [*sic*] more susceptible to improvement than the non-congenital class … the reason of that probably being that the non-congenital class suffer from the effects of damage to the brain and brain disease, whereas the congenital class … are deficient from want of development of the brain before birth, and by … subjecting them to proper educational processes, they may be improved in process of growth. (RCBDD, 1889, p. 706)

Again, drawing upon the asylum's case histories, Shuttleworth was able to construct a hierarchy of imbecile and idiot children. 'First, those capable of learning to read and write (40%); secondly, those capable of benefiting in minor degree by school instruction and discipline (45%); and thirdly, the ineducable class (15%)' (ibid., p. 708). The first two were classified as 'imbeciles' and the third as 'idiots'. In one respect this is very positive and optimistic in that it suggests that improvement is possible and such children should not be abandoned and ignored in the asylum or the workhouse. But in another regard it is much less so, because in concentrating upon a diagnosis of children's presenting personal features it brackets out consideration of other possible factors such as poverty or the system of education.

RECOMMENDATIONS FOR THE EDUCATION OF IMBECILES

On the basis of this analysis, the Commission endorsed Shuttleworth's blueprint for the 'Improvement or Education of Imbeciles' (ibid., p. 97). The aims were that imbeciles should to a degree be self-supporting, be of help to themselves and some use to their friends, and should be happy and less offensive to the community (ibid., p. 98). The means to these ends were threefold. First, their physical condition should be improved through diet and exercise. Second, their moral sensitivities should be developed by learning the difference between right and wrong, and their duty to their neighbour. Third, there would be education goals of two kinds. The preliminary element consisted of school exercises based upon 'the axiom of Seguin that the education of the senses must precede the education of the mind' (ibid., p. 99). This entailed improvement of speech, the cultivation of perceptive faculties, exercises for the hands and activities such as lessons in shopkeeping, picture and objects lessons. The second stage of industrial training followed. This involved simple housework, outdoor work in the farm and garden, sewing and certain handicrafts. In this programme the economic and political purposes are as evident as those of personal development. Shuttleworth made reference to the German 'auxiliary schools or classes' (ibid., p. 71) and as an appendix submitted a paper he had written describing 'Special classes for instruction of abnormal children in Norway' (ibid., p. 370).

While Shuttleworth may be in agreement with the pedagogic principles of Germany's and Norway's special schools and classes, he does not share their prime aim. Norway divided these pupils into four categories:

> First, those who after two or three years' special teaching can be brought back into the ordinary school; secondly, those who continue in these classes to confirmation; thirdly, those for whom these classes are found insufficient. Such after being tried for a time, are sent to special imbecile institutions; and fourthly, the utterly uneducable who, after a full trial, are dismissed to their homes. (ibid., p. 371)

Shuttleworth advocated the establishment of separate residential schools for the education of imbeciles and his views were accepted by the Commission, which included a reconstruction of his evidence (ibid., p. 710) as a quotation in the main body of the report (ibid., p. 101). Thus Shuttleworth did not appear to aspire to Norway's first two aims of either re-entry to ordinary schools or the attainment of a comparable level in the special class. Shuttleworth's goals were restricted. Inevitably, that implied a restriction upon the social experiences and potential of these pupils. Moreover, his arguments were persuasive and coherent from the Commission's perspective. He argued that there should be separate institutions because, first, the numbers of such pupils in any Elementary school would not make a class viable; second, specially skilled and experienced teachers were needed; third, they should be residential because progress depended equally upon care outside the classroom; and, fourth, the special developmental curriculum might be inappropriate to ordinary schools. He summarised his position: 'I do not think the education of imbeciles outside an institution would be efficient' (ibid., p. 711). He also advocated that a network of such institutions be established (ibid., p. 710). To be fair to the Commission, it must be remembered that there was already a tradition of segregated, institutionalised provision for the education of the blind and the deaf. Shuttleworth's proposals could be regarded as an extension of that and doubtless an improvement on such children being confined to asylums or workhouses. In this respect, the proposals must have implied some improvement in the social reproduction of disadvantages. But, at the same time, they also implied the confirmation of a status group with a particular lowly relationship to the market-place. Shuttleworth's proposals also indicate how history or tradition may influence the present.

EDUCATION OF FEEBLE-MINDED CHILDREN: WARNER'S AETIOLOGY

Dr Francis Warner's encounters with children as a paediatrician contrasted with those of a medical superintendent of an asylum for idiots and imbeciles. He presented his evidence from the basis that 'I have kept notes of cases the last ten or twelve years in connection with my work at children's hospitals and at the London Hospital ... the notes are cases of children who have been in Elementary schools and who have been admitted into the hospitals' (RCBDD, 1889, p. 698). The cases included children who had been dismissed from Elementary schools because, owing to some physical or mental defect, they had been judged incapable of being taught. The commonest group of out-patients not attending school were:

> such cases as children who occasionally have slight epileptic fits, perhaps three or four times in their life time, cases of slight chorea

[St Vitus's Dance], cases of children who suffer from repeated sick headaches, especially when attending school and who, on that ground, are exempted; children whose nerve system is completely exhausted and appears to have been so for months or years ... cases of nystagmus [oscillation of eye ball], cases of squinting; cases of myopia; cases of rickets, specially seen about the head with frequent co-incident nervous symptoms; and cases of diseased heart and lungs. (ibid.)

Such children, moreover, 'are often absent from school and from enquiries I have made in school, I believe they are often absent without any certificate at all' (ibid.). Warner gave an example he regarded as typical of many cases:

I may give an illustration of the class of child that I refer to: a little boy eight years of age, bright and intelligent in appearance, had lost both his parents; the mother died insane; he lived with his grandparents. He was liable to have such strong and sudden outbursts of passion as to be uncontrollable both at home and in the day school from which he had eventually been withdrawn as unmanageable. When removed to the country his health improved and he became good and quiet , but when he returned to London and his grandparents the quasi-epileptic outbursts of passion returned. He also suffered a few genuine epileptic fits and his younger sister also. When last heard of the child was neither being educated nor properly controlled, and although at present harmless and capable of being taught self-restraint, he is likely on arriving at manhood to be a social failure if not an absolute danger to the community. (ibid.)

Another similar case of a girl is repeated verbatim in the report (ibid., p. 105) from Warner's evidence (ibid., p. 700).

THE PART PLAYED BY ELEMENTARY EDUCATION

Warner maintained that the system of schools was the cause of children's failure for different reasons.

It is highly desirable that those engaged in conducting primary education should be aware of the common forms of mental and cerebral defect in children. If a teacher noticed that a child had a hare-lip and perhaps a little defect in his brain he would not beat that child. Children suffering from St Vitus's Dance are sometimes thrashed in school and after a few thrashings these nervous children will not attend any more. (ibid., p. 699)

Warner also believed the system of examination under the Revised Code for grant-earning purposes produced its own problems for these children:

In the first place, instead of their having to pass an examination, they should be excused from the ordinary examination … Many of them are really bright children though not capable of running through the ordinary curriculum. Some are what we term 'over mobile', they have plenty of intellectual power, but it is soon exhausted in the course of the curriculum work. (ibid., pp. 698–9)

Such children 'are not educated because they cannot be educated in large classes and they are constantly sent away from school for a year together; they may be on the books for education but they are not in school' (ibid., p. 698).

The numbers of such children he estimated as some 5 per cent:

out of 10,000 school children, probably something like five per cent out of the class to which I refer are not being educated … in our primary schools there is a class, consisting of something like five per cent, not capable of being educated under the present arrangements, and the conditions of those children are so special that they require exceptional methods of education. (ibid., pp. 698–9)

WARNER'S RECOMMENDATIONS

Warner suggested that there were two solutions to these difficulties: the first was to establish small special classes within Elementary schools and the second was to identify the children for these classes objectively. The fact that five per cent of children were not able to cope with the present Elementary school regime was in itself a sufficiently high figure to justify the establishment of special classes on educational grounds and on those of efficiency. Warner added: 'I am not speaking of London only, but of Birmingham and Liverpool and other towns' (RCBDD, 1889, p. 699).

The major difficulty in the establishment of these classes had been the absence of a means of identifying the children in need. 'Now the great drawback to dealing with this class of children hitherto has been the difficulty of picking them out' (ibid., p. 699). After spending more than ten years studying this problem, Warner believed he had devised a system whereby teachers themselves, without the services of medical officers, could identify these cases. Visiting the schools, 'the first points I note down are the signs of development as indicated by the proportions of the form and I also note any signs of defect. Now it is very common to see signs of bodily defect; you come across children with hare-lip ... Other signs are postures and movements' (ibid., p. 699). The system of identification entailed diagrams and models. He had been approached by 'the College of Preceptors, by the Education Society, by the Froebel Society and by the University of Cambridge, to give definite instruction upon this matter to those who are teachers or who are about to become teachers' (ibid., p. 699). In addition, he himself had made proposals to the London School Board. He went on to state that an ordinary student could be instructed in the system 'by half a dozen talks to him and half a dozen demonstrations in school' (ibid., p. 700). He added that he thought teachers would attend such classes voluntarily. Once identified, 'I would wish to see all such children together in small quiet classes in a classroom attached to the school under a carefully trained teacher' (ibid., p. 699).

WARNER'S CRITIQUE OF ELEMENTARY EDUCATION

Warner's evidence is at once both a critique and an indictment of the Elementary school system. First, it appears that teachers, for whatever reason, were ignoring or overlooking children with defective vision and hearing; second, children with nervous disorders were not necessarily treated with care in school; and, third, the system of payment by results, with its large, noisy classes and mechanical teaching techniques, magnified and attenuated the learning difficulties for this class of children. The report noted that, since Warner's testimony, in a survey of 2,716 children in seven schools, the British Medical Association found cases of nervousness, mental dullness, defective vision, malnutrition and signs of disease and paralysis in proportions which fluctuated around Warner's estimate (RCBDD, 1889, p. 106).

MOBERLY'S EVIDENCE TO THE COMMISSION

Warner had approached the London School Board with his system for the identification of children in need. Major-General F. J. Moberly was summoned to give evidence as chairman of the Board's sub-committee on the blind, deaf and dumb. The bulk of his nine pages of evidence concerns such children. Less than a third of one page, however, records his interrogation on the education of 'idiots' in the schools. The interrogator is not concerned about how or where such children are educated but whether a medically qualified person makes the decision that the girl or boy is to be classified as an idiot. Having established that the Board endeavours to have a 'medical man' [*sic*] on every committee of managers and that his duty is to advise the committee and not to inspect the schools, a member of the Commission remarked: 'You have at the present moment a certain number of children in your schools who are called idiots by your masters but not by a medical officer?' (ibid., p. 873). Moberly replied: 'I do not know what would be gained by the medical examination of each child. The master judges of the educability of the child' (ibid.). He goes on to remark: 'If a child is at school, it is easy to see what the condition of the child is. It is the children not at school that we do not know of' (ibid.). The Commission member persisted and revealed another problematic area when observing that 'first of all, there is a certain number that cannot be educated and those are classed among the idiots, who settles the question whether a child is an idiot? Is it the schoolmaster or a trained medical man?' (ibid.). Moberly replied that 'most of those children are at home and the visitor who schedules a child in his census is informed by the parents that they have been told that the child is not fit for school by a medical man or other authority' (ibid.). Moberly conceded that conventionally the parent's word was accepted and that a medical certificate was not a prerequisite.

There are several different inferences which may be drawn from this evidence. First, Moberly's interest and knowledge of special cases of children may have been confined to the blind and deaf. His brother, General A. S. Moberly also gave evidence to the Commission as secretary to the Workshops for the Blind of Kent. Second, Moberly may have had genuine faith in the teacher's ability to distinguish the educable from others. His choice of terminology is telling here in that while the Commission member leads on several occasions with 'idiot', Moberly replies in terms of 'children', 'cases' and 'educable'. Third, Moberly may have condoned or been ignorant of the situation in Elementary schools which Warner had outlined. Fourth, there may have been a desire on the part of the Commission member to establish the fact that idiots may be so designated without medical inspection. This, in turn, could have been a preliminary to arguing that the role of medical personnel on school management committees should be extended from that of advice to the committee to inspection of the pupils. The conversational exchange and the terminology also illustrate the struggle between the discourse of education and that of medical science to objectify the subject.

THE COMMISSION'S RECOMMENDATIONS

The Commission's report noted the effects of the Idiots Act, 1886, which facilitated and enlarged the numbers of children admitted to asylums. Until this Act, a child could only be admitted to an asylum if the parents and two doctors had been prepared to certify the child under the Lunacy Acts and thus endure the social stigma and legal disabilities which this entailed (cf., Jones, 1972; Scull, 1979). Under the Idiots Act, 1886, a single parent could apply for certification and the child could be admitted to an asylum if he or she was certified as an imbecile by one medical statement (RCBDD, 1889, pp. 92–3).

'The tentative tone of the Commissioners' recommendations about mentally defective children contrasted sharply with the assurance and detail of their proposals for the blind, deaf and dumb children' (Sutherland, 1984, p. 17). The recommendations were in two sections and directed at two classes: feeble-minded children and imbeciles. 'Feeble-minded children ... should be separated from ordinary scholars in public elementary schools in order that they may receive special instruction and ... the attention of school authorities be particularly directed towards this object' (RCBDD, 1889, p. 106). Thus Warner's criticism of the school system and advocacy of small, quiet, separate classes in Elementary schools appear to have been accepted. With regard to imbeciles, the report recommended that the school attendance officer should be required to notify all such cases and obtain a medical certificate upon their educability. 'On the receipt of such a certificate and on the application of a parent, the school authority should have the power and be required to send the child to an institution and contribute to its education and maintenance' (ibid.). Further, institutions for educable imbeciles should be carefully classed and separated. Finally, any ineducable imbeciles should be established jointly or severally by education authorities. Within institutions, imbeciles should be removed from workhouses or lunatic asylums and relocated in these institutions. In this respect, the Commission appeared to endorse Shuttleworth's typology of imbecile children capable of being taught to read and write or learning moral behaviour and also his blueprint for their education or improvement.

CONTRAST BETWEEN SHUTTLEWORTH AND WARNER

Shuttleworth's book, entitled *Mentally Deficient Children: Their Treatment and Training,* was first published in 1895. The second edition, published in 1900, was considerably enlarged and included an extensive criticism of Warner's methodology. In one sense this was anomalous, since each appeared to concentrate upon a different audience: Warner upon children's education in Elementary schools and Shuttleworth on those educable in institutions outside the Elementary system. Alternatively, Shuttleworth may have regarded Warner as detaining or deflecting pupil recruits to his special institutions. Shuttleworth's book flourished and appeared in a fifth edition in 1925. Thus for a further 30 years at least, Shuttleworth's presence was strongly felt in this field.

There is a further curiosity regarding Warner's and Shuttleworth's relative contributions to this area of work. Pritchard, who is regarded by another commentator as having produced an 'excellent study in 1963 upon which so many authors have relied for brief historical résumés' (Cole, 1989, p. 2), and by yet another as very rarely making an error of fact (Sutherland, 1984, p. 9), chooses to discuss the Commission's recommendations regarding the feeble-minded without any reference at all to Warner's evidence. He then proceeds to record incorrectly that 'the Commission did little more than repeat Shuttleworth's view that [the feeble-minded] should be educated in auxiliary schools' (Pritchard, 1963, p. 107).

The Commission seemed to accept the idea that there was a gradation or perhaps a continuum of children with mental defects. There were four classes: first, the 'weak-minded' or 'backward' (RCBDD, 1889, p. 104); second, 'those capable of learning to read and write'; third, 'those capable of benefiting in a minor degree by school instruction and discipline'; and, fourth, 'the ineducable class' (ibid., p. 97). The first class constituted the 'feeble-minded' and the second and third the 'educable imbeciles'. Warner had a clear aetiology for the feeble-minded class. These children were products of the combination of social and personal circumstances in their interactions with the dominant system of Elementary schools. Shuttleworth's aetiology was clinical. Imbeciles were the product of physiological circumstances before or after birth. Warner's prescriptions for an amelioration of the condition of the feeble-minded were a combination of modifications within the children's schooling and a closer examination of their personal and social environments. Shuttleworth's prescriptions for the educable imbeciles were physiotherapy exercises and a restricted vocational curriculum. The ineducable were to be removed from the system. Shuttleworth's children appeared to be an organic feature of society, in so far as they had their existence within society. Warner's children were a product of particular features of society.

In terms of social reproduction, Warner's position appears much more open than Shuttleworth's. Warner can be interpreted as attempting to break the mould of the reproduction of sets of disadvantages for a particular group of children and employing education as a tool to enhance life-chances and experiences. Shuttleworth's position is more restricted. For the higher grades of imbecile, he appears to attempt to enhance their future potential. But this is within a context where the ceilings of their potential and their social destinations are taken for granted. Shuttleworth's system locks his clients into an almost inevitable experience of the social reproduction of sets of disadvantages. Warner's clients need not necessarily become a particular status group but Shuttleworth's almost certainly will. Shuttleworth's recommendations for treatment reinforce the traditional mode of treatment for children who are regarded as special cases.

There are other contrasts between Warner and Shuttleworth. Warner received a traditional education in medicine and became a professor of anatomy and physiology. He published little and mostly in the form of articles in the period 1882–96. Shuttleworth also graduated in medicine in London and then took a masters degree in medicine at the University of Heidelberg. He published extensively between 1895 and 1925. From his period in Germany, he developed a strong interest in the new science of medical psychology. The difference between the two in terms of their professional work was that, from the outset, Shuttleworth worked in settings intended for the mentally defective, be it an asylum or an institution for improvable imbeciles. Warner, however, as a paediatrician, constantly saw children as out-patients or in his visits to schools where inevitably he would encounter the complete range of human potential. Paradoxically, it appears that the more traditionally trained Warner supported the more socially revolutionary ideas, whereas Shuttleworth with his immersion in a newer science appeared to support more reactionary ideas.

AN ALTERNATIVE INTERPRETATION

The foregoing, however, and particularly the differences between Shuttleworth and Warner, can be re-examined from a different theoretical perspective. One part of Michel Foucault's work attempted to explore the historical transition in so-called 'civilised' societies from the external autocratic and idosyncratic exercise of punishment to the internalised, rule-governed application of civil laws (Foucault, 1977). Two processes are central to this transition: normalisation and surveillance. Normalisation describes the process whereby individuals are distributed around a norm in 'a system of finely gradated and measurable intervals' (Rabinow, 1991, p. 20). The norm is the socially accepted standard. The norm simultaneously organises and controls the distribution, which together allocates individuals to their station. Surveillance is one of the disciplinary technologies. 'Foucault selects Jeremy Bentham's plan for the [penitentiary] panopticon as the paradigm of a disciplinary technology' (ibid., p. 18). The panopticon represents 'a particular organisation of space and human beings, a visual order that clarifies the mechanisms of power which are deployed' (ibid). From a continuous, physical but often invisible overseeing, surveillance of norms becomes a continuous and anonymous (because detached from any individual) process: 'this machine is one in which everyone is caught, those who exercise power as well as those who are subjected to it' (Foucault, 1982, p. 208).

The contrast between Shuttleworth's and Warner's views can be interpreted as evidence of the struggle between discourses seeking to objectify the subject in different ways. Shuttleworth interprets the subject primarily in medical terms and, drawing upon the science of the mind, seeks to locate the process of identification and treatment away from the public arena and into a specialist domain. Warner treats the subject primarily as a patient and here there is scope for the schoolteacher to determine an educational norm for the distribution of pupils. Moberly, as an outsider in professional terms to both medicine and teaching, stands in the middle. The dispute about the constituent elements of the norm is crucial, however, because the outcome determines the economy of distribution.

CONCLUSIONS

The Egerton Commission made recommendations for the educational provision for the blind and the deaf which quickly became the basis for Acts of Parliament. Firm recommendations for the other category were not made but deferred to the deliberations of a subsequent Departmental Committee. The Commission received conflicting evidence from leading experts on children's mental dispositions. One presented an account which was also, in part, a critique of the Elementary education system; the other account based upon a relativistic scheme of personal mental capacities was preferred. The debate, however, was to surface again in the deliberations of the Departmental Committee on Defective and Epileptic Children. These deliberations will form the next focus of attention, following an empirical diversion to explore the estimate of the number of children considered to be in this category and an account of the formation of the first special classes.

5

Estimates of the School Population Needing Special Classes and the Formation of the First Special Classes

The previous chapter set out the nature of the dispute between leading protagonists regarding the nature and origin of candidates for special classes. The dispute was such that there was no legislation for provision for those pupils, unlike the deaf and the blind. Nevertheless, these pupils continued to be a feature in the education system. At this point, therefore, two questions are pertinent: first, how large a proportion of the school population did these pupils form? This would give some measure of the extent of the difficulties; and, second, how did School Boards react to the situation in the absence of legislation? The account which follows is largely constructed from evidence presented to the Departmental Committee on Defective and Epileptic Children (DCDEC), whose report was published in 1898, some nine years after the Egerton Commission.

DEFINITION OF 'FEEBLE-MINDED'

The DCDEC felt obliged to continue to use the term 'feeble-minded' because it had been included in its terms of reference (DCDEC, 1898, p. 3). However, it made it clear that 'feeble-minded' denotes only those children who were not imbecile and who could not properly be taught in ordinary Elementary schools by ordinary methods. Further, it took the term 'defective' to include 'mentally normal children who, by reason of physical defect, cannot properly be taught in ordinary schools' (ibid.). Thus, 'defective denotes those children who are not imbecile and who, whether by reason of mental or physical defect cannot properly be taught in ordinary Elementary schools by ordinary methods'. It is important to note that with regard to the definition of 'feeble-minded' it is defined negatively rather than positively; it identifies what the subjects are not rather than

86

what they are. There are different kinds of definition. An explicit definition gives a meaning of a word or category which is independent of either. On the other hand, a contextual definition gives the 'meaning of a word by showing how it functions in a context' (Salmon, 1963, p. 92). Thus the 'feeble-minded' are defined in the context of not being 'idiots' or 'imbeciles'. The defining characteristics of the feeble-minded are not included. The existence of the definition is itself, in Foucauldian terms, the potential basis for the establishment of a dividing practice.

GERMAN AUXILIARY SCHOOLS

The first indication of the numbers of feeble-minded pupils in the school population came from Germany, where 'help' or 'auxiliary' classes were first opened in 1867. Around 1880, the German minister of education had called upon towns with more than 20,000 inhabitants to set up such classes. Admission to auxiliary classes was restricted to children who after two years in a state Elementary school had proved themselves incapable of doing the work. However, epileptics, juvenile criminals, children with deficient sight or hearing and children backward through illness or irregular attendance were excluded (DCDEC, 1898, vol. II, p. 249). Judging from the towns where returns were available, '0.95 per cent were pupils ... in auxiliary classes'. Further, from a combination of the size of auxiliary classes and from the total school population, the German government appeared to have judged that 1 per cent of children were feeble-minded (ibid., p. 5). The situation was thought to be similar in England.

ASSESSMENT OF THE POSITION IN ENGLAND

In February 1897, the Education Department had commissioned HMI in rural districts to collect information concerning feeble-minded children from the different School Boards. These returns were considered accurate and often 'the inspector seems to have verified the return with the managers' (DCDEC, 1898, vol. II, p. 200). That was not the case with the returns from the large towns: 'the numbers are somewhat vitiated by the extreme reluctance on the part of a good many Voluntary schools, especially Roman Catholic schools, to give their figures. They seem to be under the apprehension that there was a desire to withdraw their children from their schools and I had a considerable amount of difficulty in getting accurate figures' (ibid., p. 223).

TABLE 5.1
PROPORTION OF FEEBLE-MINDED PUPILS CALCULATED FROM
SCHOOL BOARD RETURNS, 1897

| School Board | Number | | Per cent |
	Total school population	Feeble-minded	feeble-minded
London Greenwich	67,690	482	0.7
London Deptford	3,987	58	1.45
Birmingham	87,500	800	0.9
Brighton	19,000	96	1.0
Bradford	10,000	117	1.1
Leicester	21,000	236	1.2
Bristol	17,818	180	0.9
Rural districts	29,446	281	0.95
Large towns	846,000	3,150	0.37

Source: DCDEC (1898, vol. I, pp. 5–6; vol. II, p. 68).

The Committee estimated that '[a]pproximately one percent of the children of the public Elementary school class appear to be feeble-minded' (ibid., p. 5). From an analysis of the data presented in the table, the Committee considered that 'the estimate … appears sufficiently probable to be adopted for practical purposes'. The statistics, however, were a product of the policies and actions of teachers and School Boards. Hence they are a reflection of the questions of how feeble-minded children may be best identified and educated. The answer to these questions may be found, first, in the circumstances which led to the establishment of particular special classes and, second, in the organisation of the special classes.

FEEBLE-MINDED CHILDREN IN OTHER URBAN AREAS

The Committee commissioned three HMI to examine the educational provision for feeble-minded children in the towns and cities in the South-West, the Midlands and the North. Information concerning Plymouth came from this source. The Inspectors' findings were fairly consistent whether they related to Liverpool, Newcastle, Leeds, Plymouth, Norwich, Aston, Reading, Merthyr Tydfil or Swansea. The first was a belief that there was a considerable underestimation of the incidence of feeble-minded children in the school population. For instance, 'In the case of Hull, it appeared to me from the scant remarks that accompanied the return that it was compiled chiefly from the School Board returns and that the clerk was not very much inclined to believe in the existence of feeble-minded children, or at any rate, to a very small extent indeed' (ibid., p. 223). Another cause of under-reporting has already been mentioned, that of an apprehension on the part of Voluntary schools that some of their pupils may be taken from them.

Second, in urban areas such as Manchester, Liverpool and Leeds there were no special classes as such, but there were industrial schools where the curricular emphasis was on practical preparation for adult work. There were five such schools in Liverpool. The returns for these schools had not been included in Liverpool's original return to HMI. However, 'the figures of those now obtained … may perhaps be of some interest. They are as follows: number on rolls in industrial schools, 849 children; defective children, 21 or 2.5 per cent' (ibid., p. 224). The inference was that feeble-minded children were squeezed from the Elementary school system into the industrial schools. The other harbours in Liverpool for some children were the so-called 'private adventure' schools. 'The private schools, judging from the reports on them by special examiners appointed by the Board, are largely a refuge for delicate children … [Returns show]: number of children on rolls of private adventure schools, 1,108; defective children, 23 giving 2 per cent' (ibid.). Such private schools would not be subject to the regime of the Code.

One industrial school wished to find out whether dullness and deafness in children were related. An experiment was undertaken. First, 'the teachers were asked to divide the children into three classes: good, fair and bad. Every child was then tested by the doctor according to their power to hear the tick of a watch held in turn for each ear, 60 inches being taken as the normal limit for that watch' (ibid., p. 226). The results are reported in Table 5.2. However crude the experiment, it appears to point conclusively to a relationship between children's assessed attainment and the sharpness of their hearing faculty.

TABLE 5.2
AVERAGE HEARING DISTANCE BY CLASS OF PUPIL

Pupil classification by teacher	Number of pupils	Percentage of pupils	Average mean hearing distance in inches
Good	89	43.8	51
Fair	52	25.6	47
Bad	62	30.5	31
TOTAL	203	100	–

Source: DCDEC (1898, vol. II, pp. 226–7).

The third finding was that in the absence of special classes, the urban Boards adopted one of three policies. The first was that feeble-minded children were retained in Standard 0 classes: 'these defective children are mixed up with dull and backward children ... in school in what is commonly called Standard 0' (ibid., p. 224). The second and third are as follows, according to the HMI: 'I find two plans going; [the feeble-minded] are either kept in Standard I – the worst of all plans to my mind, or scattered through the school according to age and physical development, which is a better plan, though not so good as special classes' (ibid.). Allied to all these three policies, was the Boards' lack of emphasis upon ensuring children's attendance at school and casual exemptions from school attendance. 'The general conclusion of the returns is that attendance is fairly satisfactory but it is not very zealously encouraged ... in Liverpool, no formal tests are attempted [for exemption from school]. The decision is sometimes left to the teachers, sometimes to the visitors ... sometimes it is left in the hands of the attendance officers who ... report to their superintendent' (ibid.).

The fourth finding appeared to go to the core of the problem. 'Out of twenty two towns from which I have returns, only six have yet practically faced the question; a few affect to disbelieve in any serious amount of defect, and the majority either regard it as insufficient to call for immediate action or have shelved the question for a time' (ibid. p. 226). In sum 'there is general public apathy on the subject' (ibid.). In the midst of this, there was an observation on teachers' attitudes. 'In talking with teachers on the subject', an HMI remarked, 'I found that many of them take a curious attitude. They seem to think that the Elementary school is the best place for these children and that three or four years in a preparatory class which is generally under the weakest teacher in the school, is the proper place for feeble-minded children. They think that so long as the children are treated with kindness, everything that is possible has been done for them' (ibid.). *Plus ça change!* (see HMI, 1990, pp. 14–15).

The fifth finding, however, may have been the root of the apathy and concerned finance. In some of the places where special classes had been established, there was considerable caution and reservation concerning incurring additional financial expenditure. In addition, there was, on occasion, a lack of sympathy on the Board's part and a desire not to be seen to be doing too much (cf., the Brighton Board, p. 108 below). On top of this, an HMI could give credit to atavistic and racist opinions such as those expressed in Birmingham:

the Roman Catholic schools are peopled very largely by Irish; Irish who have been there three or four generations – Irish who came over at the time of the famine of 1848 and have since been degrading very rapidly through drink; and the priests tell me that the effects come out in the third generation and there is no doubt that among that low class Irish population there are a considerable number of defective children. (DCDEC, 1898, vol. II, p. 224)

With options such as this in evidence, the Board perhaps felt justified in its inaction.

The sixth observation was that if the financial question could be resolved, then the apathy might evaporate. However, as one HMI remarked: 'I think unless a fairly substantial grant were given there might be a good deal of hesitation to make as much provision as is necessary in many towns' (ibid.). If the question of the grant could be resolved, then '[i]t is pretty clear that most [Boards] will be prepared to act heartily when their responsibility is brought home to them ... and would probably in all cases, when once their duty was shown and some guidance given, set up special classes.' Thus HMI believed there was a strong case for legislation in the interests of feeble-minded children, as there was for the blind and the deaf.

FEEBLE-MINDED CHILDREN IN RURAL AREAS

The Committee had again commissioned three HMI to examine the situation of feeble-minded children in a sample of rural areas in the South. The first point made was a belief that many imbecile and feeble-minded children were not recorded in the returns. 'The severely defective do not usually attend school' (ibid., p. 201). Nor did they attend any other kind of institution. Furthermore, 'the local authorities put on no pressure [to attend school] for two reasons: In the first place, I do not believe they put much pressure on anybody; and secondly, in the case of a child of that kind, they feel they would probably not be supported by the magistrates if they did' (ibid., p. 202). Exemption from attendance was usually a matter for the attendance officer. 'The attendance officer himself seems to decide ... whether a child is defective or not' (ibid.). It was only in cases where the mother and the attendance officer were in disagreement, which was very rare, that a third person was called upon. In such cases a medical certification might be demanded.

Village schools in rural areas already faced difficulties because of the small number of children, the span of children's ages and the small number of teachers. As a rule, any feeble-minded children shared classes with the other children. A change of emphasis within the curriculum to, say, manual work would be difficult because 'in cottage gardening, to do it, you must take some teacher from the work of the school, but that, in these small schools where the staff is small, is impossible' (ibid., p. 204). The only possibilities were activities such as macramé, netting or basket-making at a separate table where the teacher could keep a supervisory eye. The feeble-minded pupils were present in the class, but not a part of it in any other sense. Whatever individual attention they did receive was 'very little and often at the hands of a monitor; but they are kindly treated' (ibid., p. 201). The prevailing attitude can be seen in the following: 'Often in schools, cases are pointed out of children exceedingly dull or backward with the remark, "what that boy likes is to get away with the horses" or on the farm or the garden or something like that' (ibid., p. 203). The outcome is almost inevitable: 'The conclusion is that [the feeble-minded] receive scarcely any instruction which is likely to be of benefit to them in their future life. So far as my experience goes little trouble is taken with them' (ibid., p. 201). The only light which appears relates to Voluntary rather than Board schools. 'There seem to be indications that [the feeble-minded] were more readily admitted in Voluntary schools which I should account for by the fact that the financial pressure is greater and also that the managers have more personal knowledge of the families' (ibid., p. 202).

The dilemma which the education of the feeble-minded child in rural areas presented was skilfully articulated by the Committee's chairman. The small number in each area did not justify special resources. Was it then in the best interests of the child to be uprooted and placed in a residential institution? On balance, it was thought that the majority was better fitted for future life by living at home in family life and experiencing all the circumstances of rural life and labour among their own people. The alternative would draft them away to an institution which would neccessarily be very different in its arrangements from the ordinary rural home. All the manual work there would be of a more specialised nature and under constant supervision. Eventually, after a few years, they would return to conditions which were now unfamiliar and to people who had ceased to be friends and 'who know the returner only as having come from a "silly" school' (ibid., p. 202). Work in the countryside had to be done without immediate supervision and in a manner traditional in the neighbourhood, if it was not to be despised or suspected. The clinching argument was the belief that uprooting children would be likely to meet resistance from their parents.

However, the Committee also felt that there might be some difficult cases concerning feeble-minded children in rural areas such as related to poverty or a poor family background. Here there was an argument for a large body, such as that of the county council, which would relieve the district councils of their responsibilities in this regard. This would offer a degree of detachment from individual cases and the chance to employ better-qualified and experienced personnel for the work. Medical expertise could be drawn upon as could a wider range of industrial experience.

A MEASURE OF EFFECTIVENESS OF THE SPECIAL CLASSES

TABLE 5.3
DESTINATION OF PUPILS FROM SPECIAL CLASSES
IN LONDON AND ELSEWHERE BY NUMBER AND PERCENTAGE

Destination	Pupils from 24 specials classes in London		Pupils from 12 special classes elsewhere	
	Number	%	Number	%
Ordinary schools	193	39	65	41
Other institutions for blind, deaf etc.	38	8	16	10
Employment	49	10	29	18
Home	40	8	29	18
Dead	10	2	5	3
Unknown	163	33	16	10
TOTAL	493	100	160	100

Source: DCDEC (1898, vol. II, pp. 1254–9).

The Committee sent a survey to teachers of special classes which included a section on the future destination of pupils. There were 24 replies from teachers in London and 12 from outside London. Given that there were only 21 centres in London in 1896 and few elsewhere, the returns may be regarded as substantial. Precise analysis is difficult because of the high rate of unknown destinations in London. That may well be a simple product of the relative complexity of the London system and its detachment from the schools. The special classes in London and elsewhere share a relatively high rate in returning children to ordinary school at roughly two out of five. The return to employment in London is about half of that elsewhere. That could be a comment upon the difference between the nature of employment in the capital or it could be a product of the unknown destination factor. The variation in the rate of children whose destination is the home environment is the reverse of that of employment. That could be explained either by a difference of severity of feeble-mindedness or the relative lack of suitable employment outside London. If the categories of return to ordinary school and employment are aggregated, then special schools outside London achieve a higher success rate of six out of ten as opposed to five out of ten.

The survey also threw up another interesting observation: 'Most – about three-fourths – of the 36 teachers have noticed children who appeared to be non-educable when admitted, but afterwards turned out to be educable. Several teachers say that such cases have been common' (ibid., p. 255). Either that is a comment by teachers who are seeking to praise their personal skills, which is unlikely given the large proportion, or it is a comment upon the system of ordinary Elementary schools and its enfolding context.

REACTIONS OF INDIVIDUAL SCHOOL BOARDS: THE FIRST SPECIAL
CLASSES AND SCHOOLS

The intention in this section is to pursue empirically the problem articulated in Chapter 4 regarding the deliberations of the Egerton Commission. The expert witnesses formulated in different ways the source of the difficulties which those pupils struggling to learn faced, but the formulation was considered inadequate to make firm regulations for the School Boards. However, the fact remained that the Boards were still confronted with the problem of what measures to take on behalf of these pupils. What measures to take and what guided their thinking were therefore the two questions pursued through the evidence presented to the Departmental Committee from those Boards who had already made provision in the form of special classes or centres. These empirical data inform the analysis in the next chapter. Seven School Boards had established special classes or centres.

The First Special Class at Leicester

There are two different accounts of the origins of the first special class, which took place in Leicester. The physician to the London Hospital states in his evidence to the Committee that the chairman of the Leicester School

Board sent a child to him with a request for an examination. The chairman was frustrated because doctors would not certify the child as an imbecile so that he could be admitted to an asylum, but he could scarcely be retained in school because of his troublesome nature. The physician's judgment was that he should look for other similar cases in the town and consider setting up a special class. The physician was Dr Warner (DCDEC, 1898, vol. II, p. 32). The alternative account was offered by the inspector of the Leicester School Board, who had observed from his work in schools 'that there were some children who were not imbecile on the one hand, nor merely dull in the estimation of the teachers, on the other hand' (ibid., p. 133). The two accounts are not necessarily in conflict. What may be important, is that the inspector was working in the interests of the Leicester Board and its teachers.

On the basis of his observations in schools, the inspector asked the Board to consider the problem. The outcome was that 'we asked the teachers in the schools in the first instance to send to the office all such children as they thought ought to be in a special school. They sent about 400' (ibid.). It may be inferred from the first 'we' that the Board and the inspector were working in harmony. A committee, consisting of five members of the Board, by inspection and examination reduced the 400 to 12 children. These 12 were then examined by the inspector, and, if necessary, a doctor who was a member of the Board and the doctor who was medical officer to the Board.

The inspector described the procedures adopted in this and subsequent cases:

> The child comes to me and I notice what his age may be. Then I take a book fitted to the age of the child, if he be a normal one, and ask him to talk about the pictures and if I can get from him fairly intelligent answers, and if he count up a few numbers from objects in the pictures, and can talk about his brothers and sisters, his father and mother and also if he can read a little – a word or two, and count up to three, then I come to a judgement as to whether I ought to recommend the committee to send him to the special class or not. If I do, and the case be a doubtful one medically, I then refer him to the medical officer. (ibid., p. 134)

In this instance, medical expertise serves the interest of facilitating an educational judgment.

The 12 pupils were accommodated in the classroom of a school in the centre of the town. The central location was important as only four others were excluded because of the distance of travel. Over five years, the special class received 33 pupils and there happened to be 12 on the roll in 1897. Of the 33, seven had returned to ordinary schools and a further seven went out to work. Discounting the 12 currently in the class, these 14 constituted two-thirds of the rest. The Leicester Board appears to have done good work for its feeble-minded children.

Physical disability was not a criterion for entry to the special class. If the disabled could get to a school then the school was expected to make appropriate accommodation in its building and curriculum (ibid., p. 137).

The inspector agreed that there was probably a proportionate number of feeble-minded children in the Voluntary schools, that the Board's numbers would increase in parallel with the increase in the population, and that the central class would probably have to be relocated in classes in the north and south of the town.

There was one teacher and an assistant for the 12 pupils. 'The first teacher was chosen from the infant schools as one who was very clever in kindergarten and very sympathetic in her treatment of infants' (ibid., p. 134). The assistant had been trained by the head. Subsequently, the teacher 'has been succeeded by a similar one; but neither had any special training' (ibid., p. 135). The inspector offered little detail of the curriculum and was not asked to do so. The classroom had been adapted as far as was possible. There were 'a few desks around the walls and there are cages for doves and canaries and a tortoise is kept' (ibid.). Flowers and animal life were intended to make the room as bright as possible and the children as happy as possible. The lessons were described as 'very much shorter' and 'more manual work than in other schools'. Over time, the emphasis had shifted from 'manual work' to 'industrial work' (ibid.).

One Committee member was concerned at the low number of pupils in the special class. By questioning, he established that potential pupils were reported to the inspector either by the teachers from school or by the school visitors. The inspector accepted for admission a proportion of 'one or two out of a dozen' reported as special cases. In addition, teachers 'have not had instructions of a very formal character of the sort of children which should be recommended.' Finally, the inspector made it clear that he only called in the medical officer as a final resort and added that, in the past, doctors had made errors of judgment. He assessed children 'principally by their intelligence as judged by the answers to questions put to them … [and] I think that a good deal shows itself or does not show itself, in the face whilst the child is being examined' (ibid., p. 136).

If there is ambiguity surrounding the reason for the foundation of the

Leicester special class, the principles which oversaw admissions and the conduct of the class appear unambiguous. The criteria for admission were overwhelmingly educational and medicine played a subordinate supporting role. The class's success in this early stage is also striking. In terms of social reproduction, this is clearly an attempt to overcome whatever disadvantages the child might bring to school and only to concede that with a very small hard-core the child's condition will restrict opportunities. Moreover, the inspector made it clear that a relative judgment was usually involved: 'I think the whole question is relative. It seems to me that you cannot draw a hard and fast line between the child we specially cater for, on one side or on the other' (ibid.).

The Leicester School Board had also sought to tackle the problem of the social reproduction of disadvantages by virtue of another of its policies. With regard to children with learning difficulties, it operated what may be termed a tiered system in its Elementary schools because each school contained a Standard 0. This Standard contained children who were not progressing at their peers' rate. Such children might be 'relatively feeble-minded' in the inspector's opinion. Each of the Standard 0 classes had its own teacher but the size of the class 'very much varies with the character of the school ... There are some schools that are in almost a middle-class neighbourhood where there are very few of them indeed- only three or four out of 600 ... we have other schools in the slums where there is quite a fair class – fifteen or twenty' (ibid.). Social and economic factors tend to predominate in these children's circumstances. 'They are cases not of congenital want of development or arrested development, as in the case of some of our cases in the special class, but are cases of children who have come in as navvies' children in the building of the railways, and immigrants from country districts where they are not very well looked after, and cases of scarlet fever and arrested development along these lines' (ibid.). Thus the causal factors were economic migration and disabilities arising from living conditions. Additionally and progressively, however, Standard 0 children were not kept in isolation from other children: 'they have special provision in the smallness of the class and the care of the teacher in the ordinary schools ... but not to a very great extent. They do their writing and their arithmetic with the others' (ibid., p. 137). This must be clear evidence of an attempt to break down the process of the social reproduction of sets of disadvantages and to hinder the formation of a status group dependent solely upon the dictates of the market-place. The inspector, too, appears comfortable and confident in his relationship with the medical profession. He takes the position that judgments concerning the feeble-minded are relative and that informs his formulation of policy and his actions. He was, in fact, a graduate in medicine, from 'the London University, but I don't think it helps me very much' (ibid., p. 138).

London Board's System of Special Centres for Instruction

If the setting-up of the special class by the Leicester Board is characterised by speed and spontaneity then, in contrast, the actions of the London Board appear much more deliberate. The vice-chairman of the Board, who was also chairman of the sub-committee for deaf and blind children, stated that the establishment of special classes was the product of the conjuncture of an ethical principle and a particular child's condition. Moberly stated that 'I was aroused to the idea generally that we were responsible for all the children of London ... some years ago, and then I came upon a child ... that I could not get sent to [an asylum]. The medical officer of the Board of Guardians would not certify her as sufficiently an idiot to be sent to Darenth and they could not teach her in an ordinary school' (DCDEC, 1898, vol. II, p. 101). Subsequently, he was able to place her in a private school where she rapidly advanced to become of practical service to her mother.

Although in 1890 the School Management Committee at first accepted and then rejected his motion to open a special class in Capland Street school, in 1891 the London Board resolved, in the words of the Egerton Commission, that classes be established for pupils who 'from special circumstances would seem to require exceptional methods of education'. An experiment was agreed to set up three schools of special instruction. Mrs E. M. Burgwin who, as headmistress of a London Board school, had given evidence of her difficulties to the Cross Commission (RCEEA, 1887, pp. 113–26) was appointed Superintendent of Schools for Special Instruction. As Moberly remarked: 'We started it then systematically, engaged Mrs Burgwin and opened more than one classroom (DCDEC, 1898, vol. II, p. 101). The system expanded rapidly and the Correspondent for Special Schools in London reported that 'in March 1896, twenty-one centres for special instruction were open having a roll of 896' (ibid., p. 48). A year later, Mrs Burgwin informed the Committee that there were 1,012 on the roll (ibid., p. 101). Moberly observed that the development of the special schools was patchy geographically and estimated that, with a school-age population numbering some 800,000, London would need some 12,000 places (ibid.). This was based upon the estimate that one and a half per cent of the school population would need such education. This estimate coincided with the figure which emerged from Warner's examination of 100,000 London children between 1888 and 1896 and reported to the British Association (ibid., p. 28).

Whether by reason of Moberly's military background or by virtue of the large numbers of children involved, the solution to the problem of feeble-minded children in London's schools was conceived as the establishment of a new system of school centres and personnel. The basis of the system was the belief that 'it would be better to build one large centre with three or four class rooms than a greater number of small centres all over London' (ibid., p. 102). A map of London had been drawn up which indicated where special centres might be advantageously placed because 'it is economical to build new schools and special centres together', and because 'we have placed them in such sites that they should be more easily fed by surrounding schools' (ibid., p. 101). Only 'in the outlying districts of London, we should have one or two classrooms instead of the larger establishments we have in the more central parts' (ibid., p. 104). Finally, the system would be completed by the establishment of residential centres to overcome difficulties of travel or domestic circumstances. Thus the London Board would 'prefer an institution or arrangement for boarding out in the neighbourhood of a special class' (ibid., p. 103). It was also seeking a government grant to establish and maintain such institutions (ibid.).

The superintendent of Schools for Special Instruction had been recruited from one of the Board's schools. The process of selection of teachers for the classes was as follows: '[G]enerally a member of the committee goes to see them at work in their [London Board's] school and if they show any aptitude for the purpose, they are entertained, and then they are sent to one or other of the schools that are actually at work to see what is the process of teaching' (ibid., p. 102). Teachers who were so recruited to special classes reported that 'it is much more interesting than ordinary work and there is scarcely a teacher that takes to it that does not have a sincere affection for it' (ibid., p. 82). This was despite the fact that the Board had initially decided to limit the term of appointment to five years because teachers would be worn out by then and promotion would be out of the question. In compensation, however, the Correspondent for London's Special Schools indicated that they received higher salaries (ibid., p. 49). There was no headteacher as such in these separate centres but a 'teacher in charge'. The chain of command was such that 'the senior teacher is responsible for the centre to the Superintendent; and the Superintendent is responsible to the Board' (ibid., pp. 49–50). Thus there was a separate and different organisation of small groups of teachers without any headteachers under the control and guidance of a single superintendent. The superintendent was also able to make crucial decisions on pupils' future destinations.

The special centres were also differentiated internally. The reason given by Moberly was that 'my idea was originally to classify as much as we could because I felt there was an immense variety of children that we should have to deal with and immense variety of capacity amongst them' (ibid., p. 101). The three teachers from a special centre who gave evidence to the Committee indicated how the 79 children on the roll had been divided into classes. The prime criterion was 'their future ability of earning their living'. On this basis, about one half was considered to be 'totally self-supporting' and about four fifths of the remainder to be 'partially self-supporting'. A small rump, 'while they are not idiots, they still certainly would not be able to earn their own living' (ibid., p. 79). Within these divided classes, there were also further divisions. The most able group was divided for manual work, reading and arithmetic, although the teacher aimed at individual work as far as possible. The other two classes were divided on the basis that 'they do their manual work together' (sewing, painting, etc.) but were split up 'for reading and counting' (ibid., p. 80). One teacher had been with her class for two years, during which time 'eight had been returned to ordinary school, one to [an asylum] and three to work' (ibid., p. 79). She reported that 'the Superintendent decides who shall go to the ordinary school' (ibid., p. 81).

The London Board intended that there should be a uniformity of purpose and practice within the special centres and classes. Accordingly, shortly after her appointment and before the first schools opened in 1892, the superintendent of Schools for Special Instruction spent a period of time studying the work of the German auxiliary schools which had existed in large centres of population since the German minister of education's decision in 1880. The Committee received a detailed description of these schools (DCDEC, 1898, vol. I, pp. 249–51). Subsequently, the essence of these schools was described in the following way: pupils were not 'pronounced idiots but intellectually weak … children who, though in possession of the organic five senses, are poorly endowed in perception, memory, reason, etc.' (Klemm, 1907, p. 78). The principles upon which learning was based were activity and enjoyment. The schools had more than the usual amount of space and equipment: 'One shelf of the spacious cupboard was filled with a great number of little objects such as bells, cubes, marbles, keys, bottles and cheap playthings, each of which is there in duplicate' (ibid., p. 89). The duplicate is the device for the pupils to find the original by exercise of their faculties. Manual skills are encouraged for the sake of improved dexterity and possible future employment. The pupils' willpower is awakened and not crushed. Order and discipline are maintained and encouraged to lay the foundations for further development of a moral sense. 'The pupils' good qualities are lovingly nursed, their bad tendencies are repressed, not violently, yet firmly and consistently' (ibid., p. 82).

In almost every respect this accords with the evidence to the Committee of the three teachers in the London special centre. Thus the curriculum was differentiated as far as possible, practical activities and activities such as singing, which pupils enjoyed, were pursued. Physical punishment was very rare except for an older boy who bullied younger children, bad language or repeated insubordination. The normal punishments were isolation in the hall, in a visible place because of glass partitions, or deferment of a cherished activity. The exception was the teachers' need to adhere to the timetable: 'We admit the necessity of the timetable being rigidly adhered to as a rule, but I think sometimes, under exceptional circumstances, we ought to be at liberty to put the timetable on one side' (DCDEC, 1898, vol. II, p. 82). The clear inference from this is that the teachers in the special centres were expected to undertake their responsibilities in a particular way. The superintendent was at the pinnacle; she made important decisions and ran a tight ship.

The special centres' or classes' connection to the larger Elementary school system was through the referral of pupils to them. There were 'a great many to be tested from some schools [and] a very few from others' (ibid., p. 80) in the same catchment area. Although special centres might share premises with Elementary schools, they were separate in terms of personnel and internal organisation. The special centres tended to 'have separate playgrounds and offices [toilet blocks] and pupils do not mix at all' (ibid, p. 81). The playtimes were also structured so that the ordinary school's and the special centre's periods of recreation did not coincide.

A member of the Committee who was an HMI had visited several special classes organised by the London Board. He presented a different picture from Moberly. 'I visited twenty of the classes and in two or three cases I saw buildings that, I believe, are regarded as permanent which are very unsuitable indeed' (ibid., p. 239). One room, measuring 16 by 14 feet, contained 20 children and 10 double desks. Elsewhere, 'there are three classrooms built in the form of a tower, one above the other' (ibid.). Others had no playground. There were also difficulties with poor lighting and 'noise from the traffic outside'. The teachers 'are selected by the School Board ... as being especially bright teachers, first of all, in other schools but have had no training of any kind, I suppose, as a rule except from observing practice in another similar class' (ibid., pp. 239–40). Finally, he estimated that three-quarters to 1 per cent of the school-age pupils in the catchment areas he had visited were classified as feeble-minded and were present in the special classes.

There is evidence therefore that London's special centres and classes were developing as a system within the larger system of Elementary schools. The teachers who worked in the centres were a status group by virtue of their special recruitment and salary. Their working allegiance was not to a headteacher but through their own senior teacher to the superintendent. The superintendent, in turn, was only connected to the Elementary school system by the requirement to report to the Board and by her presence at the testing of children to be referred to the special centres. London's special centres had also developed their own document to record a pupil's progress (see Appendix 3).

There are other factors which also bolstered and encouraged the separation of the special centres from the larger Elementary school system. The assistant medical officer of the London School Board held 'that office chiefly for the purpose of deciding which children [were] more suitable for a special class and which should be relegated to the schools for ordinary children' (ibid., p. 40). He identified six main causes for the existence of feeble-minded children. The first two were malnutrition and excessive neuroticism. Both conditions might be cured and children returned to ordinary schools. The third cause was epilepsy and his experience was that there were very few such cases and mostly mild. The final three were more problematic – strumous children with glandular disorders and those suffering from paralysis or congenital syphilis. He believed that 'quite one third of the children who have been sent down to me [for examination] should not have been sent' (ibid., p. 41). In addition, official forms had been drawn up by a medical officer (see Appendix 1) which asked for comments upon the child under the headings of powers of 'observation', 'imitation', 'attention', 'memory', etc. and also particulars of family history (see Appendix 2). However, in spite of this, a child would typically be presented to him without any background history because teachers customarily wrote 'nil' against the first category 'observation' and then 'ditto' against all the remaining. The only variation was the teacher's comment to the question: 'Is the child affectionate or otherwise', where 'Yes' or 'No' or 'Fairly' might appear. He added that he thought teachers regarded dull children as a drag upon their classes and the school. Hence they just wished to be rid of them. For this reason, he added, the independent judgment of the medical officer became vital (ibid., p. 41). In any case, '[t]he opinion of the teacher should be used to aid the medical man in forming his opinion. I do not think anyone who has not had a proper medical training can properly diagnose these conditions' (ibid., p. 43). He also thought that the inspections of the special centres could be improved if the annual visit by the Education Department's inspectors was made more frequent and if they were accompanied by a medical officer. He went further to suggest that such inspections should be periodic. The Committee's chairman was quick to point to the effect of such changes: 'If there were a medical officer appointed by each Board to visit these cases, it would be necessary to have a general medical officer to oversee the process' (ibid., p. 42).

In this way, the presence of a medical officer on the London School Board was leading to pressure to expand and enlarge the role of medical officers. There was thus another nascent system with links to the London Elementary school system but with little central concern for the Elementary schools themselves.

The form of the medical officer's test of children appears extensive: 'I usually try to talk to the child and try to get out its power of observation and its memory; I watch it to see if it has any power of calculation; I test its reading, its sense of colour and sense of form, and I also keep a look out for any physical signs which I may see' (ibid., p. 41). The most reliable test of all, he found, was the child's knowledge of common objects of the home. He considered the inspector's opinion valuable because 'He tells you what naturally may be expected from a child of that age in an ordinary school, and in that way he is able to help you' (ibid.). This information was useful because the medical officer had no personal experience of teaching and children in schools. It would have been difficult therefore to dispense with the inspector's services completely. The medical officer was also very efficient in the use of his time, agreeing that the length of time taken in a test might vary: 'I think on an average it should take about five minutes; and that he 'could do about ten or twelve in an hour' (ibid., p. 43). The admission procedure outlined here contrasts sharply with that prevalent in the Leicester Board.

The Correspondent for Special Schools with the London Board indicated that the original procedure for testing candidates had been modified. '[Children] are now examined for admission to the special classes for feeble-minded children by the medical officer of the Board and the Superintendent of schools for special instruction and the Government inspector for each district is invited to be present.' Previously, however, 'the School Board Inspector and the local headteacher were also present'. The London Board changed the practice because '[i]t was thought it would not work well' (ibid., p. 47). That last phrase implies that the policy of having a school presence at the decision, in the form of the headteacher or local inspector, was never implemented beyond the planning stage. Thus two key players in the two new systems, linked only to the Elementary schools through the Board, appear to have moved quickly to consolidate their own status within the system.

While there may have been factors peculiar to the London Board's policy of establishing special centres for instruction which encouraged the growth of a system of special schools as opposed to classes, there were also factors inherent in the work which encouraged teachers elsewhere to seek the establishment of separate, special institutions. The Committee sent a survey to all teachers of special classes (see Appendix 4). There were 24 replies from teachers in London and 12 from outside the capital. Given that there were only 21 centres in London in 1896 (DCDEC, 1898, vol. II, p. 48) and few elsewhere (ibid., vol. I, p. 1), the returns may be regarded as substantial. There was overwhelming agreement among the teachers concerning admission procedure, personnel, the school site, curriculum and resources. Virtually all agreed that admission should not occur before the age of seven and after the infant stage (ibid., vol. II, pp. 79, 102). While 'most teachers are able to get trustworthy information as to character, attainments, etc., from the schools which the children attended before being admitted to special classes ... in several cases the information ... is too meagre or too superficial to be of any use. Nearly all the teachers outside of London seem to be of the opinion that an admission form is needed' (ibid., p. 256). From the evidence given by the assistant medical officer, the London Board were already using such a form (see Appendices 1 and 2).

The London Board recruited its teachers for special centres with care and rewarded them with an addition to their salary. A teacher from the Nottingham special centre observed that 'the teachers chosen for this work should be of the best – good discipliniarians, not of excitable disposition, very sympathetic, kind but *firm*', and that 'very young teachers should not be allowed to take charge of such children' (DCDEC, 1898, vol. II, p. 259). Several commented along the line that 'some course of special training be provided for teachers so that their treatment of the children may have a scientific basis' (ibid., p. 258). Thus teachers in special classes sought to establish a status group and differentiate themselves from teachers in ordinary schools.

Regarding the school site and facilities, 'seventeen of the twenty four London classes are conducted in rooms situated on the ground floor' (ibid., p. 257). This was underlined by the comment from another teacher that 'all special schools should be built apart from the ordinary schools and always on the ground floor' (ibid.). There was agreement upon this. The desire to be located on the ground floor probably had a practical basis in order not to restrict children's access. The desire for a separate building often had a different basis. Thus, 'the merits ... of the following are mentioned: A door in direct communication with the street by which children can leave and enter without coming into contact with the other children' (ibid., p. 279). Three teachers observed that the hours should be shorter and the school end earlier: 'I would suggest the advisability of assembling and dismissing special children at different times from those of ordinary schools. By doing so, defective children would not be brought so much under the notice of their more fortunate brothers and sisters, who frequently attack them and say contemptuous things to and about them' (ibid., p. 257, cf., p. 258). For the same reason, it is suggested that playgrounds and playtimes should be separated (ibid., p. 81).

The main plea regarding the curriculum is for greater flexibility. For example: 'under certain atmospheric conditions, it would be wise to substitute singing or the telling of a story for the set lesson. Again, if a child seems very unwell or very excited, manual occupation is better than any mental effort' (ibid., p. 257). In addition, '[a] little license with regard to the time-table, so that one might, without feeling that an error was committed, extend, say, a lesson in which the children were specially interested, etc., or curtail or vary one if they appeared fatigued or from any other equally proper reason' (ibid.). Thus, for sensible reasons, teachers were attempting to differentiate curricular practices in special classes.

The desire for additional resources was driven by the belief that 'As deficient children are generally incapable of comprehending abstractions it is an immense advantage to have before them things which they can actually handle as well as see, so that instruction is presented to them in a concrete form' (ibid., p. 258). Thus, 'it has been found desirable to provide toys of all kinds, particularly building bricks, soldiers, mechanical and steam working toys, spinning toys, etc., for the boys. Dolls of all sizes to dress and undress for the girls. Dolls houses, tea and dinner services. These all form excellent conversation and object lessons' (ibid.). Likewise, access to wood, woodworking tools, ingredients for cooking and the rudiments of the laundry was helpful. The one item of furniture which teachers persistently mentioned as most desirable was the single desk. 'In London, one classroom in one centre is furnished with single desks' (ibid., p. 257). The single desk offered flexibility in arrangement for the room, greater access to pupils (ibid., p. 81) and the possibility of separating children as a cautionary or disciplinary measure (ibid., p. 135). Finally, a musical instrument was needed: 'each special school should be provided with a hall, a piano (or harmonium)' (ibid., p. 257).

The London School Board may have sought to systematise its provision for feeble-minded children in its special centres for instruction. But there were, in addition, systematic features which the teachers of special classes wished to incorporate into the work and organisation of the special institutions. Thus they sought to distinguish themselves from their fellow teachers by virtue of specialist training and selection; to regularise the procedure for admitting pupils which also identified their relationship with teachers in ordinary schools; to separate their special pupils by variations in times of assembly and dismissal and by the separation of play areas; to secure a greater flexibility in the curriculum which would, in turn, guarantee an enlargement of their own scope for decision-making; and, finally, to accrue physical resources which would underpin their distinctive curriculum. In these ways, the teachers of special classes supported the creation and continuity of a system of special education.

The Committee's report observed that 'No special regulations are laid down by the Education Department for these classes ... but the School Authorities are left free to devise such arrangements as seem best' (ibid., vol. I, p. 1). The very absence of regulation permitted scope for the influence of key players such as the inspector in Leicester, the chairman of the London Board's sub-committee on the education of the blind and deaf who was also the vice-chairman of the Board itself, the superintendent of schools for special instruction and the assistant medical officer to the London Board. Each was informed by their own rational judgments, but each contributed in different ways to the establishment and consolidation of a system of special schools separate from those of ordinary Elementary schools.

Hartley Road Special Centre in Nottingham

The Nottingham School Board made a brief written submission to the Committee and its special teachers submitted the survey forms. The Board opened its first centre in April 1893. Only children over eight years of age were admitted because 'defective children below that age appear to be adequately provided for in infants' schools' (DCDEC, 1898, vol. II, p. 199). As to the admission policy, 'children for these centres can be satisfactorily selected by requiring the various teachers to submit names of children they consider suitable for such centres and requiring the Board's inspectors to report individually upon the cases submitted' (ibid.). As appropriate, 'medical experts would doubtless materially assist'. Thus, as with Leicester, the key players appeared to be the local inspectors with their educational experience. The medical officer was subordinated to that process.

The curriculum of the centres 'should be conducted strictly in accordance with the Kindergarten principles – that the instruction should be given as largely as possible in the form of directed play; and that no detailed syllabus of instruction in various subjects should be insisted upon; but the teachers (who should be specially selected for their skills as Kindergarteners) should be given fullest liberty to develop whatever aptitudes – mental or manual – their scholars from time to time evince' (ibid.). The removal of the constraints upon the curriculum and timetable is precisely what teachers who worked in special classes sought. This emerges clearly from the teachers' survey returns to the Committee.

The information which Nottingham special teachers supplied to the Committee is, for the most part, subsumed in the report of the survey (DCDEC, 1898, vol. I, pp. 254–59). The only identifiable exceptions are that there had been no special difficulty in maintaining discipline, although 'several children who had not attended a school before … had been both destructive and disorderly', but 'dangerous or violent children have invariably improved after the first few weeks through great firmness, patience and kindness' (ibid., p. 256).

Class for Afflicted Children at Brighton

The chair of the sub-committee for defective and epileptic children of the Brighton School Board told the Committee that the special class opened in September 1895. She had wished to call the class '"a class of special instruction". It has become labelled "the class for afflicted children". I have done my best to prevent it, but the office seems too strong for us' (DCDEC, 1898, vol. II, p. 68). Although described as a class, in fact it was sub-divided in two classrooms into three groups of children: blind and partially blind; deaf or suffering from ill-health; and all degrees of mental defects. There were two teachers. One was the headteacher, the daughter of a country clergyman in her forties, who had trained to teach so that she could fill any gap that might occur in the local school. She had spent six weeks in a London centre for special instruction before the class opened. The other teacher was younger. There were currently 41 pupils on the roll and, if the numbers expanded to 80, then monitors and pupil-teachers were to be appointed.

The driving-forces behind the special class were the chair of the sub-committee and the special teachers. 'The people most interested in it, so far, are the teachers and myself', she said. A major problem was to establish the extent of the need for the class. Given the size of the Brighton school-age population, and the estimate that about 1 per cent would need the special class, the 41 on the roll meant that 'there really only were, perhaps, one quarter of the children in the special class who ought to be there' (ibid., p. 69). Skilfully, the Board had had the school built in such a way that it could share facilities for baking and handicrafts with the other school classes. However, the desire to keep down costs had meant that the corridor between the two special rooms was not large enough for physical exercise. The chair was adamant that a replacement of the double desks by single ones was unnecessary as was a reduction in class size because both would increase costs. 'In fact', she declared, 'the Board are proceeding tentatively with a view to curtailing the expenses as much as possible as well as with considerations to the benefit of the children' (ibid., p. 69). In this situation, 'the teacher is very anxious indeed not to make the classes too expensive because she does not wish to prejudice the Board against them' (ibid.). Here there appears to be a policy which is finance led and under the direct control of the Board. The chair of the sub-committee remarked that her hand would be strengthened if the Education Department were to make such classes mandatory. To which the Committee chairman replied with the *non sequitur* that, if she had already accepted the existing situation, it would be very difficult to get the Board to reconsider.

By contrast, there was a seemingly open pattern of recruitment to the special class: parents could simply bring their children to the class or there might be a referral by the attendance officer or there might be an application to the Clerk to the Board. After the initial inspection by the Board's medical officer, all the children had a minimum of three weeks' experience in the class. This period was often extended because the Board met at infrequent intervals. During the period, the teacher determined whether 'she can do anything with them' (ibid., p. 68). Any tests were those of simple reading, addition of units, mental arithmetic and the writing of their names. Despite there being a medical officer on the Board, 'the admission to these classes rests entirely with the sub-committee of the Board' (ibid., p. 72). In fact, the sub-committee had rejected four children against the advice of the medical officer, on the grounds that 'the sub-committee thought they were too good and that they ought to be in ordinary schools' (ibid., p. 68).

The situation in Brighton contained curious elements. The chair of the sub-committee with responsibility had no background experience in schools, but visited the special class and even tested probationary pupils. She had recently returned to the Board after a period of 18 months' absence. Potential recruits came through three different channels and there was no mention of teachers and ordinary schools. Admission occurred after assessment in the special class and with the approval of the sub-committee. The medical officer played a subordinate role. The sub-committee appeared to be in a strong position but it is also clear that 'the office' was powerful, in matters such as the naming of the class, and that the Board itself held the upper hand through its control of finances. Thus the Chair of the sub-committee may well have been aware that the numbers in the special class might increase, but at the expense of existing resources should the Board decide against any increase in funding. Also absent from the scene is any mention of local or Government inspectors. It may well be that the chair of the sub-committee was entirely well meaning and intentioned, but lacked the experience or organising skills to pursue a policy or a campaign.

Special Classes in Birmingham

A 'member of the Birmingham School Board', who 'took a great interest in the welfare of defective children' (DCDEC, 1898, vol. II, p. 73), gave evidence to the Committee. The witness spoke confidently about the numbers of children in special classes but revised the number of defective children not in attendance at school as reported by attendance officers from 120 to 200. Likewise, the initial estimate of feeble-minded pupils in the school-age population was revised upwards from 0.146 per cent to one per cent (ibid., pp. 73, 78). The inspector for the Birmingham Division corroborated the latter in a different context (ibid., p. 224).

The Birmingham Board opened the first special class in Benson Road School in April 1894. The second started up in September 1896 in Moseley Road School. A third was on the point of opening. There were 21 pupils on the roll of the first and 18 on the second. Although aware of the advantages on paper of a large centre, 'to suit the [transport] needs of Birmingham, we require four or five moderately small centres. It would not be any use to have one large centre', even though that policy 'would not admit of the same classification as if there were one large centre' (ibid., p. 74). Both these special classes were divided into an upper and lower division.

> In the upper division the children are beginning to speak, to know their letters, to write and to draw; in the lower division, they are just as we get them when they come in. They are sometimes unable to speak and their senses are very little cultivated; and, perhaps, they are quite unaccustomed to discipline and unable to behave decently, unless they have previously been in school. (ibid., p. 75)

Given the size of the school-age population in Birmingham at that time and the estimate that 1 per cent were feeble-minded, then there should have been around 700 pupils in the special classes – considerably more than the 39 there actually were. The witness insisted on two occasions that, in Birmingham, 'teachers in the ordinary schools are not anxious to get rid of dull children and there is not any tendency to force ordinary dull children into these special schools' (ibid., p. 76, cf., p. 75). However, when a survey was taken a little later to verify the situation, it was found that the 'number of children in public elementary schools in Birmingham reported by the teachers to be mentally deficient was six hundred and thirty eight' (ibid., p. 79). That figure excludes returns from 11 denominational schools which declined to complete returns because the request had come from the Board and not the school managers. It also excludes the 200 children not in attendance at school. The sum total gives Birmingham more than the original 1 per cent estimate. As the inspector for the Birmingham Division reported, 'the majority of defective children are still mixed up with the dull or backward. They were either in Standard I or scattered about the school' (ibid., p. 224). Thus, whereas Leicester's policy toward Standard 0 classes facilitated the viability of a small special class, the absence of such a policy in Birmingham would imply that the special classes were highly selective and probably based upon geographical access as much as anything else.

At neither of the two special classes were the teachers certificated. Both, however, 'were qualified by character and by previous knowledge of the particular class with which they had to deal' (ibid., p. 74). The Board 'thought good infant teachers would be most suitable and two Board members were asked to look around and nominate a certain number of teachers for the Committee to see' (ibid.). Having selected the first, she then trained at a special centre for instruction in London. That teacher subsequently inducted other teachers as they were appointed. There was one teacher in each of the special classes. Each was also assisted by a teacher in training in the school. Given that the special class was split into an upper and lower division, a minimum of two teachers was desirable. The teachers were paid at the same level as certificated teachers because the Board had confidence in their skills (ibid., p. 74).

There was a policy not to admit children to the special classes until they were 7 years of age because infant school was considered the best environment for these pupils. The admission policy was straightforward:

> if the child is already in the elementary school, one of the special class teachers visits the teacher of the school and confers with him or her about the child. If the child is not in school at all, the special teacher visits the home of the child. We have entirely trusted to the

special teacher to tell us what children should be admitted and what should not. (ibid., p. 75)

It was established that there was a medical officer attached to the Board but there was no question that 'he should have a final voice in the selection or rejection in such cases' because 'no difficulty has ever occurred' (ibid., p. 75). It also emerged that any connection the children in the special classes had with the medical profession was casual: the medical officer of the borough asylum had paid a visit to one class and 'a lady at the Children's Hospital at Birmingham visited the children in the other class and gave us some valuable suggestions' (ibid.).

The curriculum emphasised activity: 'a good deal of the time is occupied in manual working, singing and drill. Every lesson lasts no longer that twenty minutes. Every lesson is, as it were, sandwiched with an occupation or drill or singing – something of that nature' (ibid., p. 78).

The Birmingham Board had chosen to adapt existing classrooms for its special classes, unlike a Board such as Brighton which had commissioned new buildings, although to a strict budget. The Committee believed the ideal space allowance for feeble-minded children should be 20 square feet per child – twice the allowance for the ordinary pupil. Often special classes had been constructed according to the ordinary allowance. In Birmingham, one claimed 30 square feet per child and the other, together with the one about to open, 20 square feet per child (ibid., p. 75). The Birmingham Board had, however, made some changes to the existing buildings: 'We had some structural alterations made so as to allow separate entrances for boys and girls and separate playgrounds and lavatories' (ibid., p. 74). Although the special classes were located on Elementary school sites, the Board 'would not contemplate their using the playgrounds and lavatories at the same time because the playtime can always be arranged and they are always under the supervision of their teacher' (ibid.). It emerged that this separation was a matter of principle because 'practically we have had no difficulty come from feeble-minded children among a lot of rough boys and girls in the playground' (ibid.). This advocacy of separation is supported by Boards and teachers elsewhere.

The Senior Examiner on the Committee, H. F. Pooley, pressed the witness regarding two areas: the role of medical officers in assessment and the size of the special classes. His questions, however, were not so much open as directional, in so far as they appeared to point to a model of the medical officers' involvement which was considered ideal. For example, 'Were those medical inspections confined to the physical condition of the child or did they extend to their mental state?' Again, 'Has it ever been suggested the medical officer should have the final voice in the selection or rejection of such cases?' (ibid., p. 75). The second area concerned the preference for a large centre which would facilitate classification of children, as in the London centres. It was established that the Birmingham Board had opted for two small special classes. The question then followed immediately: '[D]o you consider that preferable to having one large centre?' (ibid., p. 74). The witness replied that access to a large centre with a large catchment area would be impossible. This drew the Committee member's observation that 'that [policy] would not admit of the same classification as if you had a large centre' (ibid.). This was followed by the comment: 'Classification is scarcely possible, I presume' (ibid., p. 75). The Senior Examiner returned to the point, having established that there was probably a serious underestimation of the number of feeble-minded children in Birmingham Elementary schools: 'If this special instruction were to be provided for the whole of Birmingham, would not it be better not to have several small classes but to have a reasonable number of fairly large centres?' (ibid., p. 76). This was a question that required an affirmative response.

The situation with regard to the Birmingham Board is difficult to assess precisely. There are, however, some possible indicators. The first is the absence of the mention of local inspectors in the process. The second is that the Divisional HMI's evidence points to the fact that the feeble-minded were mixed in with other children in the ordinary schools. The third is that the Birmingham witness was simply a Board member, which may imply that there was no sub-committee which handled these matters. There is also a serious underestimation of the numbers involved on the part of the witness. An alternative view might be that the Birmingham Board was generally content with this state of affairs because the discovery of more candidates would imply more expense. Admission to the special classes was realised through the judgment of a special class teacher. As with Brighton, the teachers were only permitted to decide on admissions in situations where the Board felt in overall control of the situation and/or when it was regarded as a relatively minor concern.

Special Classes in Bristol

The Revd J. J. Martin was a member of the Bristol School Board and chairman of the committee for special classes. In fact, there was only one class, at Barton Hill School, which had opened in January 1897, but two others were planned. The Bristol Board's procedures were inchoate and its systems barely in place. The Board was not sure whether it had yet sufficient accommodation for all its ordinary school pupils. A survey indicated that there might be 260 feeble-minded pupils in the school population, but there was provision for little more than 20 in the special class. There was nobody medically qualified on the Board, so the Board asked a general practitioner who undertook occasional duties for it to examine children considered feeble-minded when thought appropriate.

There were two ways in which children for the special class were identified. On the one hand, they were 'nominated by the headteachers of the different schools. Then they [were] examined by the Board's own inspector. Then they are submitted to a medical gentleman' (DCDEC, 1898, vol. II, p. 142). On the other hand, to recruit those children not already in school, 'we simply put some information in the newspapers that this work was being commissioned' (ibid., p. 149). For the children brought by their parents in this way, 'the teacher of the defective class observes their defective characteristics and gives them a place in her class in the first place' (ibid.). Subsequently they were tested by the inspector and examined by the doctor to confirm their fitness.

There were 27 children in the special class which had opened and 20 more were expected for each of the two about to open. A return prepared in November 1895 indicated that there were '260 mentally deficient children in the Board schools alone' (ibid.). It was observed that, with a school population of 33,500, a 1 per cent estimate would yield 335 defective children. Hence many more classes were needed. Standard 0 pupils were taught in separate classes. These classes were large because 'our usual number is from twelve to twenty; but in the poorest districts from fifty to sixty' (ibid.). Pupils for the special classes were usually selected from these classes.

The special teachers 'must be well experienced in Kindergarten work. ... They were selected by the Committee on account of their special qualities – brightness, originality, good drawing qualifications, aptitude for managing children tactfully ... They are trained qualified teachers ... Two teachers were sent to London to receive a month's experience in the capital's centres for special instruction' (ibid., pp. 143, 144). Both were in their early twenties and received a small increment to their salaries. They were supported by pupil-teachers. However, because of the unruly nature of some of the pupils in the special classes, 'it would be very helpful, if we had a Superintendent or Chief Teacher who could guide them or give them instructions' (ibid., p. 147). This is a clear indication, perhaps, that difficulties were being experienced. For that reason, as well as the large number of children in need, the number of teachers and special classes needed to be increased. However, although 'the majority of the Board are in favour of special classes ... we have had some difficulty in getting classes. Some of the members thought we were trying to do too much and were opposed to it' (ibid., p. 143). 'On the grounds of expense?' the chairman enquired. 'I think so. That is a very considerable objection, as you know', the witness replied.

The curriculum was at the experimental stage and the best and most natural methods of teaching were being sought. Object lessons and drawing were emphasised. There was also much practical work. As the system developed they planned to 'form classes for laundry and cookery for the girls and woodwork for the boys' (ibid., p. 144). The aim was that pupils should become fairly independent, that girls should be useful in their homes and boys pursue some simple occupation (ibid., p. 146).

Again, because the classrooms were adapted from ordinary rooms, there was more space for each child in the smaller classes. The norm was 20 square feet. Single desks 'would be preferable for isolating pupils' (ibid., p. 144), but, again, there is the question of expense. It was felt that a residential special school would also be desirable to remove children from poor family circumstances. The fact that one had not been built, however, was 'preferable so far as the rates are concerned' (ibid., p. 145).

The witness considered that it was 'very regrettable that they use the ordinary cloak-rooms and lavatories and are not separated from the other children in any way except during the hours of study' (ibid., p. 143). The reasons given were that ordinary children distracted the feeble-minded in their play and they became inattentive in their lessons.

The question of the classification of children in special classes arose in two different contexts. The first was the view that 'classification is scarcely possible because they are so backward and ignorant' (ibid., p. 144) – a statement which compounds, if not confuses, two different ideas. The second context was when the Committee's chairman picked up the estimate of the total number of needy children. 'Eventually', he pointed out, 'you will require something like twelve to fourteen special schools ... If these consist of twenty or thirty pupils under a single teacher, then they will be entirely unclassified' (ibid., p. 149). The witness seemed confused, so the chairman went on to explain that in a single class so constituted, a single teacher would be responsible for pupils of all ages and there would be several divisions within the class and each would require special attention. The chairman therefore concluded: 'Would it not be better to build special schools which would contain three or four classes than to disperse them over a city in twelve or fourteen separate special classes?' (ibid., p. 149). The witness agreed to the question which invited a positive response.

The Committee's chairman was not averse to offering the witness advice. The witness had declared: 'We go on the principle of doing things very economically and we have found rooms [for special classes]. For instance ... we have a room originally intended for a teacher's room, and we simply turn out the teachers and put the defectives in' (ibid., p. 143). The chairman wondered whether that was not putting public funds to wrong use and added that, 'if you have not school accommodation for every child, you ought to build such accommodation and this extra class would involve no extra expense except perhaps some little planning' (ibid.). The witness demurred that this would entail the cost of securing a site. The chairman retorted that '[t]he London Board builds its special classes generally on the playground of some existing school' (ibid.). The Committee was thus not reluctant to issue and dictate its views.

The overall number of feeble-minded children also raised the question of the medical officer's involvement in their identification. It was established that the estimated number of 260 children in need had emerged from a survey of Bristol's headteachers and that '[t]he medical officer certainly did not examine those children' (ibid., p. 147). The doctor had examined the 47 children referred to him by the headteachers in consultation with the local inspector. The doctor was not a member of the Board, but the Board used his services in regard to a truant school and a boys' and girls' industrial school which were under its care. When pressed by the chairman, the witness agreed that, although there had been no disagreement up to the present between the headteacher, inspector and the doctor concerning a child's admission to the special class, 'In the case of a difficulty ... I should think the doctor's word would decide. His is the strongest position' (ibid., p. 149). The witness did not give a reason, but the Chairman accepted it as the proper thing.

The Committee's concern for the situation in Bristol is perhaps evident from the way in which it was prepared to coach the witness and give him advice as chairman of the Committee for special classes. In the Committee's view, Bristol's policy for special classes was fundamentally flawed. In its place there should be a policy for the establishment of special schools which contained a number of classes in order to classify children. Further, Bristol had been slow to survey Elementary schools; this had not occurred until November 1885. The first special class had not opened until January 1887. In the meantime, it was established that there were probably more than 250 feeble-minded children in the Board's Elementary schools, an estimate which excluded Voluntary schools. Unlike Leicester's carefully structured policy towards Standard 0 classes, Bristol's appeared to be determined by chance and by geography and consisted of classes which ranged from 15 to 60 children. As the Committee's chairman remarked: 'Bristol seems to be very full of very dull children, or very ignorant children or very untaught children' (ibid., p. 142). One vital factor which appeared to underpin this situation was the disposition of members of the Bristol School Board. This was most evident in their reservation about not wishing to be seen to do too much for these children and their reluctance to commit further burdens to the rates. For these reasons, the Committee believed Bristol needed to develop a positive system which involved a credible expert such as a medical officer. It was thought that perhaps the presence of such a figure would lend weight and legitimacy to a request for an increase in the rates. As it was, the prime players involved were the headteachers and the local inspector. A doctor was called only as confirmation of their diagnosis of a feeble-minded child.

Special Classes and the Bradford School Board

James Kerr was appointed medical superintendent to the Bradford School Board in 1893. Coincidentally, the Independent Labour Party was founded in Bradford that same year. Margaret McMillan travelled north from London to give her support to the Party. Her subsequent election to the Bradford School Board, it is claimed (Steedman, 1990, p. 41) prompted her to make Bradford her home. 'Bradford, in the last decade of the nineteenth century, became one of the most progressive school authorities' (Pritchard, 1963, p. 128). That judgment is not evident in Kerr's evidence to the Committee.

The London Board had been first to appoint a medical officer in 1890. The incumbent's duties, however, were confined to advising the Board regarding ventilation, sanitation and light in existing and new buildings (Board of Education, 1909, p. 4). Kerr's duties, however, were 'the general oversight of all matters relating to the health of all the children in all the schools under the Board' (DCDEC, 1898, vol. II, p. 17). Those duties, he added, extended to teachers and pupil-teachers.

The medical superintendent pursued his responsibilities with vigour and enthusiasm. He made a point of visiting each Board school at least three times a year and 'sometimes I visit as often as twice a week' (ibid.). There were then 28,000 pupils in the Board schools and he had personally examined 20,000. From these examinations, 'I estimated for the School Board that two per cent of the total number of children in attendance as being the number that they should supply special classes for' (ibid., p. 18). That estimate yielded a total of 350 pupils. Bradford had opened its first special class in November 1894 and four more in the year following. These five classes contained a total of 117 children. The Committee queried the basis for his 2 per cent estimate but, even if its own preferred estimate of 1 per cent was adopted, it remained clear that there was much work yet to be done.

Kerr maintained that he could immediately distinguish between children fit for the special classes and those which should go to an imbecile asylum: 'I have seen a good many children and have said straight away: "Not fit for any school under the Board" in my report to the Board or "Fit only for an asylum" or something of that sort (ibid., p. 24). Pupils were typically brought to his attention by teachers who observed that a child aged ten had been in Standard I and likely to stay there. In his experience, teachers had not 'taken the trouble to ascertain the history of a child ... They will often give you a rough idea of what the medical facts are, which, however, is scarcely worth listening to' (ibid., p. 18).

The procedures adopted for a determination of feeble-mindedness were as follows: 'I examine the child for certain physical peculiarities – the shape of the head, the ears and the eyes ... and the curved little fingers is one of my tests [which] I think is as important a test as the arched palate or lobeless ear' (ibid., p. 18). He used no test of reading, writing or arithmetic. When pressed by the Committee's chairman to describe the child's features which confirmed feeble-mindedness, he responded that 'there is a *tout ensemble* about a child that is defective that you cannot describe, but which a medical man who had had experience knows at once' (ibid.). Such a medical inspection was not merely necessary, but essential before admission to a special class. This was also in the interests of the child, because 'if it was left to the teacher, the teachers would try to get rid of all the dull children. They try to pass them through their hands' (ibid., p. 20).

The teachers in the special classes were qualified, certificated teachers who were employed by the Board and had been offered the work in the special classes on the recommendations of the school superintendent. Their salaries had been increased and 'the first one we started we sent to Nottingham and then afterwards the teachers of the next class were sent to her class' (ibid., p. 22). The teachers 'ought to be trained very thoroughly' (ibid., p. 24). Unfortunately, the medical superintendent did not have time to include their instruction in his duties.

The special classes were easily opened because 'we have just taken a classroom in the ordinary school ... made a separate entrance to it and used it' (ibid., p. 24). They were all situated on the ground floor. The aim of the classes was for the children to become independent, as far as possible, and capable of earning their own living. Examples were given of girls becoming cooks, washerwomen or tending bobbins in the spinning mill, while boys also found work sweeping in the mills (ibid., p. 20). While Kerr wished the basis of the curriculum to be 'manual and practical', '[w]e have not done any actual manual work, partly on the question of cost'. 'Do you mean Kindergarten work?' the chairman asked. Kerr appeared not to comprehend the question or the idea of 'Kindergarten work', for 'I mean wood work and so on' was his reply. 'Do you do cookery and laundry work?' another member enquired. 'No, not yet'. 'Any sloyd work or advanced sloyd work?' the Chairman asked. 'No some children do clay modelling exceedingly well', was the reply (ibid., p. 19).

The reality of the curriculum seemed far removed from the Kindergarten and similar to that in the Elementary schools: 'I have tried to get the teachers to work rationally, but unfortunately they are bound up in the idea of Standards and Codes and what not and they have the inspector after them and superintendents over them with the same ideas and it is very difficult to get them to use rational ideas' (ibid., p. 19). The witness observed that the Board's inspector visited the classes regularly: 'they [*sic*] are my chief trouble; he wants them to get on; he draws up schedules for them' (ibid., p. 23). The special classes would thus appear to follow the same regime as the larger classes in the Elementary schools: this was a feature of 'the cast iron groove' they worked in (ibid., p. 24).

Although the large size of the classes in the Elementary schools is mentioned on three separate occasions as a causal factor in feeble-minded children's difficulties (ibid., pp. 18–20), the average size of the special classes must have been nearer 25 pupils than the 20 claimed (ibid., p. 18). In addition, the special classes, although not classified, practically contained three divisions: the top division, who would return to the Elementary schools; the middle division, who would remain in the special class until they attained leaving age; and the bottom division, who should have been in the asylum for imbeciles (ibid., p. 22). But there was another class of pupil evident in the special classes, that of 'moral imbecile'. The example was given of a 'girl thieving without any purpose, silly thieving, a moral imbecile – although the police did not take that view' (ibid., p. 24). Again, 'we have a little girl who picks pockets. We have one or two moral imbeciles, you know, children who appear sharp and intelligent and you cannot say there is anything wrong with them until you begin to find out the true state of the case from the history' (ibid., p. 22). On these grounds the medical superintendent advocated the establishment of an industrial school for those who truant: 'The children are defective in some ways but not in others. In other ways they are exceedingly sharp and these truant schools could be used for them' (ibid., p. 21).

In other respects, the witness was very practical. For instance, he recommended that special classrooms be warm, that they should be spacious to facilitate physical exercise, that there should be washing facilities to encourage personal hygiene, and that classrooms should be furnished with bright pictures (ibid., p. 24). He also believed that 'it is better for the child to be mixing with the world and to rub against other people than to be isolated'. Although the special classes had been adapted with separate entrances, at his insistence the special pupils shared the playground and playtime with the other pupils in the school. He had also changed the start and finish of the day, so that all children 'are going to school and coming from it at the same time'. His reason was that in these situations 'the child is having its capacity brought out by natural means and not by artificial' (ibid., pp. 21, 25).

The London Board had appointed a medical officer and so had the Bradford Board. Both medical officers were anxious that the importance of their work should be recognised and that their influence should expand on that basis. At that point the comparison ceases. At Bradford, it is very clear that the medical officer is the gatekeeper to admission to the special classes. He is emphatic that his medical knowledge permits the identification of the feeble-minded and that it is a skill completely lacking in teachers. Indeed, if teachers were permitted such judgments, they would act perversely in their own interests in removing dull children from their classes. Clearly the children would suffer in this situation in his view. However, to all intents and purposes, the regime in the special classes appeared to run along the lines of the Elementary school curriculum. The medical officer may have changed the timings of the start and finish of the classes to coincide with those of the schools, but in the four years in which he had been in office, he had not been able to bring about any features of the 'practical', 'manual' or 'rational' curriculum he regarded as appropriate. Moreover, in one of the exchanges with the Committee's chairman, he appeared not to be aware of the meaning of a 'Kindergarten curriculum'. There appears to be a disjuncture between the medical officer's curricular aspirations and the teachers' policies and practices.

Kerr's beliefs concerning the external, physical manifestation of the internal quality of individuals' minds was then a respectable part of medical thinking (cf., Gould, 1981, pp. 30–101). It was also linked to so-called scientific theories of the differences between races, the eugenicist movement and the naturalistic basis for the detection of criminality. Kerr himself wrote in this area and was published (1905). The inadequacy of

Kerr's diagnostic techniques to distinguish between children to be classified as feeble-minded and normal was clearly highlighted by the Committee's inquiry. However, Kerr's category of 'moral imbecile' was a promiscuous classification which brought, in turn, its own internal contradiction that bright or sharp imbeciles may exist. Thus Bradford's special classes were havens simultaneously for the mentally and morally defective child. That doubtless, paradoxically, was a situation teachers in ordinary schools welcomed because it did remove pupils from their domain on the basis of criteria which were not educational. In a concluding remark to the Committee, Kerr observed that 'My own idea is that the more these [feeble-minded] children are taught to look upon themselves as part of the ordinary world, the better for them' (ibid., p. 25). It seems ironic that the 'ordinary world' gave respectability and legitimacy to such ideas as Kerr pursued so single-mindedly.

The Situation in Plymouth

The Committee's report states that a special class 'was in the process of formation in Plymouth' (DCDEC, 1898, vol. I, p. 1). The reality was that no member of the Plymouth Board had attended the meeting arranged with an HMI to discuss the formation of a special class. The HMI had thus obtained his information from the Clerk to the Board. His conclusion was: 'I do not quite know what the proposals of the Board are. At present, they are looking for buildings, but I think they are, at any rate, for the present intending to begin with one' (ibid., vol. II, p. 224). The situation in Plymouth at the time in the inspector's view was that 'there is no special notice taken of [the feeble-minded children]. I have had one or two cases where I asked the question, and they say: "We let them go up Standard by Standard; it pleases the child and he thinks he is passing the Standards, although he is not". That seems to be sensible. The whole thing is tentative' (ibid., pp. 224–5).

CONCLUSIONS

The estimate of numbers of feeble-minded children in urban and rural areas varied considerably. HMI considered that numbers were under-reported and that in urban areas, where no classes existed, industrial schools answered the challenge. Many Boards had also not yet tackled the situation and here financial considerations may be the root cause. Feeble-minded pupils in scattered rural environments also faced their own particular difficulties.

Only a small number of Boards had established special classes in this period. The London Board, which had established a system of special centres under a superintendent, was the leader in the field. However, the principles which underpinned the organisation of its system contrasted sharply with those of the Leicester Board. The basis of the London Board's examination for entry to special classes and their organisation pointed towards the separation and demarcation of pupils in special classes from their peers.

There were considerable variations in the estimations of the size of the difficulties which the Boards faced. Similarly, there were variations in admissions procedures and personnel. The empirical evidence points to the requirement for firm direction in the future. Whether this was to be forthcoming provides the basis for the next chapter and an examination of the Departmental Committee's deliberations.

6

Legacies of the Departmental Committee on Defective and Epileptic Children

In Chapter 4 the deliberations and recommendations of the Egerton Commission were discussed. There were firm prescriptions for the education of the blind and deaf but not for the third group. There was also evident a conflict of opinion between the expert witnesses. Meanwhile, as demonstrated in Chapter 5, the Boards and the pupils in their schools continued to encounter difficulties. The Departmental Committee was established to produce a solution to the conflict of opinion identified by the Egerton Commission. The witness evidence given to the Committee also provides information about how the Boards were tackling their difficulties. The intention of this chapter is to examine the way in which the difficulties were conceived of by the Committee and to explore the basis for the recommended solutions.

AN ANALYTICAL APPROACH

C. Wright Mills suggested that 'The sociological imagination enables us to grasp history and biography and the relation between the two within society'. He added the rider: 'That is its task and its promise' (1970, p. 12). The task, then, is to consider the members of the Departmental Committee on Defective and Epileptic Children, and to examine the conclusions the Committee reached in the context of the evidence it took. The 'promise' implies that the completion of the task may yield insights into the events and decisions.

As an orientation towards analysis, Weber's ideal type of authority may be taken. An ideal type is an abstraction from the social world containing the essential characteristics of social phenomena. Its prime purpose is heuristic, to facilitate the empirical study of phenomena. The concept of authority at once represents two facets which are different sides of the same coin: the right to command and the duty to obey. Thus, in Weber's view, the basis for authority or the issue of instructions is bound up with the basis for the acceptance of authority. Put in different terms,

Weber sought a mechanism to explore why groups or individuals were regarded as having the right to lead and direct others and why those who were led believed the leaders had a right to issue instructions. The core of the consideration is therefore the legitimacy of authority or, putting physical coercion to one side, the reasons why it is considered right that some issue commands or make decisions and others accept them. Weber suggested that there were three quintessential features of authority: charisma, tradition and rationality. In this way, authority may spring from the personal characteristics of an individual and those characteristics are also the basis for the recruitment of followers; or the fact that authority has been seen to reside in a particular group or family may provide the reason why subjects follow their instructions; or the basis for authority may reside in a claim to a rational principle such as the existence of codified laws which guide citizens.

The three types of authority only existed as ideal types. In the social world there is both a mixture and a movement of authority. Thus the imputation or recognition of charisma may only be the basis for authority at its very inception, which may turn into a type of traditional authority. This may be a way of examining the growth of the Christian church. In this example, however, the internal elaboration of the rules for successions and beliefs may itself provide the grounds for the rise of the sort of rationality which is considered to be objective and detached from the subjective wishes of individuals. The basis for the acceptance of rationality is the belief in its detachment. This route, in Weber's view, led to the 'iron cage' of 'victorious capitalism'. That belief, however, is not necessarily in itself evidence that ideas and practices based upon rationality are detached from the wishes or interests of individuals. Contemporarily, and presumably historically, the three types co-exist in social life. Thus the same individual may feel inspired by the personal qualities of a political figure to allegiance, while willingly accepting the duties of a son in the family and the expectations placed upon a person who works in a bank (cf., Bendix, 1960, pp. 285–431). The essence of these ideal types will now be employed in a further analysis of the development of the system of education for children considered variously dull, backward and feeble-minded.

COMPOSITION OF THE DEPARTMENTAL COMMITTEE

The Lord President of the Eduction Department established the Committee on Defective and Epileptic Children in December 1896. The recommendations of the Royal Commission on the Blind, the Deaf and the

Dumb, presented in 1889, had already become legislation for blind and deaf children. The Committee's task was to make the same possible for the feeble-minded, the epileptic and physically disabled children.

There were seven members of the Committee and an Examiner from the Education Department who acted as Secretary. The Chairman was HM Senior Chief Inspector of Schools and there was HMI. There was a Senior Examiner from the Department as well as the Examiner who acted as Secretary. Thus four members of the Committee were insiders, so to speak. Three of the remaining four, however, constituted a distinct grouping, not to say packing, of the Committee. The three consisted of the Superintendent of Schools for Special Instruction under the London School Board, the Medical Officer of the London School Board and the former Medical Superintendent of the Royal Albert Asylum for Idiots and Imbeciles, who was shortly to become Medical Examiner of Defective Children of the London School Board. The remaining member of the Committee was a Member of the Council of the Association for Promoting the Welfare of the Feeble-minded and, as such, had no direct connection with schools or the system of education.

IMPACT OF THE COMMITTEE'S REPORT

The Elementary Education (Defective and Epileptic Children) Act 1899 was largely the outcome of the recommendations of the Comittee's report. There had been previous legislation for the education of the deaf and the blind and the 1899 Act can be regarded as consolidating the other two by the inclusion of further dimensions of disability.

The Committee received evidence from 47 witnesses, the first of whom was also a member of the Committee and who undertook the important task of presenting a definition of feeble-mindedness. Other witnesses included HMI who reported upon their survey of the urban and rural situations, teachers in special classes, representatives from authorities which had set up special classes, leading neurophysiologists, medical officers and others with responsibility for imbeciles in asylums. As the preceding analysis in Chapter 5 has shown, the evidence of the witnesses revealed variations in practices, policies and motivations. The Committee's task was to consider these variations and to make recommendations for future policy and practice. In effect, its recommendations were an attempt to bring uniformity and standardisation to the variety of practices and to introduce a rationalisation to every-day school life. In Foucault's terms, the processes of normalisation – the production of a norm and the distribution of subjects around that norm – and surveillance or watchful oversight of the production and distribution, began to occur. A recommendation for a system of special Elementary education to be established thus came into being.

ROUTINE PROCEDURES OF SPECIAL EDUCATION

The system of special education was to have certain routine procedures. Children should not normally be admitted to special classes under the age of seven years and, if retained in the classes, should normally leave at 14 years of age. However, at School Boards' discretion, children might be retained until 16 years of age, but, in this case, there should be consideration whether the normally mixed classes should be segregated by sex. The initial selection of pupils was to be the responsibility of headteachers, both for the infants schools and for older scholars. HMI might also make recommendations for examination to school managers and 'if the managers fail to send such children to such examination [the inspector] should report unfavourably on the organisation of the school and make a statement of the case to the Education Department' (DCDEC, 1898, vol. I, p. 10). On presenting a child for examination, teachers were to complete an itemised form (see Appendix 1) 'stating details as to the character, capacity and attainments of the child' (ibid., p. 11). The decision whether or not to admit the child to a special class was to be made upon the result of a medical officer's completion of a certificate identifying the mental or physical grounds. The school class teacher, the medical officers of the school authority, an HMI, the special class teacher and a parent might be present at the child's examination. In addition, there were further itemised forms to be completed on admission regarding the child's family history and background (see Appendix 2), and subsequently concerning the child's progress (see Appendix 3).

The regulations specified that special classes containing more than ten children should be under the direction of a certificated teacher (ibid., p. 16). Moreover, teachers in special classes should also receive special, additional training in the course of their teaching (ibid., p. 17).

Children in special classes should enjoy the exclusive use of a suitably furnished classroom; they should not be mixed with ordinary children for any lessons; and they should be the sole responsibility of their teachers who should have no other duties. A manager should be appointed to oversee these arrangements. In this way, these children were to be set apart or distributed beyond the norm for 'ordinary' children.

The principle which was to underpin the organisation of curricular experiences was 'to alternate brain work with hand work; to take the more difficult brain work in the morning and to give short physical exercises between all lessons' (ibid., p. 17). The content and balance of the curriculum in the London Centres for Special Instruction were offered as the model. The development of manual skills for both boys and girls was to be encouraged.

The Committee's intention was to oversee the setting-up of a system of special classes with regulations and routines which controlled the selection and admission of pupils, the organisation of classes, the content of the curriculum and the qualification and training of teachers.

VARIATIONS IN ADMISSIONS PROCEDURES TO SPECIAL CLASSES

The subject upon which the Committee received evidence of the widest variation in practices was that regarding the admissions procedure to special classes. In Leicester, teachers in ordinary schools made recommendations to the Board, whose recommendations were subject to the approval of an inspector who called upon medical expertise in circumstances he considered appropriate. There was a similar procedure in nearby Nottingham. In Brighton, parents brought their children along to special classes or children were directed there by attendance officers. Children had a minimum trial period of three weeks after admittance by the special teacher and confirmation by a doctor that the source of mental defect was not physical. In Birmingham, admission was the responsibility of the special class teacher after a visit to the child either in the ordinary school or at home. In Bristol, children were recommended by ordinary teachers or brought to a special class by their parents. For these latter, admission depended upon the special class teachers' observations. For the former, it depended upon the inspector's judgment, confirmed, as appropriate, by a doctor. In Bradford, the Board's medical officer initiated the medical examination of children and presided over their admission to special classes. In London, the initial recommendation for the involvement of the ordinary school headteacher and local inspector had been replaced by admission on the judgment of an HMI, the Board's medical officer and the Superintendent of Schools for Special Instruction.

THE CHARISMATIC ELEMENT IN ADMISSIONS PROCEDURES

The effect of individual personalities may be evident in different ways in these situations. The personal qualities and judgments of the Leicester inspector are evident from the evidence he gave. His advice and recommendations appeared to have been adopted by the Leicester Board and his initiation of the special class appears little more than a rational extension of the Board's policy for Standard 0 classes. Thus the Leicester Board, in accepting his personal advice, translated a form of charisma into a tradition which became a way of working. In this way, the inspector's preference for educational criteria to take precedence over medical ones concerning admissions was accepted as rational practice.

In the case of Brighton, individual actions seemed to operate within a more restricted sphere. The witness to the Committee was drawn personally to the plight of feeble-minded children, as was the teacher of the special class. Hence a scheme had been initiated. The personal intentions of the witness had been translated into action and were accepted as the basis for the Board's action and its policy, but only in a situation where the Board felt able to retain ultimate control of resources. Hence the legitimacy of the claim was regarded as restricted to a particular area.

In both Bristol and Birmingham, the teachers in ordinary schools and the special classes were the prime players. However, the factor which appears to unite all these three examples is that provision for the feeble-minded was only at a very early stage. In all, the feeble-minded children were still largely 'mixed up with ordinary children' (ibid., vol. II, p. 224). Hence, in two at least of these instances, Committee members abandoned the format of asking questions of witnesses and instead gave policy advice about how the work in this area should develop. The inference from this may be that there exists more scope for individual initiative within a policy vacuum. Put a different way, Board members were aware of a problem which needed to be tackled. Individual Board members therefore set about tackling the problem and their solutions were acceptable as long as no significant alteration to existing policy was involved.

The Bradford case is different again. Here, rather than personal influence, doctrinal enthusiasm may have been the driving force. The medical superintendent had been appointed by the Board. Hence, the Board's support could be expected, at least initially. The superintendent took upon himself the medical examination of pupils in the context of his belief, first, in the confidence of his diagnosis of the feeble-minded child, and, second, in his estimate that 2 per cent of such children would be identified. On this basis, the number of special classes was enlarged, implying that the medical superintendent's account of the situation was accepted as a rational basis for planning. The support or the acceptance of his legitimacy, however, does not appear to have spread much further than Board members, because teachers' practices in the special classes appear to differ but little from those in ordinary Elementary schools. Perhaps the chink in the doctor's armour was his lack of knowledge of then current educational practice. Consequently, he was effectively unable to make purposeful modifications to teachers' practice.

ROLE OF THE INDIVIDUAL AND TRADITION IN THE SYSTEM'S DEVELOPMENT

The London Board's System

The London School Board had the most developed system of schools for special instruction. The superintendent of the schools was herself a member of the Committee and the Board's curricular policies were adopted as model recommendations by the Committee. The London Board had adopted a system which contained a network of schools for special instruction and special classes in ordinary schools. In each type, the supervision of the work was the responsibility of the superintendent who, in turn, was responsible to the Board. The Board had also developed its own policy and procedure: 'It was agreed that no class should contain more than twenty scholars; that no centre should be for fewer than two classes or more than five; but that if only one class could be formed in any locality, it should be conducted in the ordinary school building and not in a specially erected centre' (Burgwin, 1900, p. 255). The Board had also determined that '[n]o child was taken out of the ordinary school and sent to a centre unless it had been examined by the Board's Medical Officer and the Superintendent and had been certified by them as requiring special treatment' (ibid.).

Charismatic Phases in the London Board's System

The London Board had witnessed several charismatic phases. First, the chairman of the sub-committee for the deaf and blind children had been moved by the plight of a particular mentally defective child (DCDEC, 1898, vol. II, p. 101) to make proposals to the Board that a scheme of special classes be adopted in 1890. The proposals were eventually accepted and transformed into a policy for action. There then came the second charismatic phase with the appointment of the Superintendent of Schools for Special Instruction. The superintendent for several years had been headmistress of a central London Board school. She had recognised the force of poverty and malnutrition in children's lives and had established measures to counteract them (Horn, 1990, pp. 48–60). She had also given evidence to the Cross Commission (RCEEA, 1887, pp. 113–26). The Board's early instincts were to expose the newly appointed superintendent to the direct influence of tradition and she went on an extended tour of the German auxiliary schools before the two special schools were opened by the Board in July 1892. The superintendent's personal qualities were incorporated as a feature into the system because the newly recruited teachers were required to imitate her practices and, in turn, the centres for special instruction became the training centres for teachers sent there by other School Boards. Thus German traditional practices were transmuted through the work of the superintendent into the basis for the London Board's tradition.

Features of the London Board's System

The growth of the system of special schools was in the joint interest of both the superintendent and the London Board's medical officer. Similarly, it was in their interest that it remain within their sphere of control as far as possible. Thus, the panel to certify admissions to special classes comprised the superintendent, the Board's medical officer and an HMI. An earlier proposal to include the local inspector and a teacher from the child's ordinary school was ruled out as being too unwieldy (DCDEC, 1898, vol. II, p. 47).

The origin of the Board's policy, that all newly erected centres for special instruction should contain at least two but no more than five classes, is it be found in the Committee's belief in the idea of classification of pupils as providing optimum efficiency in the organisation of classes (ibid., pp. 73, 80, 104, 148). The London Board tried to work to a policy of classification (ibid., p. 101) and the Committee reported that '[t]he advantages in classification which are attained by three classes at a centre are so great that we recommend that, when possible, centres should be provided with at least that number of classes' (ibid., vol. I, p. 23). The policy, however, was based upon a fallacy, which will be shortly demonstrated.

There was another, perhaps crucial, reason why those involved in the London Board's special schools system should strive to have their ideas and practices widely recognised and imitated. The Committee had been told that in 1896 there were 21 centres for special instruction in the capital with a roll of 896 children (ibid., vol. II, p. 48). A year later, there were 1,012 on the roll (ibid., p. 101). The superintendent reported in 1900 that 'There are now under the control of the Board 53 centres, having a roll of 2,154 children, taught by 119 certificated teachers' (Burgwin, 1900, p. 256). The expansion in three years to more than double the number of centres and children on the roll appears impressive. However, one picture emerges if the Committee's estimate is accepted that one per cent of the school population was feeble-minded and needed special instruction; the picture is far darker if Kerr's estimate of 2 per cent (cf., DCDEC, 1898, vol. II, p. 17) of the relevant population is taken, as Table 6.1 suggests.

TABLE 6.1
CHILDREN IN LONDON ELEMENTARY SCHOOLS AND CENTRES
FOR SPECIAL INSTRUCTION (CSI), 1896–1900

Year	School-age population	Centres for Special Instruction	Number of children in CSI	Children in CSI (%)
1896	722,000	21	896	0.12
1897	727,000	21	1,012	0.13
1900	735,000	53	2,154	0.30

Sources: DCDEC (1898, vol. II, pp. 48, 101); Spalding (1900, p. 41).

In spite of the increase in numbers, if the estimate was accurate, then the London Board only had a small fraction of the estimated numbers of feeble-minded children in the centres for special instruction. In contrast, for the deaf and blind, in 1900 there were 19 centres for the education of the deaf, with a staff of just over 60 teachers and a little over 200 pupils on the roll. Similarly, there were eight day-centres for the education of the blind with 206 children on the roll. However, children attended these centres on a half-time basis with the other half spent in ordinary schools. By alternating juniors and seniors on mornings and afternoons, the capacity of the eight centres was effectively doubled (Spalding, 1900, pp. 251, 254). The inference may be that, although in terms of the size and complexity of its organisation the London Board's system of centres for special instruction may appear to have been thriving, when compared with provision for other forms of disability in children, it was struggling. When compared with a national estimate it also had a great deal of ground yet to cover.

London's 'Schools of Special Difficulty'

There is a curious fact relating to the London Board's centres for special instruction. In 1900 the secretary to the London Board presented a volume to the Paris Exhibition which was designed 'to illustrate the educational work of the School Board for London; to elucidate the problems which were submitted to the Board when it was created in 1870 and the methods by which it has endeavoured to solve them' (Spalding, 1900, p.3). The first two-thirds of the volume outline the development of the Board's policies in different areas of concern and the final part contains the details of provision in terms of children's ages, curriculum and teacher training. The policy section of the volume contains no reference to the centres for special instruction. However, it does mention 'schools which have been recognised by the Board as "Schools of Special Difficulty"; that is schools in which the pupils represent the lowest stratum of London life. These, on account of the extreme poverty or neglect of parents, and the almost complete absence of home training for the children, present serious obstacles to progress' (ibid., p. 188). In these schools, it continued, teachers were paid more because of the circumstances, and the curriculum was narrowly practical. Perhaps the source of the relative slow growth and small size of the system for special instruction in London sprang from such perceptions of the intractable source of the problems. While Moberly, as chairman of the sub-committee for the blind and deaf and as vice-chairman of the London Board, may have been 'aroused to the idea that we were responsible for all the children of London' (DCDEC, 1898, vol. II, p. 101), other members of the Board may have taken a much more cautious view. However, the individual in a system which is under threat will usually fight to maintain that system's existence. Hence, paradoxically, opposition may be a source for strength and growth.

BUREAUCRATISATION IN THE SCHOOL BOARDS

Weber also concerned himself with the process of rationalisation in modern societies (cf., Weber, 1930) and the process of bureaucratisation within modern institutions of administration (cf., Gerth and Mills, 1948, pp. 196–262). The role of specialist knowledge and the status of the officials within bureaucracies also concerned him. It may be possible to use some of the ideas involved in bureaucratisation to explore the early stages of the growth of the special education system. In a situation where there is little distinction between the status of members of a School Board, except in terms of the chair and deputy, then there is potentially more scope for the influence of individuals who may have particular ideas or goals. Individuals who have an interest, say, in the education of the feeble-minded, in order to develop ideas and policies may look towards those they regard as having the appropriate skills and knowledge in this field. Hence, Board members in Brighton, Birmingham and Bristol looked to the ordinary schools and their teachers as representative of the knowledge and skills which the new situation demanded. On the other hand, in Leicester and Nottingham, there existed specialists in the form of inspectors who wished to work with Board members to develop policies in a manner which drew upon their own knowledge and expertise. The Board members and inspectors were germane to the ordinary school system. Within this framework, policy developed with a prime focus upon the work of teachers in schools and children's skills. In this context, specialist medical knowledge was drawn upon to resolve questions which were primarily regarded as to do with schools and children and thus subordinate to them.

Impact of the Appointment of Experts to Boards

The decision to appoint a specialist such as a medical officer to the School Board changed the situation radically. By definition, the specialist enjoyed knowledge which other Board members did not. That knowledge was the reason for the specialist's presence upon the Board. Hence, any proposals put forward by the specialist were likely to be discussed by Board members not in terms of their validity or internal consistency, but rather in terms of factors external to the proposals themselves. An example would be discussion of a proposal in terms of its financial implications. While in a previous context such considerations might have been regarded as important, they could now become paramount. Similarly, a proposal for the establishment of centres for special instruction containing several classes would not necessarily be considered in terms of the argument for having several classes on the same spot, but rather in terms of the optimum location of centres geographically or their viability in terms of the size of the school population. In this way, the inclusion of individual specialists on School Boards implies a reduction of other members' influence over the development of certain aspects of policy. The imputation of charisma may have been influential in directing policies among equals, but was also ineffectual in the face of advice based upon the views of a specialist whose authority on the Board was precisely his or her specialism.

As the Boards shifted to increased bureaucracy, with the appointment of a growing number of specialists, the sphere of influence of the majority of Board members shifted. Thus, paradoxically, the appointment of a superintendent of centres for special instruction and a medical officer by the London Board may have had the reverse effect to that which was intended. Both appointments were intended to help the Board with its difficulties regarding the question of feeble-minded children and to facilitate solutions. But the very nature of their specialist proposals may have driven the Board to consider them primarily upon the grounds to which it had access, those of finance. Hence, the application of some further measures appear to have been necessary if substantial progress was to be made down this route. The extreme division of labour in this instance appears to have created its own restraints. On the other hand, a more simple division of labour such as existed in Leicester appears to have brought greater benefit to children, teachers and ordinary schools. Hence, a legacy of incorporating specialists in the Boards' work was to hive off a part of policy to those specialists, and to consider policy recommendations not in terms of proposals themselves but in the terms to which lay Board members had access. Thus financial considerations may have taken precedence, diverting attention from the work of pupils and schools.

A FALLACY AS THE CORNERSTONE OF POLICY: DEFINITION OF THE SUBJECTS

The Committee heard the evidence of those considered to be at the forefront of medical psychology at the time. They included Dr David Ferrier, Professor of Neuropathology at King's College, London; Dr Francis Warner, Professor of Comparative Anatomy and Physiology at the Royal College of Surgeons; Dr F. H. Walmsley, Medical Officer of the Darenth School for Imbecile Children; Dr Fletcher Beach, former Superintendent of Darenth; and Dr James Kerr, Medical Officer to the Bradford Board. Dr G. E. Shuttleworth, formerly Medical Superintendent of the Royal Albert Asylum for Idiots and Imbeciles, Lancaster, and shortly to be appointed Medical Examiner of Defective Children, School Board for London, was called upon to present evidence as the first witness. His task was the definition of terms. He was also a member of the Committee. In collaboration with Dr W. R. Smith, Medical Officer for the London Board, he presented a memorandum to the Committee on the definition of terms under the heading: 'Idiots, Imbeciles, Feeble-Minded and Defective Children' (DCDEC, 1898, vol. II, p. 2).

Drawing upon authoritative sources, a definition of each of the four terms was offered to the Committee. Firstly, leading medical texts were drawn upon: 'An idiot, or natural fool, is one that hath no understanding from his nativity, and therefore is by law presumed never to attain any', while psychological medicine defined 'idiocy [as] a congenital deficiency of the mental powers' (ibid.). For the second term this same authority stated that 'the word imbecility is generally used to denote a less decided degree of mental incapacity than does idiocy' (ibid.). The memorandum then went on to add that 'the term imbecile, as denoting a degree of weakness of mind less than idiot, was for the first time legally adopted in the Idiots Act, 1886 which states ... that "idiots or imbeciles" do not include lunatics and "lunatics" does not mean or include idiot or imbecile'. Finally, a conclusion of the Egerton Commission was noted: 'There is no clear line separating idiots and imbeciles; it is merely a difference of degree, not of kind. Idiocy means a greater degree of deficiency and imbecility means a lesser degree of such deficiency' (ibid.; cf., RCBDD, 1889, vol. I, p. 95).

For the definition of feeble-mindedness, the Charity Organisation Society's report on 'The Feeble-Minded Child and Adult' published in 1893 was the source (COS, 1893). 'The term feeble-minded is used to signify a lesser degree of mental weakness, while imbecility and idiocy represent the more marked degrees of the malady.' The Charity had observed that the terms 'idiot', 'imbecile' and 'feeble-minded' tended to be interchangeable in America and France but, in compensation, added: 'The definition may be vague but for practical purposes it is sufficient' (ibid.). The conclusion of this section underlined the central theoretical proposition and pointed towards the criterion of practicality.

> In weakness of mind there is every degree. At one end of the scale is the person who is not quite up to the average, who was in a lower class at school than others of his age [and] who is incapable of entertaining ideas of a moderate degree of abstractness or complexity. Beneath this class come those who are recognised as being definitely 'deficient', as being not merely below the average, but below the normal – as being more or less imbecile. The line that divides the dull or weak-minded man from the imbecile is the ability to earn a living ... when an individual fails to reach the full development of the race, the failure will be first noticed in the activities that are left over after the livelihood has been gained; hence we find that in the first degree of weakness of mind, the individual is able to earn his own livelihood, but that when that is

done, his energies are exhausted ... in imbecility, the standard of activity has sunk one degree lower. The imbecile is unable to earn his own livelihood. (DCDEC, 1898, vol. II, p. 2)

The fourth category, that of defective child, by virtue of the Committee's terms of reference 'includes both feeble-minded children and also children who come within this category by reason of physical defect or delicacy' (ibid., p. 3). In conclusion the memorandum stated: 'We recommend that the word feeble-minded be applied to children who are too mentally defective to be properly taught in ordinary elementary schools, but not so defective as to be imbecile in the sense explained above' (ibid.).

THE PRINCIPLE UNDERPINNING THE BLUEPRINT

There were two main principles which underpinned this blueprint for mentality and its diagnosis. The first was the existence of a continuum of mental weakness or deficiency; and the second was that the distinguishing criterion between the classes in the continuum was the ability to earn a living. The scheme posits four more or less broad classes of individuals and gradations within each class. Thus, the normal individual has the powers to earn a living with sufficient in reserve to pursue additional activities – a hobby, reading, attending the theatre, membership of a society, etc. The feeble-minded individual, however, has just sufficient powers to secure a living, but is exhausted in the process and consequently slumps in some stupor until the time for the next stint comes around. Someone of idiot class does not have sufficient powers 'to cut his own food without cutting his fingers ... or be trusted to go out by himself without being knocked down by passing vehicles' (ibid., p. 3). Between the idiot and the feeble-minded is found the imbecile. 'The imbecile is unable to earn his own livelihood ... fails to adapt himself to his vital environment, fails to complete the second step in his intellectual development; but he surmounts completely the first step, that which enables him to adapt himself to his physical environment' (ibid., pp. 2, 3). The 'vital environment' is that which is considered the main spring of life and is work.

The blueprint appears to be based upon certain assumptions: one is that the world of employment is based upon some natural principle and another is that the individual secures a place in the natural order on the basis of personal qualities. The blueprint contrasts with the view that the groups which have control of the materials and forces of economic production are able to create the conditions of employment and unemployment and are able to control the relationship between the employer and the employee and also, by extension, the unemployed. In terms of employment prospects, the position of the child in an impoverished family whose nominal head is an unskilled labourer, contrasts with that of a child whose family control a business of some sort or whose wealth derives from the ownership of property. Thus the criteria which distinguish the classes below the normal appear to be based upon an analysis which derives more from a social class and ownership perspective than from medical science. The attributes of the class considered to be normal are also those which distinguish status groups within society, that is, pursuit of different sorts of leisure activities. The blueprint is thus embedded in a process of the social reproduction of sets of advantages and disadvantages.

THE ESSENCE OF THE BLUEPRINT

The central idea upon which the blueprint is based is that of a continuum of mental weakness or deficiency. The degree of deficiency is established by the reference of one class to one or other of the remaining classes. Thus the feeble-minded are higher in the hierarchy than the imbecile who is, in turn, above the idiot. Such a scheme, however, while it might point to the relationship between classes, does not present criteria by which a class may be identified. Curiously, the criteria which are attempted are social and educational, such as being in a school class below the peer group, rather than to do with the nature of mental processes or the qualities of the mind.

Those concerned primarily with logic and philosophy recognise that there are several kinds of definition (Alston, 1964, pp. 10–30). Conventionally, definitions are divided into those which are explicit and those which are contextual. An explicit definition refers to characteristics external to what are to be defined as the defining features. A contextual definition defines an object or phenomenon in relation to a specific context (Salmon, 1963, pp. 92–3). The Committee's definition of the feeble-minded falls into this latter category. Thus, neither Kerr, who declared, 'There is something that eludes description in diagnosis, you must take the whole case' (DCDEC, 1898, vol. II, p. 18), nor Warner, who admitted that 'it is difficult to define what physical conditions seen, as apart from mental tests, indicate the child as unfitted for the usual methods of education' (ibid., p. 29), nor Ferrier, who considered that 'the line between the normal child, the feeble-minded and the imbecile is very vague' (ibid., p. 150), was of much help to the Committee. Beach did not offer help (ibid., p. 7) nor did Harris (ibid., p. 41). The ability-to-earn-a-living criterion is also important in the blueprint because it is the criterion used to distinguish the educable from the non-educable. This, in turn, may be linked to the shift in debates about the Poor Law previously mentioned in Chapter 3 (cf., Stedman Jones, 1971, p. 290).

THE COMMITTEE'S DILEMMA

The Committee thus faced a dilemma. Its terms of reference included a clause 'to report upon the best practical means for discriminating on the one hand between the educable and the non-educable classes of feeble-minded and defective children and on the other hand between those children who may properly be taught in ordinary elementary schools by ordinary methods and those who should be taught in special schools' (DCDEC, 1898, vol. I, p. 1). The Committee's solution, presented in its report, was to impose a series of arbitrary definitions to distinguish between the different classes and a series of procedures which would confirm the distinctions. Thus the Committee reified the abstractions of the blueprint into a set of concrete procedures.

The Committee adopted the term feeble-minded because that was used in the terms of reference. The class feeble-minded excluded those of imbecile and idiot and 'We have not attempted to formulate a technical definition of feeble-minded children' (ibid., p. 3). Feeble-minded children are described as 'those we have seen in special classes who have been tried in ordinary schools ... and shown to be incapable of receiving benefit' (ibid., pp. 3–4). This may be called definition by social convention. 'Public opinion would revolt, and rightly, against the permanent detention of these educable children in institutions ... Feeble-minded children should therefore be considered a distinct class from imbeciles' (ibid., p. 4). The Committee's propositions are thus mutually supporting: feeble-minded children are not to be in ordinary schools but they are educable because they are not imbeciles and the public would be outraged if they were detained in institutions. Therefore special classes are necessary. Social contagion is a further reason for special classes: 'The feeble-minded would take harm from association with low grade imbeciles and ought to associate with ordinary children as much as is consistent with their receiving the special and individual care that they need' (ibid.). From Foucault's perspective of normalisation, this would be an example of the separation and distribution of subjects around a norm. As with the demarcation of the sane from the insane and the process of incarceration of the latter, the role and position of specialists assume greater importance (see Foucault, 1971, pp. 33–85).

MEASURES TO IDENTIFY THE FEEBLE-MINDED AND THE NON-EDUCABLE

Identification was straightforward, in the Committee's view: 'Feeble-minded children are, in the great majority of cases, marked by some physical defect or defects discernible by the trained observer' (DCDEC, 1898, vol. I, p. 4). The precise difficulty, however, sprang from the fact that feeble-mindedness was not always accompanied by stigmata, hence: 'This is a matter which requires not only medical knowledge but some medical study' (ibid.). The Committee thus turned to the expertise of the professional group which was unable to offer discriminatory criteria in the first place and encouraged it to develop a specialism in the field. There may therefore be a correspondence between (a) the abstract presentation of the concept of a continuum of disability and distinguishing criteria and (b) the physical presence of a witness to the Egerton Commission, who was also a witness to and a member of the Department's Committee and subsequently became Medical Examiner of Defective Children for the London Board.

The Committee had also to decide upon the question of the discrimination between the educable and non-educable feeble-minded children. These fell into two groups: those not in attendance at school and those that were. For the first group neither the attendance committee nor the attendance officer was 'properly qualified to judge whether a child is imbecile or not, this being a question upon which we are satisfied from the evidence brought before us that medical knowledge is indispensable' (ibid., p. 9). The Committee therefore recommended a procedure for the appointment to the school authority of a medical officer, who was to provide a certificate of the child's fitness to attend ordinary school or special class or other institution.

The other group, those already attending ordinary school, needed no special provision until the age of 7. However, defects might be observed, either in the infant school or when older scholars failed to make progress.

138

The Committee believed there were two stages of discrimination involved: first, preliminary selection of children for admission to classes; and, second, the examination of such children. Again, a series of procedures was recommended: 'preliminary selection should be by the teachers in the ordinary schools ... of children fit for special classes rather than ordinary schools' (ibid.). For the young infant and the older scholar it should be a teacher familiar with 'the child's capacity and peculiarities'. School Authorities were to furnish nomination forms to all schools and advertise the time and place of examination. HMI might also nominate children if, in their view, managers had failed to do so. For each child to be examined, teachers had to complete an itemised form (see Appendix 1). The child should be examined by a doctor and the appropriate certificate issued. Moreover, 'the examination of the children by a medical officer should be a necessary condition of recognition of the special classes by the Department and the recommendation to the School Authority ... should be made by the medical officer' (DCDEC, 1898, vol. I, p. 11). The parent could be present at the examination. In London, an HMI should be present to be acquainted with the details of the case from the outset. Similarly, the teacher whose future responsibility the child might be, should also attend. In addition, the teacher from the ordinary school might attend.

Concerning the identification of feeble-minded children, the discrimination between the educable and the non-educable, and the process of selection, allocation and admission of pupils to special classes or classes in ordinary schools, the Committee felt able to state that: 'If the above procedure be adopted, we anticipate no great difficulty either in arriving at a decision or in enforcing it ... in doubtful cases, the Education Department who are the last resort ... have at their disposal the services of a medical adviser' (ibid., p. 12). The Committee's solution to the problems inherent in the definition and criteria for distinguishing between children was to transmute them into a set of stipulated procedures. The abstract conceptions thus became codified in a set of social practices, which is precisely what Foucault intended by the word 'discourse', his term for 'thought as a social practice' (Merquior, 1985, p. 18). Even though practitioners at the leading edge of their discipline were unable to provide rational solutions to the Committee's concerns, the medical profession was to be called upon to give the stamp of approval to decisions.

CLASSIFICATION AND THE ROLE OF THE EDUCATION DEPARTMENT

The Education Department signalled its intention to keep control of special classes. While recognising that variety may be possible, the Committee nevertheless stated that '[a] special class may be defined as one so certified by the Education Department' (DCDEC, 1898, vol. I, p. 15). Certain conditions were essential for recognition: adherence to selection and admission procedures, periodic medical inspections, exclusive use of a room and undivided attention of a qualified teacher, segregation from ordinary pupils, conformity to rules concerning class size and curricular emphasis.

The Committee expressed its preference for a collection of special classes at a centre:

> Subject to the classes being within easy reach, the centre system is approved in preference to a number of scattered single classes as giving better accommodation and better organisation. The advantages in classification which are attained by three classes at a centre are so great that we recommend that, when possible, centres should be provided with at least that number of classes. (ibid., p. 23)

In his examination of a witness, the Committee's chairman, HM Senior Inspector of Schools, declared that it would 'be better to build special schools which would contain three or more classes than to disperse them over a city in twelve or fourteen separate special classes' (ibid., vol. II, p.149). The Senior Examiner on the Committee told another witness: 'If this special instruction were to be provided for the whole of Birmingham, it would be better not to have several small centres but to have a reasonable number of fairly large centres' (ibid., p. 76). One of the replies to the survey of teachers in special classes observed that 'As far as possible no centre should consist of fewer than two classes and that children should be classified' (ibid., p. 258). The London School Board had already opted for this policy for those centres which had been or were to be built. For reasons of economy, special school classes were to be located in existing schools, but for reasons of policy any new centres for special instruction were to have a minimum of at least two classes and a maximum of five (Burgwin, 1900, p. 255). The purpose of the policy in the words of the vice-chairman of the London Board 'was originally to classify as much as we could' (DCDEC, 1898, vol. II, p. 101).

THE FALLACY OF CLASSIFICATION

The fallacy lies in the fact that there were no acceptable criteria for the classification of children, either between the major classes or within them. Members of the Committee pressed the logic of classification upon witnesses on more than one occasion. The idea figures in the report as the ideal mode of organisation of special provision. Because classification is tied in ultimately with the different classes of feeble-minded, imbecile and idiot children, and because these classes are defined contextually in relation to each other, there are no external touchstones. Hence, the Committee was obliged to translate a conceptual scheme into a code of regulatory procedures in order to impose a sense of order on the system. In the same way, at the level of special centres or special classes, the teachers sub-divided groups pragmatically in terms of the children's apparent orderliness and command of spoken and written language (cf., ibid., pp. 66–73, 78–86).

Paradoxically, the practitioners in school ignored the idealised version of classification and operated with their own version, which derived from their experience of work with children. This process of the resolution of dilemmas at the point of delivery of the policy, so to speak, has been characterised as 'Street-Level Bureaucracy' (Lipsky, 1980; cf., Ham and Hill, 1984, pp. 136–42). The special teachers operated in spite of the special system rather than because of its precepts. The dilemma experienced at the level of the School Board is evident in this exchange between the Committee's chairman and a member of the Bristol Board. The context of the exchange concerned the exploitation of child labour:

'But I think [exploitation] would be much worse in the case of these defective children' says a member of a Board. 'Would you like to make all deficient children stop at school till they are sixteen?' asks the Chairman. 'Yes'. 'For that purpose of compulsion how would you define a defective child?' 'I should have to have the assistance of an expert on that – Dr Shuttleworth, perhaps?' 'We have asked two or three experts and they say they are unable to frame a definition.' 'Is it really an insoluble problem?' 'My committee, in consultation with the clerk, say that defective children should be retained till they are sixteen, just as blind and deaf children are … ' 'The committee would decide autocratically, so to speak?' 'Where it is thought expedient by the school authority was our suggestion.' (DCDEC, 1898, vol. II, p. 147)

In this way, the fallacy which was at the core of classification produced pragmatic responses of different kinds at the level of the Departmental Committee, the School Boards and the schools.

LEGACY OF THE CONTEXTUAL DEFINITION

The most important legacy of the contextual definition of feeble-mindedness is its continuing role at the core of policy for the education of some children. The terminology of feeble-minded may have changed to that of the mentally defective, the educationally sub-normal (mild or severe), but the central problem of distinguishing these children from so-called normal children remains. More recently, the Warnock Report's terminology suggested children with 'mild, moderate or severe learning difficulties', and although the emphasis apparently shifted from a medical or psychological diagnosis to an educational one, the contextual nature of the definitions presented the same difficulty in a new form. This was embedded in one of the 1981 Act's definitions of children with special educational needs as those 'having significantly greater difficulty in learning than the majority of children of [their] age' (Section 1). Although the inadequacy of the definition was highlighted in a recent report and presented as the main reason for the failure of policy in this area (Audit Commission and HMI, 1992, p. 51), and although that same report recommended that the definition be reconsidered, the recent Bill and subsequent Act has not attempted any revision (Education Act, 1993, Part III). The government's solution is the introduction of a 'Code of Practice' to govern local authorities' practices in this regard (Norbury, 1993, p. 2). The Code, however, retains a contextual definition.

OTHER EVIDENCE PRESENTED TO THE COMMITTEE

Apart from the contribution of evidence to the Committee by the expert medical witnesses, there were three other identifiable groups: the teachers surveyed in existing special classes, and the panels of HMI who undertook surveys of rural and urban education authorities respectively.

Perspective of Teachers in Special Classes

The Committee sent a questionnaire (see Appendix 4) to all teachers of special classes. A total of 36 replied: 24 respondents were teachers in

London which at that time had 21 centres, and 12 were teachers in the other six existing special centres or classes. Hence the replies may be regarded as an extensive sample of the field.

Some questions called for factual answers, others expressions of opinion. Three-quarters of the teachers observed that children who on admission appeared non-educable, afterwards turned out to be educable. That was not an uncommon occurrence (DCDEC, 1898, vol. II, p. 255). None was able to offer a practical means of distinguishing the educable from the non-educable in order to recognise those who would be best educated in either ordinary schools or special classes. Some referred to abnormalities in children's physical appearance and movements, but '[t]here can be no infallible rule for distinguishing such cases. There must be constant revision of the classes; being with children day after day is the only sure guide' (ibid., p. 256). In this way, the teachers appeared to come to terms with the arbitrary nature of the decisions which had been made and imposed their own pedagogic criteria (cf., Lipsky, 1980).

Again, three-quarters of the teachers believed that the information relating to children which they received from ordinary teachers, while trustworthy, would benefit considerably from the addition of detailed descriptions of children's abilities and preferably in answers to a standardised form.

While the children in their classes were 'more restless, spiteful and mischievous than ordinary children' (DCDEC, 1898, vol. II, p. 256), the few who were incapable of control fell into the class of imbecile and had been incorrectly admitted. Regarding a child's progress and behaviour, teachers appeared to hold two sets of opinions: on the one hand, for those who made progress in the class, while agreeing that there were no identifiable criteria for admission, it was observed that many admitted as non-educable proved educable; on the other hand, those with intractable discipline problems were seen as children who had been wrongly admitted and were ineducable. The teachers also maintained that children's behaviour was the result of factors beyond their control: 'the children vary very much from day to day according to the weather. They are very restless and noisy during high winds, fogs or extreme heat' (ibid., p. 256).

Most believed that it was preferable for the special classes to be physically separated from the rest of the school. If this was not possible, the special children should have their own entry to the building and their own play-area. In addition, the school day should start and finish at different times from the ordinary school. These measures were proposed in the interests of the children so that they should not be subject to taunts or bullying from their peers in ordinary schools, but they were also practices which identified and demarcated subjects in the process of normalisation.

Regarding the curriculum, their main plea was for more flexibility: 'We should not be expected to adhere invariably to a time-table of work to a scheme based upon the lines of an ordinary school' (ibid., p. 259). In addition, they requested specialist equipment which lent itself to active and practical learning, with particular pleas for single desks and a musical instrument.

Finally, they thought teachers for special classes should be selected by virtue of their special qualities and that they should be provided with special training for their work 'so that their treatment of the children may have a scientific basis' (ibid., p. 258).

Summary of Special Teachers' Evidence

In sum, the teachers put forward arguments for a special school system which should recognise the different and preferably more highly trained, nature of their work, and one where the children should be separated from other children on the grounds of efficiency. There should also be modifications to the curriculum and additional resources. All these considerations implied alterations to working conditions which would further demarcate them from other teachers in ordinary schools. The whole edifice, however, was founded upon the basis that the ineducable on admission often subsequently proved educable and that there was no practical way of distinguishing the one from the other.

The teachers' practical problem was therefore to impose an order upon a system derived from arbitrariness. A reasonable inference would be that teachers in special classes, having been selected on the basis of their special teaching abilities and being in receipt of enhanced salaries, for the most part, set out to prove they were indeed special and to create a special system different from that of ordinary Elementary schools. The legacy appears to be that of a self-fulfilling prophecy, whereby the claim to have identified a particular problematic phenomenon leads to the realisation of its solution in social practices.

HMI Observations on Feeble-Minded Children in Rural Districts

Three HMI had been commissioned by the Committee to survey provision for feeble-minded children in rural districts. Their evidence was based upon returns from 28 inspectors covering 26 counties and 88 parishes, with an inclusive school-age population of 166,303 children.

Their most crucial observation sprang from the size of the rural districts' school population and the nature of village life. The feeble-minded child was not evident in sufficient numbers in any one rural district to justify the establishment of a special class. Hence the question arose whether a special class or special school should be established by a number of districts pooling their resources. On balance, this was rejected in favour of the larger county authorities establishing special residential institutions. The prime arguments for the larger authority and the residential units were, first, that the counties could build up a team of personnel with the necessary expertise while the justification for such personnel would fluctuate at district level depending on the incidence of feeble-minded children, and, second, the distance of travel probably implied that institutions should be residential for efficiency's sake. There was the added argument that the county was more likely to take a detached view of cases as its personnel were not necessarily embedded in local social life (ibid. p. 203).

This decision, however, produced the pivotal question whether the interests of the feeble-minded child were best served by living at home with his or her family and attending the local school with its known limitations in this regard – the age-range was already spread and the numbers of teachers small – or by being removed from his or her family and placed in a specialist institution with similar children, where all was geared to improving the lot of the feeble-minded.

The HMI felt that their evidence was unanimous – both the feeble-minded child and the imbecile had more to gain from being educated at a local school and staying at home than by going away: 'only a small residuum ought to go to institutions' (ibid., p. 202), and 'the great majority would be more fit for country life after passing through the ordinary school ... if they are to stay in the country ... they would get very nearly as great advantages in the country school as they would anywhere else' (ibid., p. 203).

The reason why HMI drew these conclusions was a perception of the differences between rural and urban life which appeared to correspond very much to Tonnies's conception of the distinction between community (*Gemeinschaft*) and society (*Gesellschaft*). In his conception of community, social relationships were characterised by tradition, by blood and kinship ties, by connection to land and a neighbourhood and by friendship. There was little division of labour. Society, however, was based upon economic enterprise, rationality, skill and calculation, where social relationships were largely impersonal, contractual and purposeful. The division of labour was extensive (Tonnies, 1955, pp. 42–7, 98–114; cf., Nisbet, 1967, pp. 73–9).

The residential school was based upon the ideas which underpinned this latter concept of society, because it had a specialised staff and equipment and children would necessarily be removed from the social environment of the neighbourhood:

> the larger proportion are better fitted for their future by living at home in family life and by seeing all the circumstances of rural life and labour among their own people than by being drafted away to an institution necessarily very different in its arrangements from the ordinary rural home, where [in the institution] all the manual work is of a more specialised type and under constant supervision. (DCDEC, 1898, vol. II, p. 202)

The argument seems to be that it would be harmful for the well-being of these children to be exposed to an alternative way of living and that they are best cemented into an existing traditional way of life. In addition, they would 'be returned after a few years to conditions which have become unfamiliar and among people who have ceased to be friends and who know the returner only as having come from the "silly school"' (ibid.). Also, because their work at the institution would have been under constant supervision, they would be unable to work in the traditional unsupervised manner which was customary in the rural neighbourhood.

HMI Assumptions

The views expressed by HMI seem based upon a number of assumptions. The first is that the special teaching at the institution would be successful and that its consequences would be to remove a child's knowledge of the features of his or her earlier life and environment. The second is an oversimplified view of rural life which, in spite of many external features of social sameness, was often built upon a network of subtle differences. Perhaps the most obvious shortcoming is to assume that someone working alone is unsupervised and not answerable to anyone. The reference to 'silly school' may be as much a reflection upon the way the schools were set up as it is HMI's own assessment of their popular evaluation. The rural population may have simply perceived them as yet another imposition and restriction upon their own and their children's lives.

The main point appears to be that HMI perceived a distinction between modern society, of which, presumably, they regarded themselves as a part, and the traditional rural community. Somehow, in their view, the feeble-minded became better adjusted to life in a rural community through a deficient education, than through one which might be more efficient. Earlier it had been established that curricular differentiation was particularly challenging in the small village school, with its small staff and scant equipment making individual pupil attention almost impossible (ibid., p. 201). This seems a clear example of a policy which would seek to reproduce and project the type of social relationships and expectations which were thought to exist in the past, into the future. HMI's conception of rural life appears to contrast with that of the Leicester inspector who regarded enforced migration from the countryside by virtue of poverty and ill-treatment as having created a difficulty for schools and put pressure upon the Standard 0 system (ibid., pp. 136–7). It may be a fair inference that HMI constituted an urban status group which had a particular and incomplete view of rural life. The purpose of education for the feeble-minded child in the rural countryside was not the improvement or development of personal skills – not even as they related to future employment – but the confirmation of the child in its existing status. Thus the technical device of keeping a feeble-minded child in a kindergarten class would be rejected because, as an HMI remarked: 'I think the great thing is to try to keep the child as much among children of its own age as you can, because it helps to keep up the child's self-respect and confidence' (ibid., p. 202).

The aim of education in this respect was confirmation of a child's situation rather than seeking to change or improve it. It may also have been a part of a larger syndrome, part of a larger process of modernisation and rationalisation.

HMI Observations on Feeble-Minded Children in Urban Areas

Again, three HMI had been commissioned by the Committee to survey provision for feeble-minded children in urban districts. Their evidence was based upon returns from 22 HMI who spanned the Northern, Midland and Southwest Divisions. Data were from 22 towns with a school-age population of 846,600 children.

Variations in the Incidence of Feeble-Minded Children

The evidence of HMI regarding the incidence of feeble-minded children is perhaps more reliable than that of the specialists, whose job it is to find them, and the ordinary teachers, whose task it is to teach them. The first observation by HMI was the very wide range in the proportion of feeble-minded children in the school population identified by different urban authorities. This ranged from none in Gainsborough, six in a thousand in Cardiff and eight in Hull, ½ per cent in Liverpool, Newcastle, Plymouth, Aston, Reading, Merthyr Tydfil and Swansea, to 1 per cent in Bradford, Halifax, Norwich and Birmingham. The highest incidence, of over 2 per cent, was reported from Southampton (ibid., p. 223). The second observation was HMI's view that, in spite of this range of identified incidence, the urban authorities had largely underestimated the numbers of feeble-minded children and had made little or no provision for them. Thus, 'In the case of Liverpool there are no special classes for defective children' (ibid., p. 224). The same was true for Manchester, Leeds, Plymouth and elsewhere. In addition, even in those areas where special classes existed, they were insufficient to meet the needs. HMI agreed that '[i]n Birmingham you have special classes but not sufficient for the population' (ibid.). The same was true of Bristol and Plymouth. The situation was summarised in this way by an HMI: 'Out of the twenty-two towns ... only six have yet practically faced the question. A few affect to disbelieve in any amount of serious defect and the majority either regard it as insufficient to call for immediate action or have shelved the question for a time and are waiting for a lead' (ibid., p. 226).

The reason HMI offered for the authorities' reluctance was the absence of guidance or a model to follow. There was no legislation in this area as there was for the blind and the deaf child. Hence, there appeared to be a reluctance by authorities to commit themselves to a policy which was not strictly necessary but which would entail additional financial resources. This was summarised as: 'unless a fairly substantial grant were given there might be a good deal of hesitation to make as much provision as is necessary in many towns' (ibid.). HMI reported a readiness to take action once these matters had been clarified.

The Effect of the Absence of Policy

In the meantime, there was no policy or provision for the feeble-minded children who were 'all mixed up with Standard I in school and called Standard 0'. Alternatively, 'they are scattered through the school according to age and physical development'. This was regarded as 'a better plan but not so good as special classes' (ibid., p. 224).

Criteria for Admission to Special Classes

HMI had also formulated firm opinions on admission to special classes. In the first place, they rejected the alleged expertise and experience of members of the medical profession in this area. They believed there were

148

two grounds for the rejection: first, 'experts are apt to take strong views on their own subject ... it is not wise to leave uncontrolled authority in their hands'; second, although qualified in medicine, a doctor may lack experience in these cases because of their comparative rarity: 'The doctor will not be a specialist for you cannot get a specialist to go around the country and decide in every case' (ibid., p. 225).

In the second place, HMI regarded the problem as one which had its roots in school and the classroom. Hence, 'the ultimate decision [on admission to special classes] should remain with the Department of Education or with the Department's representative ... anybody who has had a great deal of experience with these children would be a better judge than an ordinary practitioner' (ibid.). There were also practical objections to a medical diagnosis because 'very often the deficiency will not appear until the person who is forming a judgement has been in company of the child for weeks'. For this reason, HMI added, 'I should trust the opinion of a teacher or somebody in that child's company continually, sooner than I should trust the opinion of a doctor' (ibid., p. 225).

Thirdly, HMI's solutions to the problem were related to class size and the curriculum. Thus, 'twenty is a maximum number of such children to be allotted to a teacher'. Preferably, however, they were 'more inclined to eight to ten than a maximum of twenty' (ibid., p. 228). Also, in their opinion, the Department of Education should lay down certain regulations in a circular which should be a general guide outside the code for public Elementary schools. These regulations should 'allow a greater variety of teaching [and] allow a free hand outside the code' (ibid., p. 227). This action 'would be likely to draw up a better set of instructions' (ibid.). HMI in this way sought a solution to an educational problem which drew upon resources within the system rather than reaching for an authoritative solution from outside the schools' system.

HMI also pressed for the problem to be tackled within the context of the ordinary school because they perceived the consequence of the special school as that of labelling children, which compounded existing difficulties. They observed that parents were often reluctant to accept the judgments of experts because they 'are often unwilling to have their children labelled as feeble-minded or children that ought to be in special classes' (ibid., p. 227). Although 'every possible means are taken to prevent that labelling by giving the name of special classes and by attaching classes to schools rather than by having special schools which might be called "idiot schools"', nevertheless, the 'parent would rather have his child considered an ordinary child than the child of a special class' (ibid., p. 228).

149

The Stance of HMI

The cynical view would be that HMI would be expected to take this stance with regard to outsiders from the medical profession encroaching upon their own preserve. However, HMI do present both a critique and an answer to the difficulty which existed, within the realms of their existing knowledge. Thus the source and solution relate to the nature of the Code, its content and measurement, and to the demands on the teacher made by large classes. In this way, HMI point to a solution which is demonstrably within their grasp, unlike some experts from the medical profession who offer a solution in which important claims have yet to be established as fact. Moreover, unlike members of the medical profession who may regard themselves as presenting a solution to a personal, technical problem, HMI are able to relate the problem and its solution to a much wider social context; and one in which the solution itself may have social consequences; as Marx observed: 'Mankind always takes up only such problems as it can solve' (1968, p. 4).

HMI who operated in the urban areas, like their colleagues in rural districts, appeared to have a clear insight into the politics behind the provision for feeble-minded children. Unlike their rural brethren, HMI for urban areas did appear to offer a radical solution to provision for feeble-minded children and a solution in which the system of education, rather than confirming children in their particular social status, might be an opportunity to try to prevent the prospect of social labelling and the confirmation of lowly social status. Additionally, their belief that familiarity with the child was a precondition of diagnosis may also point to a more varied view of human capacities which are shaped by the social environment. If that is the case, then there is a prospect for change with a change in that environment. The HMI legacy may be the presentation of practical experience in the face of specialist, professional argument. Theirs was an expertise founded upon knowledge and experience. That expertise lost out in favour of specialist knowledge deriving from the science of medicine. In this sense, HMI constituted the 'organic intellectuals' of the Department of Education (cf., Gramsci, 1971, pp. 5–23).

PIVOTAL ROLE OF RELATIVISTIC DEFINITION AND CLASSIFICATION

The lynchpin of the Committee's deliberations was the definition of feeble-mindedness formulated by the Superintendent of the Royal Albert Asylum, Dr G. E. Shuttleworth. In his evidence to the Royal Commission on the Blind, the Deaf and the Dumb in 1889, he had argued that the distinction between the class of idiot and imbecile is 'a difference of degree and not of kind. Idiocy means a lower degradation of intellect, a greater deficiency of intellect, and imbecility means a lesser degree of such deficiency' (RCBDD, 1889, p. 705). This gradation of mental deficiency became the basis for the fourfold classification of 'idiots, imbeciles, feeble-minded and defective children' presented to the Committee by Dr Shuttleworth, one of their own members, as the first witness (see DCDEC, 1898, vol. II, pp. 1–2). The Committee accepted this gradation formula as a working definition (cf., DCDEC, 1898, vol. I, p. 3). From the working premise of a gradation of mental deficiency, there followed the logical proposition of classification. Classification implied an homogeneity within the class which would lead to efficiency in school provision and teaching. The Committee endorsed the idea of classification and recommended it as an ideal practice in its Report (ibid., vol. I, p. 23).

The Committee members, however, were not fools, in the sense of idiots, and realised the difficulties inherent in classification (see DCDEC, 1898, vol. II, p. 147). For that reason they reported that 'We have not attempted to formulate a technical definition of feeble-minded children; but we were instructed to report upon the best practical means of discriminating these children from normal and from imbecile children' (DCDEC, 1898, vol. I, p. 3). The search for the best practical means of discrimination is, perhaps, the reason why attention was directed towards the London School Board because it had the most developed system for the identification and allocation of children in need of special instruction.

ROLE OF THE LONDON BOARD

The London School Board, either through the desire to establish orderliness or because of the perceived extent of the difficulty, had established a system whereby its head or superintendent was responsible to the Board. The superintendent was responsible for the organisation and oversight of a series of schools for special instruction. Within the schools, teachers worked under the responsibility of senior teachers. These senior teachers were in turn responsible to the superintendent. The London Board had thus devised a system of schools for special instruction which was detached from the system of Elementary schools except in terms of the point of transference of pupils from ordinary Elementary schools to the special schools. Hence, in terms of the smooth running of the system, the only point which could be potentially out of the superintendent's control was that of the entry procedures. The superintendent was, however, a former headteacher of one of the Board's schools. The reason for her appointment was precisely her proven skills in the ordinary Elementary school. The procedure for the referral of children as candidates for the special schools was by the recommendation of the headteacher in an Elementary school. Given that the organisation of schools, teachers and pupils is an inexact science, there would be considerable scope for disagreement about, first, which pupil was a suitable candidate for special school, and, second, whether the pupil should be admitted or not. The grounds for legitimate disagreement between the proposing teacher and the receiving superintendent could be extensive. The debates and disputes could be protracted and, in terms of running an efficient system, time-consuming. For that reason, the superintendent may have sought a device to concentrate debates and to finalise decisions.

The London Board already had in its employ a medical officer and an assistant medical officer. This latter, in evidence to the Committee, gave his opinion that admittance to special schools should become more regularised, by requiring teachers to complete accurately a detailed form concerning the child, and that the final decision concerning the child's suitability for admission should rest with the medical officer (ibid., vol. II, p. 41). The same officer claimed that examination of the child could be systematised to occupy little more than five minutes and that ten or more examinations would be possible in an hour (ibid., p. 43). The coalition of the Board's superintendent for special schools and the medical officer was in their joint interests: the one would have a means of imposing some rationality on admissions and the other an opportunity to enlarge upon an area of professional activity. The presence of a medical officer at the examination for admission would lend an aura of authority to the decision.

PRACTICAL RESOLUTION OF THE PROBLEM OF DISCRIMINATION

The Committee's terms of reference had required it to report upon 'the best practical means for discriminating between the educable and non-educable classes of feeble-minded children' (ibid., vol. I, p. iii). Given that there did not exist an objective means for such discriminating, the presence of a member of the medical profession at the examination for admission may have proved the 'best practical' means. Perhaps for this reason, the Committee recommended that the first duty of School Authorities was that '[they] should be required to appoint medical officers to advise them as to the discrimination of defective children ... Those who already employ medical officers will presumably entrust them with the duty: and those who do not will arrange some medical man to be their officer for this purpose' (ibid., p. 37). This recommendation both confirmed and enhanced the professional position of the Boards' medical officers who had given evidence to the committee.

ROLE OF THE EDUCATION DEPARTMENT

This sort of analysis does not necessarily point towards some kind of conspiracy theory. Rather, it may point to an attempt to seek a solution to an acknowledged difficulty by the best means available. The Lord President of the Education Department had established the Committee and the terms of reference. It is not unlikely that the Secretary of the Department gave advice concerning the terms of reference to the Lord President, and the phrase 'best practical means for discriminating' may have originated here. This would imply that the Department was looking for a solution from what was regarded as the most authoritative source. This would involve the establishment of a special system of medical examiners, teachers and classes to deal with the problem. The evidence suggests that an alternative approach was available and possible: that is, the kind of analysis presented by Francis Warner, who saw the problem rooted in the nature of the economy and the social environment and the demands of the Elementary school system. In a similar vein, Leicester's inspector had demonstrated how the difficulties of the apparently feeble-minded child could be tackled from within the system of schools and the organisation of teachers. However sound that approach may have been in ideological terms and beneficial in its long-term effects – especially for the children concerned – the reality was that from the Committee's point of view it was almost a non-starter. There were two main reasons: first, it implied some interference or modification with factors to do with the economy and housing, for instance, which were well beyond the remit of the Education Department; and second, it implied some measure of direction and control over the many Schools Boards who oversaw their schools' policies and a radical change in the Elementary school system. The practical implications for changes on this scale were out of the question.

THE COMMITTEE'S SOLUTION

The Committee, therefore, may have simply turned to a system of ideas which had a general credibility and authority, and to an existing system of special schools for instruction as a means whereby the problem which faced the schools, Boards and Department could be most easily resolved. The establishment of special classes and the selection and training of special teachers was a realistic and attainable solution. It also had the merit, at least in the eyes of most teachers in Elementary schools, that it was a system designed to tackle the perceived problem as it manifested itself in schools. The alternative route would require a reappraisal of taken-for-granted practices by schools and Boards within the system.

It could be argued that the Committee's recommendation looked to a source of authority as endorsement which was outside the education system and which was based upon that traditional element associated with the high-status medical profession. While that may be true, the major source of the organisational ideas, Shuttleworth, may be regarded as pursuing innovative ideas within the new science of medical psychology. Paradoxically, however, that search for the new was occurring within a paradigm of medicine which had a very long provenance. Shuttleworth's whole career was spent within the medical paradigm of the gradation and classification of mental abilities. His purpose was, perhaps, to find a new technical means to resolve a long-established problem in medicine. Hence, Shuttleworth represented the reproduction in a different form of the ideas and associated practices of the past. He represented, as it were, the reproduction of the status quo through modern techniques. Warner is by far the more radical figure because he perceived that the practice of medicine is a product of the prevailing social environment. Hence symptoms and diagnosis may be as much social products as they are personal characteristics (cf., Mort, 1985, pp. 208–10). Shuttleworth appears to be confined in the narrow domain of presenting symptoms as the diagnosis solely of personal attributes.

ENDORSEMENT OF THE LONDON SYSTEM

The Committee's crucial decision was that of the choice of conceptual scheme and the practical procedures which were thereby entailed. The adoption of the London Board system of schools for special instruction was second order, because it followed from that first decision and appeared to exemplify in practice the central ideas of classes and classification. The endorsement of the London system also endorsed two elements of tradition: the emphasis of the special school curriculum and the training of teachers. The newly appointed superintendent of London's special schools was sent on a tour of the established German auxiliary schools. These had already been in operation for a decade and their roots went back even further (RCBDD, 1889, vol. II, pp. 370–1). The intention was that their curricular practices should be translated to the English context. Hence, the emphasis was to be upon activity, enjoyment and practical subjects. In this way, a tradition of curricular practices mutated across cultures and through generations.

With the exception of Bradford, the teachers in the new special classes spent a period of time in the London Board's special schools as a part of a process of induction into their new work. In this way, the tradition inherent in both the German system and the London system of special schools was built into the new system in different parts of the country. Thus the past became manifest in the present.

The disposition of the Committee is perhaps best summarised as pragmatic. The terms of reference presented the challenge quite clearly, that of the discrimination between the educable and non-educable of the class of feeble-minded children. At the level of ideas or theory or existing medical knowledge there was no sure answer to that question. Hence the Committee was obliged to turn to the realm of practice. Here, there was available a model of a School Board which had espoused the concept of classification and sought to make it an organisational idea in practice. For this reason, the Committee seemed disposed to recommend a series of technical procedures which appeared to resolve the problem presented at that time to ordinary Elementary schools by feeble-minded children

THE FIRST SPECIAL CLASSES FOR FEEBLE-MINDED CHILDREN: SOME CONCLUSIONS

The origin of special classes may be located within a configuration of factors which had their own roots in the past. The form which the special classes took in terms of curriculum and organisation may be located in their contemporary circumstances.

Social Background

The general background factors which led to the desire for some form of special treatment for children struggling with the demands of schooling are extensive and pervasive. They involve changes in the nature of the economy and industrial production. This entailed the migration of populations to urban areas and the increase in size and density of urban concentrations. The unequal distribution of the rewards of industrial production produced pockets of poverty and the concentration of population in poor-quality housing. The spectre of poverty and the urban masses loomed large in the 1880s. 'The discovery of a huge and swelling residuum [of the poor] and the growing uncertainty about the mood of the respectable working class portended the threat of revolution' (Stedman Jones, 1971, p. 290). By a chance of nature, the period from December 1885 to March 1886, which saw the establishment and commencement of the two Royal Commissions, also witnessed the recording of the lowest mean temperatures for decades (Drummond, 1943, p. 28). This brought outside work and the docks to a virtual standstill. There was considerable social unrest in the capital. The unrest continued through 1886 to culminate in the events of 'bloody Sunday' in October 1887, when a large mob rioted violently in the Strand and was confronted by the military forces of authority. There was extensive unease at this time at the potential threat to civil society posed by the urban poor.

Nature of the Elementary School System

In parallel with these factors, is a system of Elementary schools initiated by Voluntary bodies. The Education Act, 1870, required that there should be accommodation in Elementary schools for all children of the relevant age group. The task of the Boards was to produce the necessary accommodation. The Education Act, 1880, took the process a step further by *requiring* the attendance of all children of the relevant age group. In this way, the pressure upon the existing system increased: first, by having to expand to provide potential places for children; and, second, by having to accommodate a much wider range of pupils than previously. In the past, children had attended school because their parents had thought it desirable. Now children were compelled to attend by the authorities. Inroads were thus made into groups which were without a tradition in formal schooling and which were either unsupportive or hostile to it (cf., McCann, 1977).

The Elementary system of schools was founded upon the promise of efficiency. Thus there were large classes, few qualified teachers and more pupil-teachers. The Code which controlled the schools specified a particular curricular emphasis upon the three Rs while the mode of external examination which determined the level of payment also determined the pedagogic approach. The system was as mechanistic in its organisation as the industrial activity which surrounded it.

Emergence of the Pupil Struggling to Learn

The pressure upon the Elementary school system thus came from two prime sources: the increased numbers of pupils with a greater diversity of backgrounds and the rigid control of the content of the system by external examination (cf., Walkerdine, 1984, pp. 164–8). Within this context there began to emerge a group of children who were struggling with the demands of the system. And, perhaps not surprisingly, they made their first appearance in urban areas. That is not to say that they were not present in the rural Elementary school, but rather that the solution was different. The size of the relevant group in urban areas posed its own problematics. The accepted best estimate was 1 per cent of the school-age population and the highest was 2 per cent; the interesting question is why were there not many more? Were the elements of control sufficient to keep the lid on the system? Or was it the fact that the new system of special classes itself provided the lid for the system by removing the most intractable cases?

Pressure to Find a Solution

The Royal Commission on the Blind, the Deaf and the Dumb, began its deliberations in 1886. Following its Report in 1889, there was legislation for the education of the blind and the deaf. The position regarding the other group of children was not as clear-cut and was therefore referred to the Departmental Committee. A class of children who had been designated feeble-minded, but educable as distinguished from the non-educable, was therefore first identified in the Royal Commission of 1889, yet had to wait almost another decade before any official provision was made for them.

There is an element of chance or historical accident in the manner in which the category of feeble-minded children emerged and was handled. The Cross Commission was established in 1886 to 'inquire into the working of the Elementary Education Acts', and within a very few days the Egerton Commission was also established. However, the Cross Commission made the decision 'that the case of feeble-minded children would come more appropriately within [the Egerton Commission's] terms of reference' (RCBDD, 1889, p. 104). Hence, it was almost inevitable that a solution to the educational problem of feeble-minded children was to be sought outside the existing parameters of the Elementary schools' system.

Consequences of the Solution

From the measures of the Education Acts in 1870 and 1880 and through the two Royal Commissions reporting in the second half of the 1880s, feeble-minded children in Elementary schools came to be regarded as a problem about-which-something-had-to-be-done. That problem was sharpened by legislation for the education of the blind and deaf early in the 1890s. The Departmental Committee presented with this problem appeared to turn to what seemed the most rational and authoritative solution, even though it may have been aware that its internal logic was irrational and its solutions flawed. The consequences of that decision were both serious and long-lasting. First, it gave an important boost to the medical profession and to medical psychology and guaranteed both an important place within the new structure for special education. That boost was important because medicine was coincidentally striving to be established as an objective science (cf., McKeown, 1971; Porter, 1993, pp. 48–60). Such a public endorsement must have been an important gain. Second, however, it diverted attention away from the system of Elementary schools and any part it may have played in the production of feeble-minded children. Thus it diverted attention from the search for a solution to the difficulties of feeble-minded children within the prevailing educational context.

Nature and Role of the London Board

The model for special schools of instruction which the London Board presented may well have been opportune but it was not necessarily the optimum. The London School Board was an outcome of the Education Act 1870. The government's original scheme for the Bill had been that the administration of education in London was to be devolved upon a number of small Education Boards which were already in existence. As the Vice-President of the Council, W. E. Forster, remarked during the progress of the Bill: 'In the case of the school districts of the Metropolis we need have no provision for election, because we have already School Boards elected by the different Boards of Guardians within these school districts' (quoted in Spalding, 1900, p. 21). This proposal found disfavour and was amended to the effect that 'the ratepayers of the district should elect the School Board members' (ibid.). This proposal, however, would have been an impractical way of dealing with the Metropolis's requirements. Hence a further proposal was made and carried, to the effect that education in the metropolis was placed under the control of one Board directly elected by ratepayers. In this way, the effects of the 1867 Reform Bill had an impact upon the organisation of Elementary schools.

The London Board was thus created in 1870. The Board was unique in several respects, not least its size. On 29 November 1870, Paris was held in the siege grip of the German armies and the rest of Europe was awaiting the political outcome of Russia's repudiation of the Treaty of Paris. *The Times* leader that day, however, declared: 'The great event of today for this country, whatever may be passing on the Continent of Europe, will be the election of the first London School Board. No equally powerful body will exist in England outside Parliament, if power be measured by influence for good or evil over masses of human beings' (quoted in Spalding, 1900, p. 29).

TABLE 6.2
INCREASE IN SCHOOL-AGE POPULATION IN LONDON, 1871–85

Year	Number of school-age children	Increase (%)
1871	518,000	–
1875	571,000	10.3
1880	617,000	19.3
1885	657,000	26.8

Source: Spalding (1900, p. 41).

The size of the school-age population in London and its growth is evident in Table 6.2. The rapid rate of increase in numbers of pupils from 1871–75 was sustained until 1880. The next five years witnessed a further large proportionate increase. By virtue of the size of the school population, the number of schools and the number of district authorities, the London School Board was in a position of overseeing the work of many groups under its overall control. It tended to operate, so to speak, at one step back from direct involvement in schools. Hence, while a much smaller Board, such as that in Leicester, was subject to the same pressures of increasing pupil numbers in a similar enveloping social, economic and educational climate, it was perhaps able to feel that it was in firm control of the situation and able to execute any necessary measures at the school level. For this reason, the Leicester Board was able to put faith in its system of Standard 0 and the special class to deal with the relatively small number of dull, backward or feeble-minded children the schools were discovering. In London, the numbers of feeble-minded children being put forward by the schools made this approach almost impossible. The numbers implied that some mechanism was needed to deal with the situation, to provide an appropriate education or training for feeble-minded children, and to oversee the selection, examination and admission to schools which were different from those they had come from. The establishment of the system of schools for special instruction was an ideal solution because, under the supervision of the appointed superintendent of such schools, the number of classes could fluctuate and be as flexible in size and location as the situation demanded. The system's and the classes' detachment from the Elementary school system made that flexibility possible.

The argument concerning the impact of specialist members on School Boards has been made previously. The main effect, it was suggested, was in fact to move deliberation of proposals away from specialist grounds to those to which lay Board members had access. Not uncommonly that meant financial considerations. The performance of the London Board in selecting and admitting pupils to its centres for special instruction have been presented in detail (see Table 6.1, p. 130). In the context of an estimate of one per cent of the school-age population as feeble-minded, the London Board in 1896 had 0.12 per cent of the relevant population in its centres for special instruction and 0.30 per cent in 1900. Thus, although from the point of view of the administration of the system and perhaps also from the financial angle, the centres for special instruction may appear to have been efficient, from the perspective of children and teachers in Elementary schools that can hardly have been the case.

The Education Department's Committee appears to have turned to the London Board's model for centres of special instruction because it was apparently the most well developed, systematic and experienced system. However, the Committee may not have been aware of the pitfalls inherent in the system.

Influence of Individuals

In an analysis of this sort, it is perhaps easy to regard individual players as creatures of circumstance. Thus, there is evidence to argue that the Senior Chief HMI, the HMI and the Examiner on the Committee had made up their minds upon the direction their findings would go and were prepared to coach witnesses to these ends. Again, the faction from the London Board's centres for special instruction appear to press their own case. And in this regard Boards' medical officers emerged with an enhanced status.

There are other players, however, who have attempted to impose their ideas upon a much larger scene in order to shift the course of policy and history. The obvious player in this regard is Shuttleworth who, at the time of presenting his ideas both to the Egerton Commission and the Departmental Committee, was strictly speaking outside the system of Elementary schools. Warner is a similar figure but his ideas fell on stony ground because they may have appeared too radical. That is to say, Warner sought a revision of the system, while Shuttleworth aimed for its refinement and greater efficiency. Shuttleworth's aims constituted an enhancement rather than a threat.

The other key player, as a Departmental Committee member and the London Board's Superintendent for Schools for Special Instruction, is Burgwin. While it is evident that she was sympathetic to the general condition and prospects for feeble-minded children (cf., Burgwin in RCEEA, 1887, pp. 113–26; Horn, 1990, pp. 48–60), nevertheless she appears as facilitator of the London Board's intentions. Within this parameter, she may well have organised efficiently, but that involved restricting access to decision-making concerning admission to special classes to those who were members of that system. Whether at her own volition or that of the Board, she looked to tradition, in the form of the established German auxiliary schools, to inform the internal organisation and practices of the special classes. Thus the past rather than the future appeared to be her guiding light.

The important factors in the establishment and growth of the special school system, beyond the setting-up of the first early examples, appear to be impersonal ones which relate to the nature of the economy and to the education system. The crucial decision was to establish a special system in the first place, because from that moment it tended to take on a life of its own. The principles of Michels's iron law of oligarchy come into play (1962, pp. 70–3), in so far as officials once appointed tend to pursue their own agendas based upon their specialist expertise which can displace the original purpose of the appointment. The decisions which relate to policies for education and special schools are taken within the parameters presented by a much wider social context. Hence, the players tend to play the hand they have been dealt, rather than to ask whether the cards or the game could be changed.

OBSERVATIONS ON THEORIES

Social Reproducton

The theoretical framework within which the analysis takes place derives from a combination of Bourdieu's and Weber's work. Bourdieu proposed a theory of the social, economic and cultural reproduction of society whereby sets of advantages and disadvantages are transmitted through generations over time. A basic proposition being that social, economic and cultural forces are not neutral but arise from circumstances, actions and decisions by individuals and groups. While that may find favour as a general proposition, an important criticism is that it is ahistoric; that is to say, it does not necessarily take into account the specific circumstances prevalent at a particular point in the past. Hence, Bourdieu's basic proposition is supplemented by ideas from Weber's methodological approach, which attempted to use theoretical propositions to explore the twists and turns of what occurred in the past. Thus a model of social reproduction may be modified by reference to a particular historical context, to specific circumstances, to pressure groups and to prevailing ideas.

Special Classes and Theory

Special classes for the education of feeble-minded children is the topic which the theory is intended to illuminate and which, in turn, illuminates the theory. The central questions, then, are: why did such classes come into being? What were the prevailing circumstances? Who made the decisions? Who had control of the classes? And how were they organised?

At a general level of orientation towards seeking some answers to the questions, the theoretical framework appears satisfactory. In the first place, the political intent of the expansion of Elementary education can be gauged from Lowe's aphorism concerning the education of the people who are now the masters. From notions of efficiency and parsimony, the system of Elementary schools becomes structured around a set of basic knowledge and competence which is taken for granted as necessary by those who formulate and enact the propositions. This whole process, in turn, takes place within a particular economic context which leads to the concentration of population in urban areas with overcrowding and deficiency in basic amenities. This, then, is the social and economic background to the decisions to require local authorities to provide school places for all school-age children and subsequently to require their attendance.

Feeble-minded children are judged to be few in number relative to the total population of school-age children. Is a theory which attempts to explain the nature of schooling for the bulk of children, powerful enough to explain what happens to a group at the margin? The answer is ambivalent. On the one hand, it can point to the nature and organisation of school activities, that is, the nature of the curriculum, class size, teaching methods and examinations, and argue that these factors were responsible for the production of those who struggled or failed within the system. On the other hand, this answer raises the question: Why did the system only affect the few it did in this way? That criticism may be unfair, because it may be expecting a degree of accuracy or predictability which is not associated with similar theories. But it does raise the legitimate question of why, if the system of schools was such, were many more children not affected? There is an empirical answer, of sorts, to that question, to the effect that feeble-minded children in special classes constituted an underestimation, perhaps considerable, of children who should have been so assessed. The problem with that, however, is the accuracy of the estimate which is based upon the quality of the theory proposing it, and hence the size of the group normally considered feeble-minded.

The explanation of the origin of special classes for feeble-minded children are the increase of numbers of pupils in the decade after 1870 and the change in nature of the composition of the school cohort from 1880, when it embraced groups which had not previously attended. These, however, are second-order phenomena: the *casus belli* being the circumstances which prompted the legislation in the first place. To pursue this line, however, may be to enter a course of infinite regression.

Theory at School-Board Level

More specific answers to the questions concerning the originating circumstances and decisions relating to special classes for feeble-minded children have to be sought at a local level. Hence, from the evidence presented to the Departmental Committee, there are four different reasons available. A half of the eight Boards who had taken initiatives did so at what might be termed an *ad hoc* level; that is, the Board or a member of the Board, took an interest in the plight of feeble-minded children and became involved in setting up special classes. The Board remained in overall control and there was no separate sub-committee or recognised mechanism to supervise the conduct of special classes. The arrangements are *ad hoc*. Two Boards responded to the initiatives which their inspectors proposed. One Board pursued the policy produced by its medical officer, and the final one had a developed system which was separate from the Elementary schools and responsible to the Board.

How is this diversity to be understood? In the first place, the theory of social reproduction appears to be a background to this question offering only general propositions, and a different theoretical formula must be brought into play. Because there has to be a basis to recommend a course of action and because that basis has to be recognised as sound by those who accept it, Weber's ideal types of leadership which combine the nature of leadership and its legitimacy are explored. The School Board as a group had to make decisions. Where do the elements of personal charisma, tradition and rationality figure in such decision-making?

It is possible to argue that the element of tradition was prevalent in all but one or possibly two situations. The evidence to support this claim is that although these Boards had made a start on the establishment of special classes for feeble-minded children, they were all looking over their shoulders to the question of cost and their accountability to their communities. This was evident in the question of buildings and the numbers of teachers. In addition, there was the notion that the classes from which these children were largely drawn had brought their circumstances upon themselves. In these instances, the extent of provision was probably dependent upon the charisma or personal influence of particular members.

Rationality appeared as the basis for decision-making in the situation where a specific system had been established. The system had it own hierarchy of officers and procedures. Although the basis for the rationality was flawed, its legitimacy was nevertheless accepted as a social fact.

The final example combines tradition and rationality. In this instance, tradition is much more than an unquestioning following of procedures because this has always been the case. Rather, it is an attempt to pose the question of how a particular group of children, the feeble-minded, may be best taught within the teaching and learning parameters known to those involved. Thus the special class appears as the extreme attenuation of a tuned system.

The element of tradition is more evident in the organisation and control of special classes, particularly of the content of the curriculum. Thus the backdrop in most instances is the curriculum of the Elementary school system, and the pleas of teachers appointed to teach special classes to be allowed to alter or vary the rigid programme of lessons. In another situation, there is a form of admission to special classes based upon a dedicated form of scientific rationality, but the special class system is frustrated by the special teachers' adherence to the formal Elementary curriculum. There is the further paradox of the system initiated by rationality, but which looks to tradition to furnish its curricular emphasis.

The nature of the composition of the School Board is a further area of difficulty. Where Board members are regarded as equal in status, except for the positions of chairman and vice-chairman, then the nature of the bureaucracy within which members work is likely to determine the relative influence of traditional practices and personal skills. Both, however, are likely to be subordinated to ideas of rationality. The Board is also located within a particular social climate which envelops the relative social status of men and women. The crucial development is the appointment of specialist officers to the Board. By definition, the specialist is likely to remove an area of deliberation from the Board's purview. The important theoretical question is what factors trigger the Board to seek specialist knowledge? For instance, in the case of special classes for the feeble-minded, is it the realisation of the extent of the problem through sheer numbers? Or is it the desire to help the children once identified to the greatest possible extent? Or is it almost the reverse, the desire strictly to control and limit expenditure? Both Bristol and Brighton Board members expressed compassion for the children's condition, but hesitated to act lest they be considered to be doing too much at too much expense.

Outcome for Pupils in Special Classes

If an attempt is made to direct the theory of social reproduction of sets of advantages and disadvantages towards the actual outcomes for children from special classes, then a difficult judgment, if not dilemma, has to be resolved. Is the children's experience of a special class to be regarded as an opportunity for personal growth and skill development such as would facilitate movement away from what otherwise would have been their condition in life, that is, a change in life chances? Are special classes to be regarded as a chance to break the social mould? Or are they precisely the opposite, that is, through their selection, separation and special treatment, do they constitute a confirmation of status which is not simply different but lowly? The evidence, such as there is, points to HMI's belief that special centres separated from ordinary schools are likely to invoke the taunt of 'silly school' (DCDEC, 1898, vol. II, p. 225) and that a definite social stigma would be attached to pupils of residential, segregated special schools (ibid., p. 228). The Committee's chairman also supports that judgment, (ibid., p. 202). In part, for that reason it was considered that feeble-minded children from rural districts would be better served by staying at home and attending the local school, however imperfect that might be.

The resolution of the theoretical problem relates to the nature of the society of which the special classes are a part. Thus if society is open or in the form of a meritocracy then the development of personal skills in a special class would be advantageous. On the other hand, if society consists of configurations of status groups related to the economy, then it would more likely be a confirmation of status.

The evidence which is available points towards the instrumental success of special classes, that is, success in their own terms of measurement. The data from teachers in special classes (Table 5.3, p. 93 above) show that about two in five pupils in London and elsewhere returned to ordinary school classes. A further three in ten moved on to employment, although the success rate was twice as high outside London as in it. Special classes thus enjoyed a success rate with more than half their pupils in their own terms.

CONCLUSION

In conclusion, it can be observed that there are organic layers of problematics concerning education and the feeble-minded child. The layers are organic because they are not simply adjacent but interactive. To begin with the personal layer: this involves the accredited ideas which relate to feeble-minded children, their nature and potential; crucial here is the judgment whether they are educable or non-educable – the distinction between the categories can be as solid as the institutions which separate them. The second layer concerns the place of schools and education in society in general and whether special schools or classes are embedded in the general scheme or are set aside as something apart. This layer of schools and education has then to be located within a third layer of some conceptual view of society itself. The different layers have been identified to point to main areas of analysis. Each layer interacts with the others. Thus the ideas and concerns of society at the grand level inform the practices and judgments concerning the feeble-minded in some way. The layer of education is capable of developing ideas, theories and evidence which affect the other two.

A theory of social reproduction through generations makes a start at the general level of society. Taking this as an initial model to explore the education of the feeble-minded, the prime assumption would appear pessimistic: that is, if there are mechanisms whereby status groups and their advantages and disadvantages are reproduced over time, then the chances of success appear to be stacked against children who find their way into special classes. The optimistic side is that the empirical evidence, however slight, points towards some fairly high level of success for these classes in terms of returning children to ordinary classes or to employment. Hence, it would be fair to conclude that, on the whole, the presence of special classes neither confirms nor enhances social disadvantages, but may alleviate them to some degree.

7

Discourses of Normalisation and Classification

This chapter charts the category of feeble-minded from the deliberations of the Education Committee through the permissive Elementary Education (Defective and Epileptic Children) Act, 1899, to the requirements of the Mental Deficiency Act, 1914. The growth of provision for the mentally defective pupil is outlined as is the considerable variation in ascertainment by Local Education Authorities. The continuing effects of the inadequate definition are shown. Finally, the last section tackles the issues that have been identified as unresolved in the study.

'FEEBLE-MINDED' AS A CATEGORY

Writing in 1899, George Shuttleworth observed that he had taken the opportunity in the second edition of his book to include an account of the DCDEC's deliberations. The first point was that the term 'feeble-minded' had 'acquired in this country a special significance' (Shuttleworth, 1900, p. 13). He explained how, 'according to American usage, this term has long been employed to include all degrees and types of congenital defect from that of the simply backward boy or girl ... to the profound idiot' (ibid., p. 12). However, the term 'feeble-minded', if tracked through its connotations in the Egerton Commission, the Departmental Committee and subsequent legislation in 1899 and 1913, had become a specific category. This process had occurred through the supervision and watchfulness – the surveillance – of the Education Department.

As has previously been argued, the Egerton Commission took as its starting point for its definitions the assumption that there was a gradation of deficiency from the classes of imbeciles to idiots. The prime task was 'directed towards ascertaining how many of them are capable of education' (RCBDD, 1889, p. xcii). Its recommendations were that there should be 'a careful classification and separation ... of educable imbeciles [who should then] be sent to a special institution' (ibid., p. cvi). The assumption was, as with the blind and deaf, that the educable imbeciles would be accommodated in institutions outside the Board's district. The feeble-minded children, however, seemed to be regarded by the Commission as either at the top end of the continuum of deficiency or beyond it. The recommendations for their education were also different and unclear, if not contradictory.

First, the Commission accepted that there was a category, and that 'the case of feeble-minded children would come more appropriately within our terms of reference' (ibid., p. civ). The Commission justified this by declaring that 'we have received evidence that there are a great many backward children in our Elementary schools who require a different treatment to that of the ordinary children' (ibid.). At this point, the concept of feeble-minded children and backward children appear to refer to the same phenomenon.

Second, the recommendations for the education of these children contain different elements. Thus, at one point, there is 'the recommendation of auxiliary schools for such classes' (ibid.), but at another point it is suggested that 'feeble-minded children should be separated from ordinary scholars in public elementary schools ... [to] receive special instruction' (ibid., p. cvi) Whether deliberate or otherwise, the confusion arises from whether there should be schools for special instruction or classes for special instruction within ordinary schools. Both models emerged in practice.

SEPARATION OF THE DULL AND BACKWARD FROM THE FEEBLE-MINDED

Evidence presented to the Departmental Committee a decade later separated the dull and backward child from the feeble-minded. First, the Medical Officer of the Darenth School for Imbecile Children stated that there was a class of child that may be called dull but was not, at the same time, defective. Thus: 'I should consider that a defective child has some functional or organic derangement of the brain cells. I should consider that a slow child was slow because its mental operations were slow; that it was a normal child but spoke slowly because it thought slowly, to put it in simple language' (DCDEC, 1898, vol. II, p. 120). Second, there is the evidence of the Physician to the London Hospital. In five different instances, he pointed to the fact that a judgment of dullness or backwardness in a child derived from the evidence presented by a teacher.

This could take the form of a mismatch between a pupil's performance in arithmetic or reading, where one was extremely weak (ibid., p. 37), or the instance of neglected and undernourished children (ibid., p. 35), or the very well-behaved child who is struggling academically (ibid., p. 33). He emphasised in his evidence that a judgment of feeble-mindedness could only be reached by the medical officer with the benefit of information given by the teacher with knowledge of the child.

The third witness, the Medical Superintendent to the Bradford School Board, identified a category of dull child who improves spontaneously as it were. Thus: 'There are a certain number of very dull children from about seven to eight years of age that I leave a year and they polish up, they brighten up wonderfully' (ibid., p. 20). The alternative explanation was that of a failure to respond to school discipline which both hindered the pupil's attainment and masked potential. The child who 'had pulled the cat's head off' was one such (ibid.). The evidence of these witnesses thus distinguishes dullness and backwardness in a pupil from feeble-mindedness. This latter condition, in their view, could only be properly ascertained through a medical examination.

THE LEGAL DEFINITION

Parliament approved the EE(DEC) Act in August 1899. Section 1(1) defined the category of children subject to the Act and separated them from the dull or backward. The Act stated that:

> A school authority ... may, with the approval of the Education Department, make such arrangements as they think fit for ascertaining – (a) what children in their district, not being imbecile, and not merely dull or backward, are defective; that is to say, what children by reason of mental or physical defect are incapable of receiving proper benefit from the instruction in the ordinary elementary schools, but are not incapable by reason of such defect of receiving benefit from instruction in such special classes or schools as are in the Act mentioned. (62 and 63, Vict. c.32, 5.1(1))

The third subsection specified that for the purpose of ascertainment 'a certificate to that effect by a duly qualified practitioner approved by the Education Department shall be required in each case' (ibid.,1(3)). It further prescribed that '[t]he certificate shall be in such form as may be prescribed by the Education Department' (ibid.). The legislation thus established the category of mentally defective child which was distinguished from the dull and/or backward child. Moreover, classification or ascertainment was only possible through the medium of a medical practitioner, approved in advance by the Education Department. In addition, while the practitioner was obliged to follow the procedure prescribed by the Education Department, the Department retained the authority to vary that procedure as it thought fit.

PASSAGE OF THE BILL THROUGH PARLIAMENT

Contributions to debates on the Bill in both Houses produced important insights. In the Commons the School Board for London was regarded as the Bill's initiator: 'The London School Board ... has paid the very greatest attention to this subject – in fact, I think it may be regarded as the promoter of this special legislation' (PD, vol. LXXV, c. 936). In the Lords, the Lord President of the Council, having observed that 'the details of the Bill are based upon the recommendations of the Departmental Committee' – three of whose seven members were employed by the SBL – confirmed that the term 'mentally defective' referred to 'those who are feeble-minded and ... not merely dull and difficult to teach'(PD, vol. LXXIII, c. 395). Most importantly, in further debate in the Lords, Earl Egerton, as he had become, regretted that the Bill did not oblige school authorities to appoint medical officers to 'advise on the discrimination of these children'. The Lord President of the Council replied that 'These are matters which ... are better left to the Education Department than provided for in the Bill' (PD, vol. LXXIV, c. 1126). He gave three reasons for this opinion: no child would be admitted to a special class who did not fall within the definition given in the first section; the Education Department would only approve medical practitioners 'conversant with such cases'; and the Department reserved to itself the final decision whether a case was suitable or not.

The Department's determination to keep a tight control over the whole process of ascertainment was emphasised by the Vice-President of the Council in debate in the Commons. A member of the House attempted to move an amendment to the effect that 'public control should go with public money' and the decision concerning admission to a special class be devolved to the school authority, as was the case with blind and deaf children. (PD, vol. LXXV, c. 936). The Vice-President replied that 'he could not accept the Amendment and pointed out that the money in question was subject to the public control of the Education Department' (ibid., c. 937).

Provisions of the Act

In 1899, the Board of Education (BoE) replaced the Education Department, becoming the sole central authority for primary, secondary and technical education alike. The EE(DEC)A gave the school authority the power to ascertain which children were mentally defective or epileptic, and the power to make provision for the education of such children either in special classes in Elementary schools or in special schools established for that purpose. The approval of the Education Department was required for both variants. School authorities were also permitted to provide guides or conveyance for such children who might also be boarded out or transferred to a school in another authority.

Quantification of Mentally Defective Pupils

From the time when the education of feeble-minded children became a matter of concern to the Egerton Commission in 1889 through to the deliberations of the Departmental Committee on Defective and Epileptic Children in 1898, the prime means of establishing the numbers of special schools, classes and pupils ascertained as feeble-minded was through an examination of the evidence presented by witnesses to the Committee and a survey of the minute books of the School Boards. In addition to those special classes or schools which have been identified, a member of the Committee confirmed that in 1899 others were in operation in Birmingham, Bolton, Burnley and Bury (Shuttleworth, 1900, p. 163). Classes were also arranged to open in Liverpool and Manchester. (This conflicts with evidence given by an HMI with overall responsibility for schools for defective pupils to the Royal Commission on the Care and Control of the Feeble-Minded (RCCCFM) in 1908, which restricts the special classes to five towns prior to the 1899 Act and conspicuously omits mention of Bradford and Brighton (Eichholz in RCCCFM, vol. II, p. 206).)

The *Report of the Board of Education, 1899–1900* includes information on schools for the blind (BoE, 1901, p. 152) and the deaf (ibid., p. 153). From that point onwards, however, the Board also published details of the education of defective and epileptic children. There is no reason why mentally defective children and epileptics should be considered jointly except in the instance where the mentally defective child is also epileptic. Their joint consideration arose from the fact that, together, they constituted the residuum of children regarded as educable but for whom the Egerton Commission was not able to make firm recommendations regarding their education.

During the period 1900–7, the Board of Education published statistics of public education in which mentally defective and epileptic children were presented jointly. In 1909 separate statistical returns were presented for each. In that year the commentary for Table 32 on epileptic children indicated that they had been ascertained as such 'within the meaning of the EE(DEC)A'. Under section 1.1(b) of this Act, epileptic children are defined as children who 'not being idiots or imbeciles, are unfit by reason of severe epilepsy to attend the ordinary public elementary schools' (BoE, 1908, p. lvi). The commentary for the preceding Table 31 on mentally defective children indicated that these children too had been ascertained in accordance with the provisions of the Act.

Table 7.1 shows that the first certified school for epiliptic children was established in 1904 and had ten pupils on the roll. The expansion to six schools over the next five years indicates that the numbers of epileptic pupils may have become stable following a steep initial rise. It is also worth noting that the provision of places exceeds the numbers of ascertained cases throughout.

TABLE 7.1
CERTIFIED SCHOOLS FOR EPILEPTIC CHILDREN, 1903–14

Date	Number of schools	Number of places	Number on roll
1903–4	–	–	–
1904–5	1	56	10
1905–6	4	222	164
1906–7	4	222	183
1907–8	4	252	216
1908–9	5	331	265
1909–10	6	464	351
1910–11	6	464	377
1911–12	6	464	395
1912–13	6	475	441
1913–14	6	496	474

Source: Board of Education, *Statistics of Public Education in England and Wales* (1903–14).

The fact that there were no ascertained epileptic children on roll up to 1904 means that Table 7.2 is a record of schools for mentally defective children. Because the BoE publication in 1908 contained retrospective statistics, it is possible to build up a complete picture from 1900 to 1914 by combining Table 7.2 and Table 7.3.

TABLE 7.2

CERTIFIED SCHOOLS FOR DEFECTIVE OR EPILEPTIC CHILDREN, 1900–3

Date	Number of schools	Number of places	Number on roll
1900–1	79	3,325	2,965
1901–2	96	4,041	3,843
1902–3	111	5,218	4,927

Source: Board of Education, *Statistics of Public Education in England and Wales* (1900–3).

TABLE 7.3

CERTIFIED SCHOOLS FOR MENTALLY DEFECTIVE CHILDREN, 1903–14

Date	Number of schools	Number of places	Number on roll
1903–4	119	5,404	5,672
1904–5	144	7,816	7,948
1905–6	145	8,229	8,737
1906–7	146	8,764	9,205
1907–8	147	9,596	9,870
1908–9	150	10,511	10,649
1909–10	155	11,211	11,713
1910–11	159	11,738	12,150
1911–12	167	12,420	12,572
1912–13	177	13,095	13,226
1913–14	179	13,836	13,651

Source: Board of Education, *Statistics of Public Education in England and Wales* (1903–14).

Trends in the Statistics

Two trends are worth noting. First, the initial rapid increase of special schools between 1900 and 1903, an increase of more than 70 per cent in the system, produced an excess of places over pupils on the roll. Second, between 1904 and 1913, although special schools continued to increase in number by more than 60 per cent, there was an excess of numbers of pupils on the roll over official provision. Therefore, it took almost a decade for the enlarged special school system to regain its initial position. Finally, all the statistics are for special schools. They remain silent regarding special classes. (The same HMI's evidence also noted that by 1905 almost two-thirds of county boroughs 'have made no attempt to deal with their defectives ... The non-county boroughs, with only one exception, made no provision of any kind' (RCCCFM, 1908, vol. II, p. 206). He also estimated that only one-eighth of children who ought to be in special classes were actually in them.)

This situation is confirmed by another source which demonstrates that LEAs (Local Education Authorities) were slow to adopt the permissive measures of the EE(DEC) Act, 1899, in spite of the Board of Education Chief Medical Officer's sanguine observation in his *Annual Report* that 'An increasing number of Local Authorities has adopted this Act' (1911, p. 208).

TABLE 7.4
LEA ADOPTION OF EE(DEC) ACT, 1899

Year	Number of LEAs	Percentage of LEAs	Number of schools/centres	Average pupil attendance
1902	47	14	119	4,672
1906	87	26	144	7,948
1910	142	43	155	9,205
1911	175	53	169	11,309
1913	183	56	177	12,245

Source: Chief Medical Officer of the Board of Education, *Annual Report for 1913* (London, HMSO, 1914, p. 213).

IMPLEMENTATION OF THE MENTAL DEFICIENCY ACT, 1913

The Mental Deficiency Act, 1913, left the powers and duties of the LEAs the same as under the EE(DEC) Act, 1899, but made compulsory the ascertainment of all mentally defective children in their respective areas and ascertainment and notification of children considered to be ineducable. In order to ascertain the mentally defective child, it was necessary to have some scheme or principles by which to measure and assess children. In spite of the inconsistent, inaccurate and fallacious nature of the definition and scheme of mental attributes espoused by the DCDEC, that definitional scheme became the basis, first, for the Board of Education's encouragement of LEAs to ascertain mentally defective children and, second, the basis for their compulsion to do so in the Mental Deficiency Act, 1913. Thus, the Chief Medical Officer for the Board of Education could typically include in his *Annual Report* that 'medical examination of such cases makes it possible to assert definitely whether a child is imbecile, feeble-minded, merely dull and backward or retarded by reason of general physical defect' (1911, p. 209). Again, writing more boldly at a later time, the Chief Medical Officer could declare:

> speaking generally, and from the point of view of classifying the various forms of mental abnormality, it may be said that there are five groups of children as follows:
>
> i.   the child that is mentally normal
> ii. the dull or backward child
> iii. the feeble-minded child
> iv. the imbecile child
> v.   the idiot
>
> The overwhelming majority of children are happily in the first group … Nor need we consider here the last two groups of imbecile and idiot children who are ineducable. (1913, p. 231)

Two facts about the classification strike the reader: first, there is no attempt at gradation for the 'overwhelming majority' of 'mentally normal' children and, second, 'idiot' is used as a term complete in itself without the attribute 'child'.

If the second quotation sets out the supposed gradations in the scheme of classification, then the first emphasises that 'medical examination' can 'assert definitely' the child's classification.

ACHIEVEMENT OF CLASSIFICATION

How was classification to be achieved? Existing medical knowledge and tests provided a ready answer:

175

In selecting tests the medical officer who has a knowledge of children, will have no difficulty in framing his own tests, which should aim not so much at scholastic acquirement or precision, as at

i. a common and practical knowledge on the part of the child of the relationships of time, space and matter in his own environment.

ii. medical observations, including physical condition, acuity of senses, equilibrium and muscular control and the special physical stigma of mental defect.

iii. motor and sensory response, emotions, intellect, will-power and memory. (Chief Medical Officer, 1911, p. 208)

One inference from this list is that it appears to combine some of the sort of practical tests advocated by the Leicester inspector with those accepted in the medical profession. The prevalence and proof of stigmata is accepted and recommended even though its advocates, such as the Bradford Board's medical officer, could furnish neither proof nor explanation. A second inference, and a crucial one, is that the test almost seems to boast that 'the aim is not so much at scholastic acquirement or precision'. In other words, it claims that the proper test for educational potential lies outside the sphere of education and derives from the realm of medicine. Thus the overseeing of the norm for the distribution of pupils is to be medical rather than educational.

In his report for 1910, the Chief Medical Officer regarded 'the psychological and educational tests of Binet and Simon ... barely sufficient to enable a definite decision' (1911, p. 208). By 1912, however, there was a firm recommendation that 'the Binet–Simon method of testing the intellectual age of the child should be used' (1912, p. 231).

The Chief Medical Officer first set out a scheme for medical examinaton to classify mentally defective children as an Appendix to his report for 1908 (see 1909, pp. 208–12). He continued to reproduce and recommend the scheme in his subsequent reports.

OTHER OUTCOMES

In one instance at least, because the 1889 legislation specifically excluded 'dull and backward' children from special classes, the actual numbers of pupils in such classes were reduced by a quarter. The evidence of the vice-chairman of the Leicester Authority presented to the Royal Commission on the Care and Control of the Feeble-Minded (RCCCFM, 1908, vol. I,

p. 161) records this occurrence. The retention rate in the special classes increased as the proportion of pupils returned to Elementary schools declined. The return rate subsequently became very small. In the face of these events, the Leicester Authority early in 1903 decided to retain 'one centre including classes for both boys and girls, worked in accordance with the Act; and three classes for backward children ... without special grant' (ibid., p. 162).

MENTAL DEFICIENCY ACT, 1913

The Education (Administrative Provisions) Act, 1907, gave local education authorities 'the duty to provide for the medical inspection of children immediately before, or at the time of, or as soon as possible after their admission to a public elementary school' (7, Edw. VII, c.43, 13(b)). The permissive aspect of the EE(DEC) Act, 1889, was replaced by the comprehensive Mental Deficiency Act, 1913. The intention of the Act was to make further and improved provision for the care of the feeble-minded, adult and child alike, and others judged mentally defective, and to amend the Lunacy Acts. It was now made the duty of each education authority 'subject to regulations made by the Board of Education' to ascertain 'the case of all defective children over the age of seven' (3 and 4, Geo. V, c.28, 2(2)). Thus, the Board of Education retained its central role in ascertainment and there was confidence that all the cases could be ascertained. Further, a Board Minute specified the form of certification and the fact that the qualified practitioner must be approved by the Board (Wormald and Wormald, 1914, p. 10).

The following year, the Elementary Education (Defective and Epileptic Children) Act, 1914, was enacted (4 and 5, Geo. V, c.45). This separated responsibility for provision for adults from that for children over 7 years of age. The local education authority was given responsibility for provision for such children and the Act confirmed the role and responsibilities of the Board of Education in the process of ascertainment and placement (cf., Moulton, 1919, pp. 221–5).

CONTINUING IMPACT OF THE DEFINITION

One of the consequences of the absence of an adequate definition of feeble-minded was that there was considerable variation in the discovery of such children in different parts of the country. Table 7.5 reveals the variaton between different counties and urban areas and Table 7.6, the variation within a county in 1909. Table 7.7 demonstrates that in 1913 the situation had deteriorated, with even wider variations. This variation, however, was not regarded as problematic but rather as confirmation of the findings of the RCBDD, 1889. Commenting upon the data in Tables 7.5 and 7.6, the Chief Medical Officer wrote: 'It is interesting to note that these returns as a whole compare somewhat closely with the estimates made by the Royal Commission, based upon examination in a few typical areas' (1910, p. 206). 'In conclusion', his report stated,

> following the data of the medical investigators, we may say that in England and Wales the number of feeble-minded children may be expected to be, in the areas urban and rural, 0.7 per cent of the number of children on the school registers, falling as low as 0.28 per cent in a northern colliery district and rising as high as 1.12 per cent and 1.24 per cent in urban areas. Generally speaking, therefore, the percentage of feeble-minded children in any community varies from 0.25 per cent to upwards of 1.0 per cent. (1910, p. 207)

TABLE 7.5

PROPORTION OF PUPILS ASCERTAINED AS MENTALLY DEFECTIVE
IN COUNTY AND URBAN AREAS, 1909

Counties		Urban areas	
Name of area	*Percentage*	*Name of area*	*Percentage*
Hertfordshire	2.50	Grimsby	2.60
Norfolk	1.19	Huddersfield	2.10
Northumberland	0.57	Hereford	1.96
Oxfordshire	0.47	Rowley Regis	1.51
Berkshire	0.45	South Shields	0.52
Devonshire	0.45	Northampton	0.50
Surrey	0.40	St Helens	0.37
Gloucestershire	0.39	Plymouth	0.34
Staffordshire	0.37	Clitheroe	0.34
Warwickshire	0.31	Bradford	0.31
Somerset	0.25	Manchester	0.31
Derbyshire	0.24	Kingston-upon-Hull	0.26
Shropshire	0.18	Bristol	0.20
Lancashire	0.11	Dover	0.15
Dorset	0.11	Batley	0.06
Glamorganshire	0.10	Newcastle-upon-Tyne	0.05

Source: Chief Medical Officer of the Board of Education, *Annual Report for 1910* (London, HMSO, 1911, p. 206).

The explanation for the variation which both the Royal Commission and the Board's Chief Medical Officer proposed is that the rate is variable. The conclusion is thus built into the original premise. Hence the circular definition of feeble-mindedness produces a replica in the data which derive from its application. The data, however, are accepted and even celebrated as proof of the original definition! Thus the abstract ideas, however erroneous, take on a reality in the social world. The ideas' application produces its own unquestioned 'facticity'. In Foucault's terms, power and knowledge are concatenated dialectically: knowledge produces power and power produces knowledge (cf., Foucault, 1982, pp. 216–26).

TABLE 7.6

NUMBER OF BOYS AND GIRLS EXAMINED AND THE PROPORTION ASCERTAINED AS MENTALLY DEFECTIVE IN DISTRICTS OF THE COUNTY OF WORCESTER, 1909

Education district	Boys			Girls			Total		
	Exam-ined	Axcer-tained	%	Exam-ined	Ascer-tained	%	Exam-ined	Ascer-tained	%
Yardley	1,107	17	1.5	1,298	10	0.77	2,405	27	1.1
Halesowen	676	8	1.2	665	3	0.45	1,341	11	0.82
Stourbridge	763	13	1.7	762	4	0.52	1,525	17	1.1
Kidderminster	497	5	1.0	508	1	0.2	1,005	6	0.6
Rock	89	2	2.2	97	–	–	186	2	1.08
Bromsgrove	472	6	1.3	528	2	0.38	1,000	8	0.8
Redditch	616	28	4.5	589	29	4.9	1,205	57	4.7
Droitwich	261	2	0.8	300	–	–	561	2	0.36
Pershore	320	20	6.2	306	4	1.3	626	24	3.8
Evesham	380	6	1.6	335	1	0.3	715	7	0.98
Shipston-on-Stour	98	3	3.06	68	1	1.5	165	4	2.4
Upton-on-Severn	353	10	2.8	326	5	1.5	679	15	2.2
Malvern	329	6	1.8	342	8	2.3	671	14	2.09
Martley	292	6	2.05	316	2	0.63	608	8	1.3
Tenbury	155	2	1.3	110	4	3.6	265	6	2.3

Source: Chief Medical Officer of the Board of Education, *Annual Report for 1910* (London, HMSO, 1911, p. 207).

179

TABLE 7.7

PERCENTAGE OF MENTALLY DEFECTIVE CHILDREN DISCOVERED AT
ROUTINE MEDICAL INSPECTIONS, 1913

Area	Percentage	Area	Percentage
Cambridgeshire	0.5	*Towns (continued)*	
Herefordshire	0.5	Glossop	0.3
Lincolnshire (Holland)	0.5	Kendal	0.3
Surrey	0.5	Ramsgate	0.3
Westmorland	0.5	Stockton-on-Tees	0.3
Cumberland	0.4	Acton	0.3
Staffordshire	0.4	Kettering	0.3
Oxfordshire	0.36	Waterloo-with-Seaforth	0.3
Nottinghamshire	0.3	Huddersfield	0.28
Sussex, East	0.3	Northampton	0.29
Northumberland	0.23	Leyton	0.25
Cornwall	0.21	Chester	0.21
Bedfordshire	0.2	Brighton	0.2
Denbighshire	0.2	Derby	0.2
Salop	0.2	Salford	0.2
Suffolk, West	0.2	Stockport	0.2
Norfolk	0.19	York	0.2
Yorkshire (E. Riding)	0.13	Colchester	0.2
Lincolnshire (Lindsey)	0.12	Maidstone	0.2
Gloucestershire	0.11	Widnes	0.2
Durham	0.1	Tottenham	0.2
Essex	0.1	Liverpool	0.18
Kent	0.1	Preston	0.16
Radnor	0.1	Stoke-on-Trent	0.16
Dorset	0.07	Shipley	0.16
		Lincoln	0.15
Towns		Haslingden	0.13
Sunderland	4.3	Morley	0.13
Bath	1.7	Heywood	0.11
Clitheroe	0.9	Dewsbury	0.1
Halifax	0.8	Newcastle-upon-Tyne	0.1
Chesterfield	0.7	Southend-on-Sea	0.1
Abertillery	0.7	Bacup	0.1
Hereford	0.6	Hornsey	0.1
Lewes	0.59	King's Lynn	0.1
South Shields	0.5	Rawtenstall	0.1
Wolverhampton	0.5	Richmond	0.1
Harrogate	0.5	Enfield	0.1
Scarborough	0.47	Rochdale	0.09
Kingston-upon-Hull	0.43	Hindley	0.09
Portsmouth	0.36	Walthamstow	0.09
Newport (Mon)	0.34	Wrexham	0.07
Todmorden	0.32	Nelson	0.06
Bristol	0.3	Nottingham	0.05
Carlisle	0.3	Cardiff	0.04
Great Yarmouth	0.3	Gloucester	0.03
Batley	0.3	Tynemouth	0.02

Source: Chief Medical Officer of the Board of Education, *Annual Report for 1913*
(London, HMSO, 1914, p. 210).

THE CATEGORY OF 'MORAL IMBECILE'

The 1913 Act also evinced rationalisation of care provision for the feeble-minded. Different types of provision were proposed in institutions with local or national catchments (3 and 4, Geo.V, c.28, s.35–41). 'Colonies for the feeble-minded ... organised on a large scale and on modern, economic lines were preferred' (Wormald and Wormald, 1914, p. 43).

The Mental Deficiency Act identified four 'classes of persons who are mentally defective' (3 and 4, Geo. V, c.28 1.1). They were defined as 'idiots', 'imbeciles', 'feeble-minded persons' and 'moral imbeciles'. This latter category was defined as 'persons who from an early age display some permanent mental defect coupled with strong vicious or criminal propensities on which punishment had little or no deterrent effect' (ibid., 1(d)). The moral imbecile had been identified in evidence presented to the DCDEC, as already discussed, and featured extensively in evidence to the RCCCFM, 1908. The category had also become entangled in the eugenicist movement. Francis Galton had produced *Hereditary Genius* in 1869, and 20 years later *Natural Intelligence*. Briefly, he applied Mendel's Law to the human race and claimed that it held equally well for the inheritance of both physical characteristics and mental abilities. Just as blond-haired parents could expect to produce blond-haired children, so intelligent parents could expect to produce intelligent children. Particular abilities could also be transmitted: children of statesmen became statesmen and those of musicians became musicians. However, the negative side was equally possible: the criminal produced children with criminal tendencies and the children of the feeble-minded would almost certainly be defective. From 1900 onwards, the social movement of eugenicism mushroomed (see Barker, 1993, p. 197). However, 'The attention of Edwardian eugenicists was remorselessly shifting from the qualities of the great and the good to the defects of degenerates and the residuum' (ibid.). It has been argued that the growth and interest in eugenics sprang, in part, from the interests of the group of professional occupations whose status and income came from the sale of their services as experts. Thus the Eugenics Society was 'a forum in which a distinctive aspect of middle-class ideology could be advanced: namely, the view that social problems could be resolved through scientific knowledge and technological formulae' (Ray, 1983, p. 213) – an illustration, in Foucauldian terms, of scientific discourse in the service of objectification of the subject.

THE PUTATIVE LINK BETWEEN CRIME, MORAL DEGENERACY
AND FEEBLE-MINDEDNESS

Much evidence presented to the RCCCFM, 1908, attempted to demonstrate a link between crime, moral degeneracy and feeble-mindedness. The Director of Education for Bolton submitted a commentary upon 38 cases brought before magistrates between 1887 and 1905 for non-attendance at school. Here, all the children had been ascertained as feeble-minded as had one or other of their parents. However, in only four of the cases was a link with crime established. Mothers and daughters were frequently described as 'immoral woman' or 'immoral girl'. Rarely was this the case with fathers and sons (RCCCFM, 1908, vol. II, pp. 69–70).

The Salvation Army also submitted evidence which summarised 577 cases of feeble-minded women received into the Army's rescue homes over a period of three years. Here the evidence linked feeble-mindedness with crime, unemployment, pauperism and drink. Over a third of the sample had given birth to illegitimate children. Moral imbecility appeared clear to assessors in these cases. But what judgment of the fathers of the children? None (see Mort, 1985, pp. 206–7). Finally, for those illegitimate offspring for whom particulars were available, no less than a quarter were judged 'of average intellect' (RCCCFM, 1908, vol. II, pp. 572–604).

LEGAL DEFINITIONS

If the concept of moral imbecile has its problematics as demonstrated earlier, then the concepts of idiots, imbeciles and feeble-minded persons are equally problematic. As with the definitions given in the DCDEC report, the three concepts are defined in relation to each other. Thus 'idiots [are] so deeply defective in mind … as to be unable to guard themselves against common physical dangers. Imbeciles … [have] mental defectiveness not amounting to idiocy … Feeble-minded persons [have] mental defectiveness not amounting to imbecility' (3 and 4, Geo. V, c.28, 1(a), (b), (c)). The definitions, as previously argued, are problematic and inadequate precisely because they lack external reference points. Without a firm touchstone, the application of the definitions proves a continuous source of difficulty and contention. Two examples will serve to illustrate that difficulty. A witness to the RCCCFM, who had served a total of 21 years on a School Board and local authority and who was a medically qualified practitioner, stated that 'in the case of defective children, there is no sharp dividing line but a merging of one degree of deficiency insensibly into another' (RCCCFM, 1908, vol. II, p. 162). The *Oxford English Dictionary* gives two meanings for 'insensible': not appreciable by the senses or unintelligible. To paraphrase the witness, the distinction between the types of defective was neither understandable nor understood by the existing state of medical knowledge.

The second example illustrates the duration of the difficulty. The Mental Deficiency Act, 1927, revised and shortened the definitions of the three types by omitting reference to their aetiology. Their contingent definition was retained as was the reference to social competence (17 and 18, Geo. V, c.33, 1(a)–(d)). A senior assistant medical officer to an Education Committee, who was also certifying medical officer to a county mental deficiency authority, having set out the Act's definitions goes on to write that:

> To enable us to make a diagnosis of mental deficiency in any particular case, there must first of all be some clear conception of what it means. It is defined in the Act as a 'condition of arrested or incomplete development of mind'. How is this to be estimated? As practical diagnosticians we are not concerned with its ultimate basis … whatever the anatomical or physiological causes or concomitants of their condition, it is by their mental 'fruits' that we have to know them. (Herd, 1930, p. 7)

In this way, a key figure in the classification and certification of both children and adults first admits the lack of concern with and yet also the importance of the basis of the patient's condition, but then resorts to a metaphor to explain the possible diagnosis.

PERSISTENCE OF INADEQUATE DEFINITIONS

Dr A. F. Tredgold, a neurologist at the London Hospital, gave expert medical evidence to the RCCCFM between 1905 and 1908; he was a member of the Wood Committee of Inquiry into Mental Deficiency and Education, 1924–29, and a member of the Brock Committee of Inquiry into Sterilisation, 1932–33. In 1908, his textbook *Mental Deficiency* was published, 'which in a much revised form, is still in use' (Potts, 1983, p. 183). Tredgold defined mental deficiency by the hybrid term 'amentia', which yielded a taxonomy of 16 clinical variations each of which varied by degree from feeble-mindedness to imbecility and idiocy (ibid., p. 185). The potential for the use of the contingent definition was considerable.

How was social competence to be judged? 'There may be said to be two criteria of social normality. One is his capacity to fill his place adequately as a social unit earning his own living and managing his own affairs. ... The second criterion is that he must conform himself to the working moral standards of the community of which he is a member' (ibid., pp. 7–8).

The normative nature of these judgments is palpable. The judgments have endured intact since the DCDEC report in 1898. Both constitute clear examples of the process of normalisation, the distribution of subjects around a norm.

UNRESOLVED ISSUES

At this point, it is evident that there are a number of factors in the study as a whole which call for further understanding or explanation. These are: the triumph of the London School Board's system of special classes over Leicester's model; the separation of pupils from their peers into special centres or special classes; the persistence of inadequate definitions of the feeble-minded and others; the control and overseeing of the special system exercised by the Education Department; and the stress upon a medical examination for admission to special classes.

How may Foucault's thinking help with the problems outlined? While no definitive answers may emerge, it certainly presents a different terrain to till and one which may yield ideas for further empirical work.

The Function of the Medical Examination

The medical examination appeared early in the deliberations of the DCDEC. The report recorded a range of different procedures for admission to special classes which could involve variously teachers, headteachers, board members, HMI, local officials, parents and doctors. The subsequent legislation in 1899 specified a medical examination in all cases.

The insistence upon a medical examination celebrates and confirms a particular discourse. That discourse was evident in the conflicting evidence presented to the Egerton Commission and the DCDEC. Within the preferred discourse, the classification and distinction between degrees of mental disability are not called into question. Rather, the basis for the examination remains invisible and watchful supervision is directed towards the objectified subject. So long as attention is concentrated upon individual cases and the completion of documentation, then the internal inadequacies of the underpinning theory remain unchallenged and are, to a degree, irrelevant to the social realisation of the examination.

The medical examination also serves to restrict permissible discourses. The co-existence of conflicting discourses is perilous and hazardous because the triumph of any particular one is not necessarily within the control of the particular discourse. Hence, in terms of social action, there needs to be an alliance or alliances between players who span different discourses. For this reason, the physical presence of three members in the employ of the London School Board on the DCDEC represents more than a simple co-operation between the Education Department and the Board, which was regarded as an initiator of the 1899 Act; it represents the preference for a discourse which would suffuse the whole system. The medical examination preference displaces the discourses of teachers, officials, parents and others. The classification in the 1899 Act of the feeble-minded child as separate from the dull and backward child may be judged as the realisation of the dominance of a particular medical discourse.

The Function of the File

The disputes between the discourses which derived from different branches of medical science were evident in the Egerton Commission. No concrete measures emerged from the Commission. The acceptance of a particular discourse, whatever form it might take, was a precondition for recommendations and implementation of measures for the education of feeble-minded children and educable imbeciles. Thus, in spite of evidence in the DCDEC report which demonstrated the theoretical inadequacies of the formulation of degrees of mentally defective children, stress was laid upon the form of documentation of cases, the regulation of files and the format of reports. Again, the objectified subject was to come under the watchful supervision of a discourse whose knowledge and power would remain invisible.

The Surveillance of the Education Department

The debates in Parliament concerning the 1899 Bill are also indicative. Both the Lord President and Vice-President of the Education Department rebuffed amendments which would have taken supervisory control of medical examinations to ascertain feeble-minded pupils out of the domain of the Department to the level of the Boards or education authorities which they were to become. The Education Department stressed its control over the public system through its rights to approve the appointment of medical practitioners, the schemes proposed at local level, and, ultimately, individual cases themselves. The evidence presented by the Leicester medical practitioner to the RCCCFM (1908, pp. 161–2) perhaps points to the need for this degree of control, particularly in the early stages of the establishment of the national system. Thus Leicester pointed to the invisible part of the discourse which was inadequate and to the deleterious consequence, in educational terms, of trying to separate out practically the feeble-minded from the dull and backward children.

The need for continuing policing of the discourse of feeble-mindedness was also evident from the continuing medical debate concerning 'the stigmata of degeneration' (Binet and Simon, 1914, p. 115). An HMI reported on a Congress on the Education of Feeble-minded Children in Germany and stated that: 'It is to be noted that no mention was made of the so-called physical signs commonly referred to in the examination of feeble-minded children in England' (Eichholz, 1902, p. 595). Evidence to the RCCCFM contained several such references to stigmata (cf., RCCCFM, 1908, vol. II, pp. 2–3, 122, 168, 197, 472).

The London Board's Development of Files

The Superintendent of Special Schools for the London County Council, first appointed to SBL in 1894, as a part of her evidence to RCCCFM in 1908, submitted a sample of six of the special forms developed by London for use in the course of medical examination of pupils prior to admission to special schools. Children were thus transformed first into pupils, by the Elementary education system, and then into cases by the files of the examinations (RCCCFM, 1908, vol. I, pp. 485–91). In a similar vein, the HMI responsible for inspection of the special schools for defective pupils submitted in evidence to the Royal Commission samples of five of the forms developed by the Department of Education relating to the working of the EE(DEC) Act, 1899 (RCCCFM, 1908, vol. II, pp. 685–91).

The Board of Education's continuing control over medical inspections is clearly stated in the Education Act, 1907 (13(b)) and relates specifically to the ascertainment of mentally defective children over the age of seven in the Mental Deficiency Act, 1913 (2(2)(a)) and in the Elementary Education (Defective and Epileptic Children) Act, 1914 (1.1).

The Episteme and the Inadequate Definition

It must be acknowledged, however, that there is a positive advantage in theoretical inadequacy or imprecision for those responsible for the administration of a system at either national or local level. Such imprecision gives scope for manipulation and manoeuvre of policy in the direction considered desirable. That may be the explanation for the seeming underprovision of school places for the ascertained feeble-minded in the period 1900–13.

Foucault's concept of episteme may indeed provide a useful theoretical framework for the future empirical investigation of a form of thought which, although admitted inaccurate, nevertheless was taken as the basis for planning and organisation. Foucault rejected the lineage of Cartesian rationality and was highly suspicious of claims to universal truths, as the debate with Chomsky illustrates (see p. 30 above). His injunction rather was that 'What we have to do, is analyse specific rationalities' (Foucault, 1982, p. 210). Foucault elaborated his ideas concerning the nature of an episteme in the concluding stages of *The Archaeology of Knowledge*:

> The episteme is not a form of knowledge ... which, crossing the boundaries of the most varied sciences, manifests the sovereign unity of a subject, a spirit, or a period; it is the totality of relations that can be discovered for a given period between the sciences when one analyses them at the level of discursive regularities. (1974, p. 191)

The form which analysis of the episteme takes is 'a questioning that accepts the fact of science only in order to ask the question what it is for that science to be a science ... not its right to be a science, but the fact that it exists' (ibid., p. 192). There is already an account of an aspect of the development of primary education from such a perspective (Walkerdine, 1984, pp. 153–202). This work looks at the relations between developmental psychology and a child-centred pedagogy and particularly at how Piaget's theoretical propositions became inserted into early childhood education. In brief, the pedagogy produces both teachers and pupils as subjects.

The Economy of Normalisation

If this aspect of a consideration of discourse offers some account of the persistence of seemingly inadequate definitions, the continuing exercise of control and oversight by the Board of Education, and why the London School Board's system became the model for the national system,

Foucault's ideas concerning the normalisation of punishment may help with others. Here he argues that punishment flows from a display of failure to attain the expected norm. The idea of norm provides the link between ideas which are apparently incompatible. Hence feeble-mindedness as an inability to attain the norm for mental activity can be linked conceptually with an apparent failure to attain the norm of conduct. For this reason, the moral imbecile can be accommodated in an overarching scheme. Moreover, the evidence for lapsed or unattained norms of morality comes in particular forms. The most obvious example is the mothering of children outside marriage, drunkenness, criminality and reckless conduct. All these are visible to the watchful supervision of authority. Similar conduct occurs in different contexts but, because it remains invisible, it also remains unsanctioned publicly.

The normalising surveillance classifies and separates cases from one another. Classification furnishes precision, while separation prevents contagion and facilitates treatment. Thus the discourse includes the logic for the separation of cases, who happen to be children, into special classes or special schools. The discourse, as in Leicester, which posits that they are children before they are cases, produces a discourse of inclusion with other children.

In this way, Foucault's ideas permit a reshuffling of ideas and events. This, in turn, offers different insights into social phenomena. While Marx's and Weber's philosophical anthropology may present an account of the total context within which ideas and events occurred, Foucault's concentrates more sharply upon how thought becomes a social process in the context of the school, clinic and asylum.

THE DISCOURSE OF CLASSIFICATION

Unifying Discourse of Classification

There have been several strands in the study as a whole: the nature and growth of Elementary education; the overseeing of Elementary education by the Education Department and government ministers; the deliberations and recommendations for educational provision for children considered dull, backward and feeble-minded by those regarded as leading experts in the field; and the practical implementation of measures for such children by School Boards and local authorities. The discourse of classification can be regarded as a common concern which brings all four together but where, for each, classification has a different focus of attention.

Discourse, in Foucault's terms, simultaneously has a foot in the camps of the abstract and of the empirical. The contradictions and discontinuities within any particular discourse permit analysis to free itself from transcendental notions of telos, structure and rationality.

The discourse of classification, presented schematically in diagrammatic form (see Figure 7.1) brings together the practical and pedagogical concerns of Elementary school teachers with the theoretical dispositions of acknowledged experts in provision for dull and backward children, which in turn interact with the practical and pedagogic measures adopted by bodies responsible for provision for such children in school. The whole discourse, in turn, falls within the ambit of the Education Department.

FIGURE 7.1
THE DISCOURSE OF CLASSIFICATION

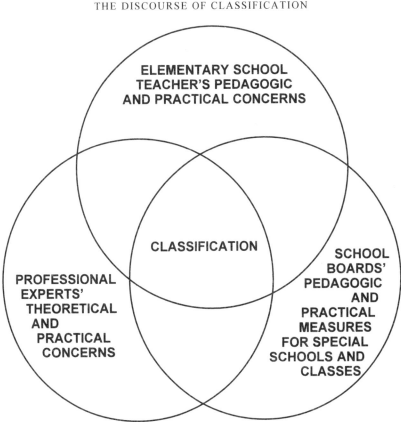

ELEMENTARY SCHOOL
TEACHER'S PEDAGOGIC
AND PRACTICAL CONCERNS

CLASSIFICATION

PROFESSIONAL
EXPERTS'
THEORETICAL
AND
PRACTICAL
CONCERNS

SCHOOL
BOARDS'
PEDAGOGIC
AND
PRACTICAL
MEASURES
FOR SPECIAL
SCHOOLS AND
CLASSES

THE RING MASTER: THE EDUCATION DEPARTMENT

Concerns of Teachers in Schools

The Education Acts of 1870 and 1880 made the system of Elementary education comprehensive in the sense that school places were to be made available for all children of the appropriate age and all children were expected to attend. The system, however, was predicated upon payment by results. Hence teachers were subjected to a policy which constrained pedagogic principles in terms of what rightly should be taught and how it could be taught most effectively. The two consequences of this have been summarised: 'The passing of the 1870, 1877 and 1880 Acts had caused a large influx of new pupils into the elementary schools. Many of these children were utterly ignorant. They clogged up the schools and yet had to be coached and crammed for grant-earning purposes, instead of being dealt with according to their needs' (Barnard, 1961 edn, p. 171). One effect of this, in turn, was to subject pupils to 'over-pressure' of instruction. There are literally hundreds and hundreds of references in the witness evidence presented to the RCCEA in 1886, 1887 and 1888 to over-pressure (cf., RCEEA, 1888, pp. 107–12). Several witnesses openly linked over-pressure with the nature of the system itself. For example, a London headteacher declared that 'I certainly think there is over-pressure in my school ... I attribute the over-pressure to the system of payment by results' (ibid., 1887, p. 115). In the view of one commentator, 'The child was literally sacrificed to the system' (Smith, 1931, p. 269).

The freedom to classify pupils for teaching purposes was perceived by headteachers, teachers and chairmen of School Boards alike as offering a solution to the difficulty. The root of the difficulty in the organisation of schools was the link between the scholastic expectations of each Standard and the child's age. Several witnesses remarked upon 'marked differences of attainment among children of the same Standard so much so that some children for the purposes of organisation should be taught in a Standard higher than that of their chronological age'. Teacher witnesses repeatedly called for greater liberty to classify pupils for teaching purposes (cf., RCEEA, 1888, pp. 101–7). Thus there was the plea that '[c]hildren should be classified according to their power and capability for learning' (ibid., p. 104).

While headteachers may have been divided between granting teachers complete liberty to classify pupils or the responsibility being shared jointly between teachers and school managers, there was little absence of support for classification itself. While the system of Standards inhibited the effective organisation of schools, if the 'liberty of classification were allowed, the instruction in every subject would produce better results' (ibid., p. 104). Again, 'if freedom of classification were allowed, a better classification for teaching purposes would be obtained' (ibid., p. 105). The support for classification was thus on the grounds of the more efficient organisation of the schools, the opportunity for more effective teaching and the overall improvement in pupil attainment. There was, however, no mention of the mechanisms to achieve classification or its boundaries.

Classification as an Organising Mechanism for Practice

The root meaning of classification is that of placing individuals or objects in groups or classes. It is specifically a dividing process. Without a definition of a group or criteria for demarcation between groups, then the extent of the process and the number of groups cannot be determined objectively. However, it is clear that the discourse of classification was a mechanism whereby teachers were able to organise the cognitive, physical and practical demands with which the system of Elementary education confronted them, and to marshal ideas and arrangements which might alleviate those demands.

Classification as an Organising Mechanism for Theory

The leading experts who contributed their professional expertise, initially to the RCBDD in 1889 and subsequently to the DCDEC in 1898, appear to have taken the notion of classification as the starting point simultaneously for their cognitive analysis and practical organisation. Thus Shuttleworth stated in his evidence that 'Idiocy means a lower degradation of intellect, a greater deficiency of intellect, and imbecility means a lesser degree of such deficiency' (RCBDD, 1889, p. 705). In turn, this hierarchy of imbecile and idiot children could be transposed into different classes of children who were capable of benefiting from instruction to various degrees. Broadly, Shuttleworth conceived three classes of children: 'Firstly, those capable of learning to read and write (40%); secondly, those capable of benefiting in minor degree by school instruction and discipline (45%); and thirdly, the ineducable class (15%)' (ibid., p. 708). Once classified, Shuttleworth advocated separate residential institutions for educable imbeciles and idiots. The justification for separation was a mixture of cost-effectiveness, class viability, teacher skills, care outside the classroom and the special developmental curriculum (ibid., p. 711). The Commission endorsed Shuttleworth's blueprint for the 'Improvement of Education of Imbeciles' and

191

incorporated his relativistic definition of a hierarchy of mental deficiency into the main body of its recommendation (ibid., p. 95).

Francis Warner also made classification his starting point, albeit that his classification was broader and the boundaries of classes more permeable since the causal factors were regarded as much social as personal in origin. This broader classification was endorsed by a British Medical Association's survey of almost 3,000 children (ibid., p. 106). Warner advocated small, quiet, separate classes within Elementary schools for what the Commission was to describe as 'feeble-minded children'. Feeble-minded children were classified as the top echelon in the hierarchy of imbeciles and idiots. In creating this classification, the Commission also made firm recommendations for the measures to be taken for the children's education: 'Feeble-minded children ... should be separated from ordinary scholars in public elementary schools in order that they may receive special instruction and the attention of school authorities be particularly directed towards this object' (ibid., p. 106). Thus the discourse of classification was to migrate from the deliberations of professional experts to become an officially endorsed mechanism underpinning policy, planning and practice for the education of children considered dull and backward.

Classification as an Organising Mechanism for Administration

The London School Board provided the model for the early organisation of special schools and classes. This was acknowledged by the fact that other Boards arranged for teachers appointed to work in special classes to visit the London classes before starting their teaching. The London Board placed the idea of classification at the heart of its provision for children considered dull, backward and feeble-minded. The Board developed the policy that newly erected centres for special instruction should contain at least two but no more than five classes. The belief in the idea of classification was reinforced by the belief that it provided optimum efficiency in the organisation of classes (cf., DCDEC, 1898, vol. II, pp. 73, 80, 104, 148). The Board further developed its policy and subsequently stated that 'The advantages in classification which are attained by three classes at a centre are so great that we recommend that, when possible, centres should be provided with at least that number of classes' (ibid., p. 23).

The idea of classification, perhaps because it was germane to the Elementary school teacher's notion of classification, was also evident in the thinking of teachers working in special classes. HM Inspectors had undertaken a survey of teachers in special classes for the DCDEC. A report of their survey observed that, 'As far as possible, no centre should consist of fewer than two classes and that children should be classified' (ibid., p. 258).

One Board also used the idea of classification in what it regarded as the interests of the scholar. Thus a member of the Bristol Board reported that pupils regarded as feeble-minded were required to stay at school until they were 16 years old, as were the blind and deaf, in the interests of avoiding exploitation on the part of unscrupulous employers (ibid., p. 147). That same witness asked the Committee's chairman for a definition which would permit his Board to distinguish the feeble-minded pupil from the others. The Chairman replied: 'We have asked two or three experts and they say they are unable to frame a definition' (ibid.). The experts, one by one, confirmed the impossibility of the translation of the idea of classification into a formula empirically to distinguish pupils and formulate classes. Thus, Shuttleworth (ibid., vol. II, p. 2), Warner (ibid., p. 29), Kerr, Medical Superintendent to the Bradford Board (ibid., p. 18), Ferrier, Professor and Physician to King's College Hospital (ibid., p. 150), Beach, late Medical Superintendent of the Darenth Schools for Imbecile Children (ibid., p. 7), and Harris, Assistant Medical Officer to the London Board (ibid., p. 41), all admitted their inability in this matter.

Commitment to Classification

There were seven members on the DCDEC. Three were Inspectors or Examiners in the Education Department (four if the Committee's secretary is included); two were employees of the London Board, the Board's medical officer and the superintendent of the Board's schools for special instruction; a further member was to join the London Board shortly as its assessor of defective children; and the final member represented the Council for Promoting the Welfare of the Feeble-Minded. The chairman of the Committee was the Chief HMI with responsibility for schools in the Metropolitan District. In his General Report for 1893, he commented upon the 'excellent classes of schools ... established by SBL [School Board for London] for special instruction for children [with] mental ... infirmity' and the schools' 'able superintendent' (PP, 1894, vol. xxx, p. 92).

In spite of the empirical deficiency, the idea of classification afforded an organising principle for the thinking of Elementary school teachers, teachers in special classes, members of the Education Department responsible for the overseeing and smooth running of the Elementary school system and members of the largest School Board in England with responsibility for the administration of the most developed system of centres for special instruction. The commitment of the London Board to the idea of classification is manifest from the witness evidence of the vice-chairman of the London Board, also chairman of its sub-committee for defective children (DCDEC, 1898, vol. II, p. 101), and from the evidence of its superintendent of schools for special instruction to the Egerton Commission (RCBDD, 1889, p. 115). Similarly, the chairman and vice-chairman of the DCDEC pressed the idea of classification as an organising principle upon witnesses summoned to present evidence (cf., DCDEC, 1898, vol. II, pp. 76, 101, 149, 258).

The status and advance of the discourse of classification in one way may be measured objectively over time. In the digest of evidence to the Egerton Commission in 1889, classification figures only as a reference within the larger headings of over-pressure, teachers' grievances and the organisation of schools. In the Education Department's report almost ten years later, classification has secured its own heading with a battery of references (ibid., p. 265).

The Education Department's Surveillance

The fact that the Education Department had technical responsibility, through its link with government, for the imposition of the rules and procedures which regulated the system, put it in a position of commanding oversight of the mechanisms operating within the system. Thus, in Foucauldian terms, the Departmental gaze exercised an educational surveillance throughout the system of special schools and classes. The Departmental gaze, while recognising that variety was possible, nevertheless laid down that: 'A special class may be defined as one so certified by the Education Department' (DCDEC, 1898, vol. I, p. 15). Certain conditions were stipulated as essential for recognition: adherence to selection and admission procedures, periodic medical inspections, exclusive use of a room and the undivided attention of a qualified teacher, segregation from ordinary pupils, conformity to roles concerning class size and curricular emphasis. All these conditions were subsequently codified in an Education Department Minute of the Committee of the Council on Education in February 1900 (PP, 1900, vol. lxiv, pp. 1–26). In residential schools, the principle of the panopticon also figured: the Minute stipulated that '[a] dormitory must be supervised by means of a window in the bedroom of the officer in charge ... Doors must be open at night' (ibid., p. 7). The Minute also highlighted the dividing practices to be followed in day schools – separate classroom, playground, offices, lavatory, entrance and passage, stating that: 'Children must not for any lessons be mixed with the children of the ordinary public Elementary schools' (ibid., p. 6).

The London Board's Surveillance

In the course of the development of its own schools for special instruction, the gaze of the London Board had led to patterns and regulations of procedures for admission to special classes. These had included the development of standardised forms to be completed by teachers and headteachers requesting the examination of pupils for admission to special classes and by medical officers in the course of their examination. The Education Department adopted the system of standardised forms for requests for admission to special classes, medical inspections and assessments. Thus the procedures for recognition, inspection, assessment and admission of pupils to special classes became gradually bureaucratised.

The Normalising Economy of the Examination

The normalising judgment and hierarchical surveillance are most evident in the process of examination.

> In this slender technique [of examination] are to be found a whole domain of knowledge, a whole type of power. In [the examination] are combined the ceremony of power and the form of experiment, the deployment of force and the establishment of truth. At the heart of the procedures of discipline, it manifests the subjection of those who are perceived as objects and the objectification of those who are subjected. (Foucault, 1977, pp. 184–5)

The fact that the abstract formulations and the empirical implementation of the discourse of classification were inconsistent and irrational is irrelevant in a context where the surveillance and gaze of the Education Department is paramount throughout the system, and where the surveillance and gaze such as that of the London Board prevails at the local level.

If the ideas and procedures entailed in the discourse of classification are not so much concerned with the education of children considered dull, backward and feeble-minded as with the objectification of subjects, the transformation of private, personal histories into public, official files, then how are they to be understood? Does the Education Department's gaze figure in a larger canvas? Is the discourse of classification a feature of a larger process?

THE DISCOURSE OF ELEMENTARY SCHOOL EDUCATION

Lewis A. Dexter has published extensively in journals and elsewhere on the subject of mental deficiency and has frequently raised the questions of how such deficiency can possibly be assessed accurately and why it should be identified from a whole range of human capacities as a social problem (cf., Dexter, 1964, n. 1). Ultimately, Dexter maintains that the school's organising principle around academic performance is arbitrary and especially so in a context professing democratic equality. Dexter would be supported in his claim that educational knowledge and the content of the curriculum is arbitrary from another quarter (Bourdieu, 1971b, 1977). It can be argued most compellingly, however, that the pedagogic organisation of Elementary school education around the 3Rs was far from arbitrary.

While in the past there have been cultures or civilisations whose members have been familiar with reading, writing and mathematical calculation, as in Egypt, Greece or Rome, these activities were confined to a particular segment of the population. If the commitment to a belief in natural science is the characteristic which primarily distinguishes the modern, industrial society from the agrarian, then it follows that those with power and control in such a society would wish to make available as many individuals as possible to contribute to the applied or technological processes in industrial society (see Gellner, 1988, 1992). Hence, the 3Rs form simultaneously a part of the essence of modern society but also become the basis upon which Elementary education, intended for the first time for most of the country's children, is rationally organised on an instrumental basis. The 3Rs thus represent the discursive dimension of modern industrial, capitalist society. Other segments of British education, such as the traditions of the grammar and so-called public schools, persisted relatively unchanged precisely because their origins were not in modern, industrial society. Hence the organisation of Elementary school education around the principles of the 3Rs was far from arbitrary.

CHANGE IN CONCEPTUALISATION OF THE LABOUR FORCE

There is dispute concerning the process of transition from an agrarian economy to industrial capitalism. Neither of the rival materialist conceptions of history, the Malthusian and the Marxist, is regarded as providing a satisfactory explanation of the agricultural revolution from the fifteenth century onwards and the later demographic revolution (see Smith, 1991, pp. 139–47). However, if the Malthusian emphasis upon demand within the economy and population is combined with that of the Marxist emphasis upon supply, then some more satisfactory explanation becomes possible to one commentator (Banks, 1989, pp. 294–309).

Both Marx and Weber have underlined the essential place of a pool of wage labourers in a capitalist system. According to Marx, 'Capital presupposes labour and wage labour presupposes capital. One is a necessary condition of the other; they mutually call one another into existence' (1957, p. 635). Hence the existence of a pool of labourers, who were not only able to dispose of their labour but were also obliged to do so to survive, was quintessential to capitalism. Weber, however, drew attention to the capitalist's organisation of labour: 'All the peculiarities of Western capitalism have derived their significance from the capitalist organisation of labour ... . Exact calculation – the basis of everything else – is only possible on the basis of free labour' (1971, p. 22).

The rationalist fundamentalist view (cf., Gellner, 1992, pp. 2–8) which led to natural science also led to a rational perception of the capabilities of the members of the labour force. Thus, in the transition from agrarian to industrial society, there emerged a transformation in perception of the labour force from a homogeneous group of people with exploitable, naturally endowed work-skills to a heterogeneous class of individuals with skills and capacities which could be developed by employers in the pursuit of maximising profit. This point has been elaborated:

> Traditional pre-capitalist conceptions viewed the domestic population as a largely unchangeable given from which an effort was made to squeeze as large a surplus as possible; the emergent modern conception of the labour pool viewed it as a modifiable and manipulable human material whose yield could be steadily enlarged through improvements in use and organisation, rationally designed to transform qualitatively its value as an economic resource. (Scull, 1979, p. 38)

Instead of a reservoir for tax and work purposes, the domestic population was regarded increasingly as an industrial labour force (cf., Donzelot, 1980, pp. 70–82).

The endeavour to rationalise the industrial labour force highlighted at least two social groups which were problematic: the unemployed who were able-bodied as distinct from the aged, infirm and children (cf., Polanyi, 1957, p. 94; Stedman Jones, 1971, pp. 281–314). This question was, in turn, bound up with the parochial provision of relief which interfered with labour mobility; the other group were those considered mad or insane. As Foucault has pointed out, this group changed from being accepted and tolerated within society to being exported and incarcerated. The institution of the workhouse would bring both groups into conjuncture: 'It rendered problematic the whole question of what was to be done with those who could not or would not abide by the rules of the house – among the most important of whom were the acutely disturbed and refractory insane' (Scull, 1979, p. 40).

THE PROCESS OF RATIONALISATION, DEMOCRACY AND THE EDUCATION OF THE DISABLED

The process of rationalisation, as discussed earlier, at one and the same time produces or leads to several different social phenomena which are conflicting rather than harmonious. On the one hand, rationalistion, as evident in industrial processes, demands differentiation within the labour force so that optimum skills and profit may be developed. The process of differentiation, however, produces a hierarchy of skills, expertise and authority within members of the labour force. This case has been presented in detail (Bowles and Gintis, 1976, pp. 53–101). The process also strips out the uniqueness of individual human beings; the processes of assessment, judgment and normalising transform individuals into subjects, cases, pupils and render them notes in files. On the other hand, the very process of normalisation in its creation of subjects and cases also points up the similarities shared by groups of human beings. Thus one strand of rationalisation leads to industrial activities and organisations underpinned by capitalism, but another germane strand leads to the discourse which is able to articulate the distinction between a social class in itself and a social class for itself (cf., Marx, 1967, pp. 88–94). Rationalisation simultaneously produces social hierarchy, normalisation and demands for equality and emancipation.

Both these strands manifest themselves in the system of Elementary education. On the one hand, there is the pressure for development and differentiation within a system based upon a particular form of pedagogy: the demands of efficiency and surplus value require the maximisation of the potential of members of the labour force. These factors alone suggest that a particular segment, such as the disabled, should not be excluded unnecessarily or arbitrarily. On the other hand, the process of normalisation and the pursuit of the idea of equality lead to demands that there be Elementary education for those hitherto excluded – the blind, the deaf, the dumb, the dull and the backward.

THE PLACE OF EDUCATION IN THE KNOWLEDGE–POWER, POWER–KNOWLEDGE THESIS

Some of Foucault's works are described as 'archaeologies' and involve examinations of the social and historical conditions of the emergence of discourses and their relationship to institutional powers. Foucault's thesis is that knowledge and power are concatenated: forms of power are permeated by knowledge and forms of knowledge are imbued with power relations. He produced the term power–knowledge to suggest that power and knowledge are twin sides of a single process. Thus he writes that: 'Power produces knowledge ... Power and knowledge directly imply one another. There is no power relation without the correlative constitution of a field of knowledge, nor any knowledge that does not presuppose and constitute at the same time power relations' (1977, p. 93).

There is, however, no shortage of commentators seeking to point up the shortcomings of the power–knowledge thesis (cf., Merquior, 1985, pp. 108–18; Dews, 1989, pp. 73–6; Barker, 1993, pp. 76–84). The criticisms are twofold: that the thesis remains incomplete and unfinished in both theoretical and empirical terms. What is conspicuously absent is an exploration of the impact of science and technology.

At the heart of Foucault's key texts, such as *Madness and Civilisation, The Birth of the Clinic, The Order of Things* and *Discipline and Punish*, is an account of the transformation of knowing or learning how to know. The new form of knowing makes or constitutes the subject, the patient, the case. The transformation is a kind of hyphen simultaneously connecting and distinguishing one social order from another. Through the institution of forms of examination of what is known, bodies such as doctors, scholars and lawyers are given the right to exercise power over their subject-objects.

The form of educational examination is precisely the hyphen in education in medieval and modern societies. In the Middle Ages, Aries has shown how, from the configuration of learning and examination surrounding the universities, there emerged the object of this whole

199

apparatus, the child (1973, pp. 172–82). At that time, the examination was primarily social, inquisitorial, oral, subjective and qualitative. The industrial era and Elementary school education witnessed the transformation of the examination to the personal, written, objective and quantitative. From this 'second epoch of examinatorial power [emerges] the psychologised child, the differentiated child who is variously labelled from genius to defective or gifted to special needs' (Hoskin, 1990, p. 48).

THE SOCIAL ECONOMY OF THE DULL AND BACKWARD CHILD

An important theoretical point has been observed in the proposition that a form of systems theory is possible which is not based upon teleology (Hall, 1989, pp. 552–4). The proposition is that social evolution is best conceptualised as a form of adaptation to circumstances:

> It is 'normal' to try and adapt to circumstances. It also makes us realise that Parsonian theory is a powerful tool in comprehending much of the historical record precisely because many civilisations were 'systems' which found ways in which ... to preserve their basic structure. (ibid., p. 554)

Foucault has observed that 'for the past 150 years the proclamation of the failure of the prison has always been accompanied by its maintenance' (1977, p. 272). He then proceeds to ask what is the use of these social phenomena which are constantly criticised. Why does the penal system appear to maintain delinquency, to encourage recidivism, to transform the occasional offender into an habitual delinquent and to organise a closed milieu of delinquency? Merquior has dismissed all this as tiresome rhetoric and thereby, as with the power–knowledge hyphen, 'so discharging himself from further thought on the matter' (Hoskin, 1990, p. 49). Foucault's view has a lengthy provenance in the sociological commentary upon crime (cf., Durkheim, 1933, p. 102; Marx, 1963, pp. 167–8; Lemert, 1972, pp. 26–61; Lemert and Gillan, 1982, pp. 30–41). In Foucault's view, 'the prison ... is not intended to eliminate offences, but rather to distinguish them, to distribute them, to use them' (Foucault, 1977, p. 272). The economy of offences, publicly tried and punished, is a mechanism which, first, distinguishes the normal, law-abiding citizen from the offender and, second, produces a hierarchy of offences by distinguishing between offenders. Foucault subsequently elaborated this point in detail (ibid., pp. 40–8).

In the economy of offences, the reform, re-education dimension is rhetorical. The reality is the identification of those convicted as a hierarchy of wrong doers and deserving of punishment. The economy of punishments also simultaneously identifies the unconvicted as morally sound citizens. The solution to the problem of recidivism is not simply irrelevant to the process but it is also potentially damaging to the whole system itself.

There is an array of different practices, procedures and outcomes in courts of law. These are tolerated because the crucial part of the process is the public examination and treatment of offenders. So in education, the ability to classify the dull and backward child is irrelevant, and from that it follows that the internal logic of schemes of classification is irrelevant. The crucial part of the process is the public examination and treatment of cases.

The hierarchy of mental deficiency is the basis for an economy of mental disability. The important stages in the process are the objectification of the subject, identification, labelling and placement. For the sake of supposed accuracy and fairness, the process must be undertaken publicly according to the rules and prescribed procedure. The dull and backward children, struggling to learn in Elementary schools, were the perverse product of the system because they confirmed the rectitude of the system even though they failed within it. Their failure was the system's success. The dull and backward children were thus the perverse validation of the whole system.

The proposals and structure of the education of dull and backward children were a significant feature within the larger canvas of Elementary school education. This, in its turn, was linked in an important way to the nature of industrial society itself. The discourse of Elementary school pedagogy and that of the economy of mental disability both had their roots in rationalisation. Rationalisation, in its turn, was the basis of modern society.

8

Conclusions

THE ELEMENTARY SCHOOL SYSTEM

The Elementary school system was conceived of and developed within a context of social, economic and industrial change. These changes brought people from rural surroundings to growing centres of population in towns and cities where there was industry, business and work. The extension of compulsory education to the whole age cohort, the nature of the school curriculum and of the teaching profession within a system policed by the Code of payment by results, created the context for the production of the dull and backward pupil, particularly in the urban context. Table 3.1 presents the outline of growth of numbers of pupils in Elementary schools which more than doubled between 1870 and 1880. The numbers of pupils on the roll in Elementary schools increased to 5.6 million in 1889 and 6.1 million in 1914. Over the whole period the ratio of pupils to each teacher, including qualified, assistant and pupil-teachers, was as follows: in 1870, 60.7:1; in 1890, 49:1; in 1899, 46:1, and in 1914, 36:1 (Board of Education, 1900, p. 104; Ministry of Education, 1951b, p. 247). Thus the size of classes fell gradually over a period of 45 years but still remained large.

The establishment of the Royal Commission on the Elementary Education Acts in 1886 can be understood as a response to the difficulties which the system faced in its early stages. However, evidence presented by HMI, members of School Boards and teachers themselves supported the view that class size, teaching methods and the pressure from the Code of payment by results combined to create the conditions for the emergence of the dull and backward pupil. The extensive debate concerning over-pressure can be interpreted in this way.

BACKGROUND TO THE DULL AND BACKWARD PUPIL

While some of those with knowledge of the work in Elementary schools pointed to the features of the system itself as the creator of the dull and backward child, there were others who acknowledged other background features. Thus in her evidence to the RCEEA, Mrs Burgwin, in her capacity as headteacher of an Elementary school under the London Board, gave ill-health, malnutrition, poverty and poor housing as important causes (RCEEA, 1886, pp. 115–17). She also introduced a system of cheap and even free meals for pupils on the school premises (Horn, 1990, pp. 48–60). In addition, she pressed for school facilities where children could bathe and their clothes be washed and dried (ibid.). Margaret McMillan worked for precisely these same goals during the period of her association with the Bradford School Board in the 1890s (Steedman, 1990, pp. 195–7).

As this study shows, HMI frequently reported upon the unsatisfactory environmental factors in Board schools. Narrow windows set high in walls admitted very little light in certain circumstances, while petroleum lamps added their fumes to the classroom atmosphere without shedding much illumination. The quality of pupils' eyesight was also a concern to many School Boards. The evidence in this study shows that the first task which Boards set their medical officers on appointment often was the construction of a device to test all pupils' eyesight. This was the case in Bradford, London, Reading and Aldershot. Table 5.2 also reveals an HMI's concerns over the quality of children's hearing in urban environments.

THE EGERTON COMMISSION

The establishment of the Egerton Commission can be regarded as a response to the new, comprehensive nature of the Elementary school system. When attendance at school was not compulsory, then children with disabilities could rest freely outside the system. As Chapter 4 reveals, the terms of reference of the Commission were increased from the initial concern for the education of the blind to include the deaf and dumb and finally the defective and epileptic child. If the status of this last group is not accurately reflected in the report's use of the ampersand in its title, then it more certainly is in the fact that it occupied a mere 15 pages of reference and recommendation in a total of 107 pages. There already existed models for the education of the blind and the deaf and the Commission's recommendations relatively quickly became the basis for Acts of Parliament. The educational provision for the dull, backward, feeble-minded or defective child remained problematic.

THE CONFLICT BETWEEN WARNER'S AND SHUTTLEWORTH'S
EVIDENCE

Chapter 4 sets out the detail of the conflict in evidence which Warner and Shuttleworth presented to the Commission regarding the nature and aetiology of mental deficiency. (Epilepsy, which had been tagged on to the terms of reference, was scarcely mentioned there or subsequently.) Warner and Shuttleworth were called to give evidence as leading experts.

Dr Shuttleworth was Medical Superintendent of the Royal Albert Asylum for Idiots and Imbeciles, Lancaster and had previously taken a higher degree in the new science of the mind at Heidelberg University. Shuttleworth espoused a relativistic definition: 'Idiocy means a lower degradation of intellect, a greater deficiency of intellect, and imbecility means a lesser degree of such deficiency' (RCBDD, 1889, p. 705). The condition, in his opinion, originated in the womb or early infancy or childhood (ibid., p. 670). The Egerton Commission accepted and endorsed Shuttleworth's conception of a hierarchy of mental deficiency which made itself evident very early in natural life, by repeating his evidence in the main body of the report (p.95). If the starting point for a diagnosis of mental deficiency is that it is a condition evident within the individual almost from the start of life, then the prognosis is likely to be very restricted. Such was the case, in Shuttleworth's mind, because it was only possible to train the imbecile and higher forms of idiot in special conditions.

Warner was a paediatrician with a traditional medical training, and a professor of anatomy and physiology at a London college. Warner presented his evidence on the basis of notes which he had kept over ten or more years concerning children who had come under his care as patients in hospital or outpatients in clinics. He identified a group of children expelled by reason of inability to progress in Elementary schools as those with sight defects, tuberculosis and symptoms of malnutrition and exhaustion. He also added that he considered the Elementary school system, in part at least, responsible for the condition of such children by virtue of the mechanical and large-scale nature of instruction and by the physical mistreatment of such children by their teachers.

Leaving on one side any clinical judgment between the merit of Shuttleworth's and Warner's views, with the detachment which the passing of more than a century brings, it is possible to identify the important differences between the two. On the one hand, Shuttleworth conceived the phenomenon as one capable of precise diagnosis and treatment and with firm boundaries around it in medical terms. Warner, on the other hand, conceived the phenomenon as a critique of the nature of society and the Elementary school system. The attractiveness of Shuttleworth's conception to those who had to take political and administrative action is that of a clearly boundaried problem or difficulty with remedial action which relates to the perceived problem. Warner's conception, however, pointed to originating causes and factors which were well beyond and outside the system of Elementary education. The remedial measures which Warner's conceptions called forth were much broader and more radical in political and administrative terms. Perhaps Warner's conceptions were literally unthinkable and unacceptable.

Haec est regula recti. In Foucauldian terms, what is the difference between the norms of the political economy of distribution around which the subjects are arranged in each conception? Shuttleworth's norm centres around medical knowledge. The subject is objectified in the form of a case through the mechanism of a medical examination. The practice divides the subjects from their peers and confirms simultaneously their condition as a personal property. As a medical specialist, Shuttleworth's conceptions create special cases to be identified by the expert.

Warner's norm is different and more complicated. One strand is that of the physician's goal to restore the patient to normal life. Although Warner's subject may become objectified in the form of a case established through examination, the qualities displayed by the examination are by no means regarded as fixed or permanent. In Warner's conception, the economy of distribution may be affected and changed by social, economic and educational factors which lie beyond the characteristics of the particular case. Another strand, and perhaps the more important one, is Warner's recognition that the examination is a basis of the economy of cases and for that very reason must be tackled with caution. It is also clear that a range of experts may contribute to the examination. An obvious addition is that of the schoolteacher. Hence, as Warner's goal may be restoration to normal life, the examination norm may be as much educational and social as medical. The case is a patient, literally, one suffering, whose condition must be diagnosed and changed. The patient is more than a case distributed around a medical norm.

THE DEPARTMENTAL COMMITTEE

Legislation for the education of children designated mentally defective did not follow from the Egerton Commission's report as it did for the blind and deaf. Legislation took place in 1899 following the deliberations of the Departmental Committee on Defective and Epileptic Children. While the absence of legislation following the Egerton Commission may be an indication of the uncertainty on the part of politicians and the Education Department whether to accept Shuttleworth's or Warner's opinions, as Chapter 5 relates, these pupils were still evident in the Elementary education system as the evidence of HMI in urban and rural areas demonstrated. A very small number of School Boards also established their own special classes.

The contrast between the Leicester and the London School Boards, summarised in Chapter 5, is illuminating. Leicester's approach and particularly its incorporation of a Standard 0 mechanism corresponded closely to Warner's critique and is based upon an educational norm.

The London Board, however, based its policy and practice upon Shuttleworth's norm. First, a system of special centres was established which was divided from the rest of the Elementary school system; this was by virtue of the fact that the teacher responsible for the conduct of each centre was responsible to a superintendent of special centres of instruction who reported to the Board's sub-committee concerned with deaf, blind and mentally defective pupils. The Board also accepted that the medical examination could separate pupils suitable to enter special centres from other pupils. Thus pupils became objectified as special subjects. The centres consisted of a minimum of three classes wherever practicable. This was based upon the pursuit of the principle of classification which was itself based upon the assumption of a detectable hierarchy of differences, or deficiencies, between pupils. The system also transformed the subjects into cases, through the practice of writing notes about each 'case' on standardised forms. There were forms for admission, family background and progress in the classes (see Appendices 1, 2 and 3).

The category, feeble-minded children, was regarded as representing the highest echelon in the hierarchy of mental deficiency from imbecile to idiot. Egerton had recommended that 'feeble-minded children … should be separated from ordinary scholars in public elementary schools in order that they may receive special instruction' (RCBDD, 1889, p. 106). The location of the phrase 'in public elementary schools' makes precise interpretation of the whole ambiguous. Nevertheless, the London Board quoted that same passage from Egerton in its minutes to justify the policy of segregating pupils and centres of special instruction from other schools (cf., Ch. 5). Thus the dividing practices were based upon Shuttleworth's norm and were reinforced by the accepted practices for provision for the blind and deaf.

COMPOSITION OF THE DEPARTMENTAL COMMITTEE

There were seven members of the Departmental Committee: three members – two HMI and one Examiner – represented the Education Department, and three represented the London Board in the persons of Shuttleworth, shortly to join the Board as chief assessor for admission to its special classes, the superintendent of its centres of special instruction and the Board's medical officer. The seventh member represented a charity concerned for the feeble-minded.

THE DEPARTMENTAL COMMITTEE'S DELIBERATIONS

The Committee took evidence from those considered to be at the forefront of the science of the mind at the time and accepted the relativistic definition of a hierarchy of mental deficiency (cf., Ch. 6). This acceptance occurred despite the Committee's chairman acknowledging the definition's inadequacy and his declaration to a witness that there was no certain way of distinguishing the mentally defective pupil from other pupils (cf., Ch. 7, p. 193 above).

The Committee also accepted the main principles of the London Board's organisation of centres for special instruction as the basis for the blueprint which other Boards should adopt. At the centre of the blueprint was the idea of the hierarchy of mental deficiency. The classification of pupils in accordance with their degree of mental deficiency was the central idea in the practical organisation of the centres and their internal arrangements. Thus the blueprint recommended that the centres should contain a minimum of three classes. If the definition of deficiency was problematic, then so too was classification (cf., Ch. 7, pp. 190–5 above). Admission to the special classes should be on the basis of a medical examination conducted by an expert. The norm of distribution thus became palpably medical, although the justification for discrimination was presented as educational. Attendant upon the examination was the completion of standardised forms of the details of diagnosis.

SUBSEQUENT LEGISLATION

The Elementary Education (Defective and Epileptic Children) Act, 1899, set out the framework within which education authorities could make provision for mentally defective pupils. The Elementary Education (Defective and Epileptic Children) Act, 1914, obliged education authorities to make provision. This Act followed closely after the Mental Deficiency Act, 1913, which had included both children and adults. At the heart of each of these sets of legislation there persisted the relativistic definition of the hierarchy of mental capacities and the organisational principle of classification. This form of definition endured and a commentator upon the Mental Deficiency Act, 1927, who was also medical officer to an Education Committee and certifying medical officer to a county mental deficiency authority, acknowledged these definitional inadequacies but discounted them on the grounds that his tasks were primarily practical ones (Herd, 1930, p. 7).

LEAs were slow to adopt the permissive measures of the 1899 Act as Table 7.4 demonstrates. In 1902, 14 per cent of LEAs had made provision and that rose to 56 per cent in 1913, which perhaps explains the need for the subsequent legislation.

The impact of the relativistic definition can be seen in Tables 7.5, 7.6. and 7.7 in the variations in policy and practice by the LEAs. The evidence revealed variations in the proportion of pupils ascertained as mentally defective between the Education Districts within a single county in 1909. There were also variations in proportions between county and urban areas revealed in 1909 and 1913.

SURVEILLANCE OF THE EDUCATION DEPARTMENT

At several points the Education Department controlled events through its ability to lay down the details of codes of practice which Education Authorities were obliged to follow. In the Parliamentary debate on the 1899 Act, the Department's remit to oversee was pointed to as a safeguard for public interests. Thus the Department was able to insist upon a medical examination for admission to special classes, to specify the personnel and procedures of the examination, to lay down the principle of classification for the organisation of classes, to determine the qualifications of teachers in special classes and the numbers of pupils in the classes. A code of precise regulations and a principle of classification were needed in the context where the foundation of the system, the very definition upon which it was based, was inadequate in distinguishing between children's educational capacities and prescribing for their treatment. The code of practice provided the regulation for the system because the principles upon which the system was based were in themselves incapable of providing the logical basis for action.

THE DISCOURSE OF CLASSIFICATION

The principle of classification provided the focus which could unite the interests of different groups of participants within the education system of which special classes were a part. First, teachers in the Elementary schools subscribed to the idea of classification as a measure which would bring order to the organisation of their teaching and their classes. Second, the School Boards which first tackled the question of the teaching of dull, backward and defective children, needed a principle which would identify the objects of their concern. Special schools and classes could be confidently established and organised if different sorts of pupils could be distinguished and classified one from another. Third, the professional group within medical circles which developed the classification system were also interested in its outcome. The professional concern was to develop a basis of medical knowledge which would help distinguish between cases. The espousal of the principle of classification and its adoption as an organisational factor for the establishment of special classes by School Boards and its pursuit by teachers in school, constituted proof of the veracity and validity of the concept of classification. Thus the idea of classification was reified in the Boards' establishment of special classes. Fourth, the Education Department, although apparently standing above the practical details of Boards' and schools' organisations, nevertheless supported the principle of classification as a device bringing order to a particular part of the system for which it had ultimate responsibility. Reification was therefore in the interest of the Department of Education and the other parties involved.

THE DISCOURSE OF ELEMENTARY SCHOOL EDUCATION

The placing of the 3Rs at the centre of the organisation of the code controlling the Elementary school system was not arbitrary. The 3Rs represented, simultaneously, the basis upon which industrial and economic changes were achieved through scientific developments and the means by which different parts of the work-force could be educated to achieve the new skills demanded by industrial and economic changes.

THE NORM OF THE 3RS

Haec est regula recti. The 3Rs became the norm of the system of Elementary school education. The norm of the 3Rs was the basis for the economy of the distribution of pupils. Along the terrain of such a norm, there are bound to be those who succeed and those who fail. The aim of the norm and the process of normalisation is precisely the distribution of its subjects in serried order around it. The dull and backward children struggling to learn in Elementary schools were the perverse product of the system because they confirmed publicly the rectitude of the system, even though they failed within it. Their failure was the system's success. The dull and backward children were thus the perverse validation of the whole system.

The proposals and structure of the education of dull and backward children were a significant feature within the larger picture of Elementary school education. This, in its turn, was linked in an important way to the nature of industrial society itself. The discourse of Elementary school pedagogy and that of the economy of mental disability both had their roots in rationalisation. Rationalisation, in its turn, was the basis of modern society.

A NOTE ON THEORY

The combination of Bourdieu's ideas regarding social reproduction and Weber's on status group formation, has facilitated the organisation of a great deal of information which centred upon the system of Elementary schools and the consequences for different groups of children with disabilities. The ideas surrounding Foucault's concepts of normalisation and the objectification of the subject have also permitted the organisation of material and practices regarding the growth of special schools for backward pupils.

The analytical strategy of narrative and criticism, however, laid bare (see Ch. 6) the issues which this form of theorising could not tackle. Foucault's concept of episteme was of help here. Its essence may best be illustrated, first, by the fact that, when Foucault and Chomsky discussed publicly the concept of human nature, while Chomsky sought to develop the notion that it consisted in what distinguished human beings from other species, Foucault posed the different problem of how human nature had been constructed by different social groups at different points in history (cf., p. 30). Second, it is evident in Foucault's injunction that rather than rationality we should seek to understand rationalities (Foucault, 1982, p. 210). Third, the form which the analysis of an episteme takes is 'a questioning that accepts the fact of a science only in order to ask the question what it is for that science to be a science' (ibid., p. 192). Thus it was possible to accept the irrationality of a relativisitic definition of a hierarchy of mental deficiency and to present an explanation of its existence by the application of another form of rationality.

Appendices

Appendix 1
DCDEC Proforma for Admission to Special Class

Form A: *To be filled up by Teacher of Ordinary School sending Child to be Examined with a view to Admission to Special Class*

1. Name of child and address
2. Age
3. How long has the child attended school?
4. What is the appearance of the child – stupid or bright?
5. Is the child: 1) Obedient; 2) Mischievous; 3) Spiteful?
6. Are the habits of the child correct and clean?
7. Are the propensities of the child peculiar or dangerous?
8. What is the mental capacity of the child?

      1. Observation
      2. Imitation
      3. Attention
      4. Memory
      5. Reading
      6. Writing
      7. Calculation
      8. Colour
      9. Special tastes

9. Is the child affectionate or otherwise?
10. Has the child any moral sense?
11. Have you any other information bearing on the case?

12. Has the child been in regular attendance?
    If not, state why.

    Signed..

    School..

    Department..

    Date..

N.B. In filling up this Form avoid general terms such as 'fair', 'moderate', &c., and say in the simplest terms what the scholar can do.

Source: DCDEC, vol. I (1898), p. 11.

Appendix 2
DCDEC Proforma of Family History for Children Admitted to Special Class

Form B: *Particulars of Family History of Child admitted to Special Class.*

1. What is the bodily and mental condition of the parents?
2. Are they temperate or otherwise?
3. Family History:–

(Living) Present age		Present State of Health	Age at Date of Death		Cause of Death	Year of Death
Father,	alive, aged		Father,	died, aged		
Mother,	alive, aged		Mother,	died, aged		
Brothers	alive, aged alive, aged alive, aged alive, aged alive, aged		Brothers	died, aged died, aged died, aged died, aged died, aged		
Sisters	alive, aged alive, aged alive, aged alive, aged alive, aged		Sisters	died, aged died, aged died, aged died, aged died, aged		

4. Has any near relative, dead or living, suffered from Insanity, Fits, Consumption, Scrofula, or any other hereditary disease?
5. When was the mental deficiency of the child first observed?
6. To what cause is this mental deficiency attributed?
7. Is the child subject to Epileptic or other Fits?
8. From what illness has the child suffered?

9. Has the child received any special treatment?
    If so, where?
10. Is the child improving or otherwise?
11. When did the child commence to walk?
12. When did the child commence to talk?

Name and address of person giving the above information

Date

Source: DCDEC, vol. I (1898), p. 13.

Appendix 3

DCDEC Proforma for Progress of Children in Special Class

Form C. *Particulars as to Progres of Child in Special Class*

Name of School
Name of Scholar
Date of Birth
Date of Admission to Special Class

	PROFICIENCY IN				YOUR OPINION AS TO		NUMBER OF ATTENDANCES AT SPECIAL SCHOOL
	Reading	Writing	Number	Handwork	General Intelligence: Knowledge of Form, Colour &c.	Character, Health and Conduct	
At time of admission							
6 months after admission							For 1st six months
1 year after admission							For 2nd six months
1½ years after admission							For 3rd six months

| PROFICIENCY IN | | | | YOUR OPINION AS TO | | NUMBER OF ATTENDANCES AT SPECIAL SCHOOL |
Reading	Writing	Number	Handwork	General Intelligence: Knowledge of Form, Colour &c.	Character, Health and Conduct	
2 years after admission						For 4th six months
2½ years after admission						For 5th six months
3 years after admission						For 6th six months
3½ years after admission						For 7th six months
4 years after admission						For 8th six months
4½ years after admission						For 9th six months
5 years after admission						For 10th six months

N.B. In filling up this sheet, avoid, as far as possible, general terms such as 'very fair', 'moderate' &c., but say in the simplest words possible what the scholar can do.

Signed

Teacher of class

Source: DCDEC, vol. I (1898), p. 14.

Appendix 4
DCDEC Survey of Teachers in Special Classes

The following questions were addressed to teachers of special classes:

1. At what ages are children generally admitted into your Class? (Leave this unanswered if your Class has been opened under a year.)
2. In what proportions would you distribute under the following heads the children that are now in your Class?
   (a) Likely to be self-supporting when they leave school
   (b) Likely to be partially self-supporting
   (c) Not likely to be self-supporting.
3. How many crippled or very delicate children, but of average intelligence, have you in your Class?
4. Are there any scholars whose sight or hearing are so defective that you cannot deal with them properly? If so, how many?
5. How many children have left the Class since you have had the charge of it?
   Of these:–
   (a) How many have gone to the ordinary school?
   (b) How many to institutions?
   (c) How many to work? (Say what kind of work.)
   (d) How many have stopped at home under the care of parents &c. but have done no particular work?
   (e) How many have died?
   (f) How many unknown?
6. Have you noticed children who appeared to be non-educable when first admitted, but afterwards turned out to be educable? Have such cases been common?
7. What, in your opinion, are the best practical means of distinguishing between the educable and non-educable classes of feeble-minded children, and also of distinguishing between those children who may properly be taught in an ordinary elementary school and those who should be taught in special schools?
8. (a) Can you as a rule obtain trustworthy information as to 'family history'?

218

(b) When the answers about family history seem untrustworthy, do you leave blank the 'family history' in the history and 'progress book'; or put down what you are told; or guess at the truth?

9. Do you get trustworthy information from the teachers of the schools from which your scholars come? Is the form in which this information is supplied satisfactory, or do you suggest any other?

10. What is the usual and what is the longest distance between the homes of the scholars and your school? Do the scholars come to school by themselves? Have they to cross any crowded thoroughfares? Do you know of any cases of street accidents to your scholars?

11. (a) Have you had any special trouble in maintaining discipline?

(b) Have you had any experience of children who could not be brought under control, i.e., who, in spite of all your efforts, were too restless and noisy or disorderly for work in a room in which other children are taught?

(c) Have you had any experience of dangerously violent children, or of children with any very repulsive habits? Have cases of this sort been common? Have you been obliged to exclude any children on account of the above reasons?

(d) (a) How many children have you generally under your care?

(b) Have you found your Class too large?

(c) How many children in a special class can be taught by a single-handed teacher?

12. Is the room (or rooms) in which you conduct your Class on the ground floor? How is it furnished? Point any special merits or defects in the room or in the furniture.

13. What standard is reached by your most advanced scholars in (a) Reading, (b) Writing, (c) Arithmetic, (d) Needlework, (e) Drawing, (f) Manual work other than Needlework or Drawing?

14. Do you keep a book to show details of the progress made from time to time by each of your scholars? If so, in what form?

15. Have you any suggestion which you wish to bring before the Committee?

16. Name of teacher (or teachers) giving the above information.

Source: DCDEC, vol. II (1898), pp. 254–5.

Bibliography

ACTS OF PARLIAMENT

53 and 54, Vict., c. 43, Education of Blind Deaf-mute Children (Scotland) Act, 1890

56 and 57, Vict., c. 32, Elementary Education (Blind and Deaf Children) Act, 1893

62 and 63, Vict., c.32, Elementary Education (Defective and Epileptic Children) Act, 1899

7, Edw. VII, c.43, Education (Administrative Provisions) Act, 1907

3 and 4, Geo. V, c.28, Mental Deficiency Act, 1913

4 and 5, Geo. V, c.45, Elementary Education (Defective and Epileptic Children) Act, 1914

17 and 18, Geo. V, c.33, Mental Deficiency Act,1927

7 and 8, Geo. VI, c.31, Education Act, 1944

PARLIAMENTARY DEBATES (PD)

PD, vol. CLXV, 1862

PD, vol. LXXIII, 1899

PD, vol. LXXIV, 1899

PD, vol. LXXV, 1899

PARLIAMENTARY PAPERS (PP)

PP, 1875, xxiii, Selection of Civil Servants (Playfair)

PP, 1884, xiii, Select Committee, Ministerial Responsibility for Education

PP, 1894, xxx, General Report for Metropolitan District and for East Central Division

PP, 1896, xxvii, General Report for Metropolitan District

PP, 1897, xxv, Special Reports on Education
PP, 1898, xxiii, General Report for East Central Division
PP, 1900, xx, General Report for East Central Division
PP, 1900, lxiv, Minute of Committee of Council on Grants for Defective and
Epileptic Children

SECONDARY SOURCES

Abercrombie, N., Hill, S. and Turner, B. S. (1988) *Dictionary of Sociology*,
London, Penguin Books.
Abrams, P. (1982) *Historical Sociology*, Shepton Mallet, Open Books.
Adamson, J. W. (1930) *English Education 1789–1902,* Cambridge,
Cambridge University Press.
Alston, J. (ed.) (1992) *The Royal Albert: Chronicles of an Era*, Lancaster,
Centre for North-West Regional Studies, University of Lancaster.
Alston, W. P. (1964) *Philosophy of Language*, Englewood Cliffs, NJ,
Prentice-Hall.
Andreski, S. (1964) *Elements of Comparative Sociology*, London, Weidenfeld
& Nicolson.
Aries, P. (1973) *Centuries of Childhood*, Harmondsworth, Penguin Books.
Armytage, W. H. G. (1964) *Four Hundred Years of English Education*,
Cambridge, Cambridge University Press.
Audit Commission and HMI (1992) *Getting in on the Act: Provision for
Pupils with Special Educational Needs: The National Picture*, London,
HMSO.
Ball, S. J. (ed.) (1990) *Foucault and Education: Disciplines and Knowledge*,
London, Routledge.
Ball, S. J. (1990) Management as Moral Technology: A Luddite Analysis, in
S. J. Ball (ed.), *Foucault and Education: Disciplines and Knowledge*,
London, Routledge.
Ball, S. J. (1994) *Education Reform: a Critical and Post-Structural
Approach*, Buckingham, Open University Press.
Banks, A. J. (1989) An Effective Demand Conception of History, *British
Journal of Sociology*, 40, 2, pp. 294–309.
Barker, D. (1893) How to Curb the Fertility of the Unfit: The Feeble-minded
in Edwardian Britain, *Oxford Review of Education*, 9, 3, pp. 197–211.
Barker, P. (1993) *Michel Foucault: Subversions of the Subject*, London,
Harvester Wheatsheaf.
Barnard, H. C. (1947, revised edn 1961) *A History of English Education From
1760*, London, University of London Press.

Barnett, C. (1986) *The Audit of War: The Illusion and Reality of Britain as a Great Nation*, London, Macmillan.

Beechey, V. and Donald, J. (1985) *Subjectivity and Social Relations,* Milton Keynes, Open University Press.

Bendix, R. (1960) *Max Weber: An Intellectual Portrait*, London, Methuen.

Binet, A. and Simon, T. (1914) *Mentally Defective Children*, London, Edward Arnold.

Board of Education (1900–14) *Statistics of Public Education in England and Wales, Education Statistics*, London, HMSO, published annually.

Board of Education (1901) *Report of the Board of Education, 1899–1900,* vol. III, London, HMSO.

Bottomore, T. and Outhwaite, W. (eds) (1993) Commentary, in Karl Lowith, *Max Weber and Karl Marx*, London, Routledge.

Bottomore, T. B. and Rubel, M. (eds) (1963) *Karl Marx: Selected Writings in Sociology and Social Philosophy*, Harmondsworth, Penguin Books.

Bourdieu, P. (1971a) Systems of Education and Systems of Thought, in M. F. D. Young (ed.), *Knowledge and Control: New Directions for the Sociology of Education*, London, Collier-Macmillan.

Bourdieu, P. (1971b) Intellectual Field and Creative Project, in M. F. D. Young (ed.), *Knowledge and Control: New Directions for the Sociology of Education*, London, Collier-Macmillan.

Bourdieu, P. (1977) Cultural Reproduction and Social Reproduction, in J. Karabel and A. H. Halsy (eds), *Power and Ideology in Education*, New York, Oxford University Press.

Bourdieu, P. and Passeron, J. C. (1977) *Reproduction in Education, Culture and Society*, London, Sage.

Bowles, S. and Gintis, H. (1976) *Schooling in Capitalist America: Educational Reform and the Contradictions of Economic Life*, London, Routledge.

Burgwin, E. M. (1900) The Physically and Mentally Handicapped, in T. A. Spalding, *The Work of the London School Board*, London, King.

Burke, P. (1980) *Sociology and History*, London, Allen & Unwin.

Bryant, J. M. (1994) Evidence and Explanation in History and Sociology: Critical Reflections on Goldthorpe's Critique of Historical Sociology, *British Journal of Sociology*, 45, 1, pp. 3–19.

Charity Organisation Society (COS) (1877) *Report on the Education and Care of Idiots, Imbeciles and Harmless Lunatics*, London, Charity Organisation Society.

Charity Organisation Society (COS) (1893), *The Feeble-Minded Child and Adult*, London, Swan Sonnenschein.

Chief Medical Officer of the Board of Education (1911, 1913, 1914, 1917) *Annual Report for 1910, 1912, 1913, 1916*, London, HMSO.

222

Cole, T. (1989) *Apart or a Part? Integration and the Growth of British Special Education*, Milton Keynes, Open University Press.

Collins, R. (1971) Functional and Conflict Theories of Educational Stratification, *American Sociological Review*, 36, pp. 1002–19.

Copeland, I. C. (1991) Special Educational Needs and the Education Reform Act, 1988, *British Journal of Educational Studies*, 39, 2, pp. 190–206.

Copeland, I. C. (1993) Is there a Sociology of Special Education and Integration? *European Journal of Special Needs Education*, 8, 2, pp. 1–13.

Curtis, S. J. (1948) *History of Education in Great Britain*, London, University Tutorial Press.

Dahrendorf, R. (1958) Out of Utopia: Towards a Re-orientation of Sociological Analysis, *American Journal of Sociology*, 44, 2, pp. 102–19.

Davis, K. and Moore, W. (1945) Some Principles of Stratification, *American Sociological Review*, 10, pp. 242–9.

Deem, R. (1978) *Women and Schooling*, London, Routledge & Kegan Paul.

Dent, H. C. (1970) *Century of Growth in English Education*, London, Longman.

Department for Education (DFE) (1994) *Code of Practice on the Identification and Assessment of Special Educational Needs*, London, DFE.

Department of Education and Science (1978) *Special Educational Needs, Report of the Committee of Enquiry into the Education of Handicapped Children and Young People*, London, HMSO.

Dews, P. (1979) The Nouvelle Philosophie and Foucault, *Economy and Society*, 8, 2, pp. 127–71.

Dews, P. (1984) Power and Subjectivity in Foucault, *New Left Review*, 144, pp. 72–95.

Dews, P. (1989) Foucault and the Frankfurt School, in L. Appignanesi (ed.), *Ideas from France: ICA Documents*, London, Free Association Books.

Dexter, L. A. (1964) On the Politics and Sociology of Stupidity in our Society, in H. S. Becker (ed.), *The Other Side: Perspectives on Deviance*, New York, Free Press.

Digby, A. and Searby, P. (1981) *Children, School and Society in Nineteenth Century England*, London, Macmillan.

Donald, J. (1985) Beacons of the Future: Schooling, Subjection and Subjectification, in V. Beechey and J. Donald (eds), *Subjectivity and Social Process*, Milton Keynes, Open University Press.

Donzelot, J. (1980) *The Policing of Families: Welfare versus the State*, London, Hutchinson.

Drummond, A. J. (1943) Cold Winters at Kew Observatory 1783–1942, *Quarterly Journal of the Royal Meteorological Society*, 69, pp. 19–37.

Durkheim, E. (1933) *The Division of Labour in Society*, trans. G. Simpson, New York, Free Press.

Durkheim, E. (1952) *Suicide: A Study in Sociology*, trans. J. A. Spaulding and G. Simpson, London, Routledge & Kegan Paul.

Durkheim, E. (1956) *Education and Sociology*, trans. S. D. Fox, London, Collier-Macmillan.

Eaglesham, E. J. R. (1967) *The Foundations of Twentieth Century Education in England*, London, Routledge & Kegan Paul.

Eco, U. (1992) *Interpretation and Overinterpretation*, Cambridge, Cambridge University Press.

Edmonds, E. L. (1962) *The School Inspector*, London, Routledge & Kegan Paul.

Education Department (1898) *Report of the Departmental Committee on Defective and Epileptic Children* (DCDEC), 2 vols, London, HMSO.

Education Department (1900) *Minute of the Committee of Council on Education, 26 February 1900, Providing for Grants on Account of the Education of Defective and Epileptic Children*, London, HMSO (PP, 1900, vol. lxiv).

Eicholz, A. (1902) Report of the Congress on the Education of Feeble-Minded Children. Held at Augsburg, April 10–12, 1901, in *Board of Education, Special Reports on Educational Subjects*, vol. 9, *Education in Germany*, London, HMSO.

Elders, F. (ed.) (1974) *Reflexive Water: The Basic Concerns of Mankind*, London, Souvenir Press.

Engels, F. (1969) *The Condition of the Working Class in England*, St Albans, Panther Books.

Evans, K. (1975) *The Development and Structure of the English Education System*, London, Hodder & Stoughton.

Evans, R. J. (1997) *In Defence of History*, London, Granta.

Flew, A. (ed.) (1984) *A Dictionary of Philosophy*, London, Pan Books.

Ford, J., Mongon, D. and Wheelan, M. (1982) *Special Education and Social Control: Invisible Disasters,* London, Routledge & Kegan Paul.

Forster, W. E. *Hansard*, vol. cxix, p. 438, quoted in T. A. Spalding (1900), *The Work of the London School Board*, London, King.

Foucault, M. (1971) *Madness and Civilisation: A History of Insanity in the Age of Reason*, London, Tavistock.

Foucault, M. (1973) *The Birth of the Clinic: An Archaeology of Medical Perception*, trans. R. Howard, London, Routledge.

Foucault, M. (1974) *The Archaeology of Knowledge*, trans. A. M. Sheridan Smith, London, Tavistock.

Foucault, M. (1977) *Discipline and Punish*, trans. A. Sheridan, London, Allen Lane.

Foucault, M. (1980a) Power/Knowledge in C. Gordon (ed.), *Selected Interviews and Other Writings 1972–77*, London, Harvester Press.

Foucault, M. (1980b) Truth and Power, in C. Gordon (ed.), *Selected Interviews and Other Writings 1972–77*, London, Harvester Press.

Foucault, M. (1980c) Prison Talk, in C. Gordon (ed.), *Selected Interviews and Other Writings 1972–77*, London, Harvester Press.

Foucault, M. (1982) The Subject and Power, in H. L. Dreyfus and P. Rabinow, *Michel Foucault: Beyond Structuralism and Hermeneutics*, Brighton, Harvester Press.

Foucault, M. (1990) *The History of Sexuality, Vol. I: An Introduction*, trans. R. Hurley, London, Penguin Books.

Gellner, E. (1988) *Plough, Sword and Book: The Structure of Human History*, London, Collins.

Gellner, E. (1992) *Postmodernism, Reason and Religion*, London, Routledge.

Gerth, H. H. and Mills, C. W. (1948) *From Max Weber: Essays in Sociology*, London, Routledge & Kegan Paul.

Glass, D. V. (1954) *Social Mobility in Britain*, London, Routledge & Kegan Paul.

Goldthorpe, J. (1991) The Uses of History in Sociology: Reflections on some Recent Tendencies, *British Journal of Sociology*, 42, 2, pp. 211–30.

Goldthorpe, J. (1994) The Uses of History in Sociology: A Reply, *British Journal of Sociology*, 45, 1, pp. 55–77.

Goode, W. J. (1967) The Protection of the Inept, *American Sociological Review*, 32, pp. 5–19.

Goodson, I. and Dowbiggin, I. (1990) Docile Bodies: Commonalities in the History of Psychiatry and Schooling, in S. J. Ball (ed.), *Foucault and Education: Disciplines and Knowledge*, London, Routledge.

Gordon, C. (ed.) (1980) *Power/Knowledge: Selected Interviews and Other Writings 1972–77, Michel Foucault*, London, Harvester Wheatsheaf.

Gordon, P. (1974) *The Victorian School Manager: A Study in the Management of Education 1800–1902*, London, Woburn Press.

Gordon, P. and Lawton, D. (1978) *Curriculum Change in the Nineteenth and Twentieth Centuries*, London, Hodder & Stoughton.

Gould, S. J. (1981) *The Mismeasure of Man*, London, Penguin Books.

Gramsci, A. (1971) *Selection from the Prison Notebooks*, trans. and ed. Q. Hoare and G. N. Smith, London, Lawrence & Wishart.

Green, A. (1990) *Education and State Formation: The Rise of Education Systems in England, France and the USA*, Basingstoke, Macmillan.

Gutting, G. (1994) *The Cambridge Companion to Foucault*, Cambridge, Cambridge University Press.

Hall, J. A. (1989) They Do Things Differently There, or, the Contribution of British Historical Sociology, *British Journal of Sociology*, 40, 4, pp. 544–64.

Halsey, A. H., Floud, J. and Anderson, C. A. (eds) (1961) *Education,*

Economy and Society, London, Collier-Macmillan.

Ham, C. and Hill, M. (1984) *The Policy Process in the Modern Capitalist State*, London, Harvester Wheatsheaf.

Harris, J. S. (1955) *British Government Inspection: The Local Services and the Central Department*, London, Constable.

Herd, H. (1930) *The Diagnosis of Mental Deficiency*, London, Hodder & Stoughton.

Hindess, B. (1973) *The Use of Official Statistics in Sociology: A Critique of Positivism and Ethnomethodology*, London, Macmillan.

HMI (1990) *Education Observed: Special Issues, A Survey by HMI*, London, HMSO.

Hobsbawm, E. J. (1969) *Industry and Empire*, Harmondsworth, Penguin Books.

Hoggart, R. (1958) *The Uses of Literacy: Aspects of Working Class Life with Special Reference to Publications and Entertainments*, Harmondsworth, Penguin Books.

Hollis, P. (1987) *Ladies Elect: Women in English Local Government 1865–1914*, Oxford, Clarendon Press.

Holman, R. (1978) *Poverty: Explanations of Social Deprivation*, London, Martin Robertson.

Horn, P. (1990) Elizabeth Miriam Burgwin: Child Welfare Pioneer and Union Activist, *Journal of History of Education*, 14, 3, pp. 48–60.

Hoskin, K. (1990) Foucault under Examination: The Crypto-Educationalist Unmasked, in S. J. Ball (ed.), *Foucault and Education: Disciplines and Knowledge*, London, Routledge.

Hurt, J. (1972) *Education in Evolution: Church, State and Popular Education 1800–1870*, London, Paladin.

Hurt, J. S. (1988) *Outside the Mainstream: A History of Special Education*, London, Batsford.

Jarman, T. L. (1953) *Landmarks in the History of Education*, London, John Murray.

Jenkins, K. (1995) *On What is History? From Carr and Elton to Rorty and White*, London, Routledge.

Jones, D. (1990) The Genealogy of the Urban School Teacher, in S. J. Ball (ed.), *Foucault and Education: Disciplines and Knowledge*, London, Routledge.

Jones, K. (1972) *A History of the Mental Health Services*, London, Routledge & Kegan Paul.

Jones, K. and Williamson, J. (1979) Birth of the Schoolroom, *Ideology and Consciousness*, 6, pp. 59–110.

Jones, R. (1990) Educational Practices and Scientific Knowledge: A Genealogical Reinterpretation of the Emergence of Physiology in Post-

Revolutionary France, in S. J. Ball (ed.), *Foucault and Education: Disciplines and Knowledge*, London, Routledge.

Katz, M. B. (1976) The Origins of Public Education: A Reassessment, *History of Education Quarterly*, pp. 381–407.

Kekewich, G. W. (1920) *The Education Department and After*, London, Constable.

Kenway, J. (1990) Education and the Right's Discursive Politics: Private versus State Schooling, in S. J. Ball (ed.), *Foucault and Education: Disciplines and Knowledge*, London, Routledge.

Kerr, J. (1905) Physical Inspection, *Journal of the Royal Sanitary Institute*, 26, pp. 47–58.

Klemm, L. R. (1907) *European Schools*, New York, D. Appleton.

Knight, J., Smith, R., and Sachs, J. (1990) Deconstructing Hegemony: Multicultural Policy and a Populist Reponse, in S. J. Ball (ed.), *Foucault and Education: Disciplines and Knowledge*, London, Routledge.

Lawson, J. and Silver, H. (1973) *A Social History of Education in England*, London, Methuen.

Leese, J. (1950) *Personalities and Powers in English Education*, London, Arnold.

Lemert, C. C. and Gillan, G. (1982) *Michel Foucault: Social Theory and Social Transgression*, New York, Columbia University Press.

Lemert, E. M. (1972) *Human Deviance, Social Problems and Social Control*, 2nd edn, Englewood Cliffs, NJ, Prentice-Hall.

Lipsky, M. (1980) *Street-Level Bureaucracy*, New York, Russell Sage.

Locke, J. (1965) *An Essay Concerning Human Understanding*, Vol. I, London, Everyman,.

Locke, R. (1984) *The End of Practical Man: Entrepreneurship and Higher Education in Germany, France and Great Britain, 1880–1940*, London, Cassell.

Lowe, R. (1980) Primary and Classical Education, in D. A. Reeder (ed.), *Educating Our Masters*, Leicester, Leicester University Press.

Lowith, K. (1993) *Max Weber and Karl Marx* (ed. T. Bottomore and W. Outhwaite), London, Routledge.

Lukes, S. (1975) *Emile Durkheim, His Life and Work: A Historical and Critical Study*, Harmondsworth, Penguin Books.

Marsden, W. E. (1977) Education and the Social Geography of Nineteenth-Century Towns and Cities, in D. A. Reeder (ed.), *Urban Education in the Nineteenth Century*, London, Taylor & Francis.

Marx, K. (1957) *Capital*, 2 vols, London, Dent.

Marx, K. (1963) The Social System of Capitalism, in T. B. Bottomore and M. Rubel (eds), *Karl Marx: Selected Writings in Sociology and Social Philosophy*, Harmondsworth, Penguin Books.

Marx, K. and Engels, F. (1967) *The Communist Manifesto*, Hardmondsworth, Penguin Books.

Marx, K. (1968) *Preface to a Contribution to the Critique of Political Economy*, first published in 1859. Reprinted in K. Marx and F. Engels, *Karl Marx and Frederick Engels: Selected Works*, London, Lawrence & Wishart.

Marx, K. (1973) *The Eighteenth Brumaire of Louis Bonaparte*, in D. Fernbach (ed.), *Surveys from Exile*, Vol. II, Hardmondsworth, Penguin Books.

McCann, P. (ed.) (1977) *Popular Education and Socialisation in the 19th Century*, London, Methuen.

McClure, S. (1970) *One Hundred Years of London Education 1870–1970*, London, Allen Lane.

McKeown, T. (ed.) (1971) *Medical History and Medical Care: A Symposium of Perspectives*, London, Oxford University Press.

McKeown, T. and Record, R. G. (1962) Reasons for the Decline of Mortality in England and Wales during the Nineteenth Century, *Population Studies*, 16, pp. 94–122.

Meadmore, D. (1993) The Production of Individuality through Examination, *British Journal of Sociology of Education*, 14, 1, pp. 59–74.

Merquior, J. G. (1985) *Foucault*, London, Fontana Press.

Michels, R. (1962) *Political Parties: A Sociological Study of the Oligarchical Tendencies of Modern Democracy*, New York, Free Press.

Mills, C. Wright (1970) *The Sociological Imagination*, Harmondsworth, Penguin Books.

Ministry of Education (1945) *Statutory Rules and Orders No. 1076, The Handicapped Pupils and School Health Service Regulations*, London, HMSO.

Ministry of Education (1951a) *Education 1900–1950: The Report of the Ministry of Education for the Year 1950*, London, HMSO.

Ministry of Education (1951b) *Education and Statistics of Public Education for England and Wales, 1900–1950*, London, HMSO.

Morris, R., Reid, E. and Fowler, J. (1993) *Education Act 93: A Critical Guide*, London, Association of Metropolitan Authorities.

Morrish, I. (1970) *Education Since 1800*, London, Allen & Unwin.

Mort, F. (1985) Sexuality: Regulation and Contestation, in V. Beechey and J. Donald (eds), *Subjectivity and Social Relations*, Milton Keynes, Open University Press.

Moulton, H. F. (1919) *The Powers and Duties of Education Authorities*, London, William Hodge.

Murphy, J. (1971) *Church, State and Schools in Britain, 1800–1970*, London, Routledge & Kegan Paul.

Nisbet, R. A. (1967) *The Sociological Tradition*, London, Heinemann.

Norbury, B. (1993) (Under-Secretary, DFE), 'SEN and the Current Bill on Education', conference address, Bournemouth, EDPEC.

Owens, G. and Birchenall, P. (1979) *Mental Handicap: Social Dimensions*, London, Pitman Medical.

Peterson, A. D. C. (1952) *A Hundred Years of Education*, London, Duckworth.

Platt, J. (1981) Evidence and Proof in Documentary Research: Some Specific Problems of Documentary Research, *Sociological Review*, 29, 1, pp. 31–52.

Polanyi, K. (1957) *The Great Transformation*, Boston, MA, Beacon.

Porter, R. (1993) *Disease, Medicine and Society in England 1550–1900*, 2nd edn, Basingstoke, Macmillan.

Potts, P. (1983) Medicine, Morals and Deficiency: The Contribution of Doctors to the Development of Special Education in England, *Oxford Review of Education*, 9, 3, pp. 181–96.

Pritchard, D. G. (1963) *Education and the Handicapped 1760–1960*, London, Routledge & Kegan Paul.

Quiller-Couch, A. (1917) *Memoir of A. J. Butler*, London, Longmans.

Rabinow, P. (ed.) (1991) *The Foucault Reader*, Harmondsworth, Penguin Books.

Ray, L. J. (1983) Eugenics, Mental Deficiency and Fabian Socialism, *Oxford Review of Education*, 9, 3, pp. 213–22.

Reeder, D. A. (ed.) (1980) *Educating Our Masters*, Leicester, Leicester University Press.

Ritchie, J. M. (1930) *Concerning the Blind*, Edinburgh, Oliver and Boyd.

Rose, N. (1979) The Psychological Complex, Mental Measurement and Social Administration, *Ideology and Consciousness*, 5, pp. 5–68.

Rosen, G. (1971) Historical Trends and Future Prospects in Public Health, in T. McKeown (ed.), *Medical History and Medical Care: A Symposium of Perspectives*, London, Oxford University Press.

Rowntree, S. B. (1910) *Poverty: A Study of Town Life*, London, Macmillan.

Royal Commission on the Present State of Popular Education in England and Wales (1861), London, HMSO.

Royal Commission on Elementary Education Acts (RCEEA) (1886), *First Report*, London, HMSO.

Royal Commission on Elementary Education Acts (RCEEA) (1887), *Second Report*, London, HMSO.

Royal Commission on Elementary Education Acts (RCEEA) (1888), *Final Report*, London, HMSO.

Royal Commission on the Blind, the Deaf and the Dumb, &c. of the United Kingdom (RCBDD) (1889), *Report*, London, HMSO.

Royal Commission on the Care and Control of the Feeble-Minded (RCCCFM) (1908), *Report*, Vols I and II (Radnor Report), London, HMSO.

Rubinstein, D. (1969) *School Attendance in London 1870–1904: A Social History*, Hull, University of Hull Publications.

Rubinstein, D. (1977) Socialisation and the London School Board 1870–1904: Aims, Methods and Public Opinion, in P. McCann (ed.), *Popular Education and Socialisation in the 19th Century*, London, Methuen.

Rutter, M. and Madge, N. (1976) *Cycles of Disadvantage: A Review of Research*, London, Heinemann.

Salmon, W. C. (1963) *Logic*, Englewood Cliffs, NJ, Prentice-Hall.

Sarup, M. (1982) *Education, State and Crisis: A Marxist Perspective*, London, Routledge.

Sayer, A. (1992) *Method in Social Science: A Realist Approach*, 2nd edn, London, Routledge.

Scott, J. (1990) *A Matter of Record: Documentary Sources in Social Research*, Cambridge, Polity Press.

Scull, A. (1979) *Museums of Madness: The Social Organisation of Insanity in Nineteenth Century England*, London, Penguin.

Selleck, R. J. W. (1968) *The New Education: The English Background 1870–1914*, London, Pitman.

Shuttleworth, G. E. (1900) *Mentally Deficient Children: Their Treatment and Training*, 2nd edn, London, H. K. Lewis.

Silver, H. (1983) *Education as History*, London, Methuen.

Simon, B. (1960) *Studies in the History of Education 1780–1870*, London, Lawrence & Wishart.

Simon B. (1965) *Education and the Labour Movement 1870–1920*, London, Lawrence & Wishart.

Skeggs, B. (1991) Challenging Masculinity and Using Sexuality, *British Journal of Sociology of Education*, 12, 2, pp. 127–39.

Smart, B. (1983) *Foucault, Marxism and Critique*, London, Routledge.

Smellie, K. B. (1937) *A Hundred Years of British Government*, London, Arnold.

Smith, D. (1982) Social History and Sociology – More Than Just Good Friends, *The Sociological Review*, 30, 3, pp. 286–308.

Smith, D. (1991) *The Rise of Historical Sociology*, Cambridge, Polity Press.

Smith, F. (1931) *A History of English Elementary Education 1760–1902*, London, University of London Press.

Spalding, T. A. (1900) *The Work of the London School Board*, London, King.

Spencer, F. H. (1938) *An Inspector's Testament*, London, English Universities Press.

Spinley, B. (1953) *The Deprived and the Privileged*, London, Routledge & Kegan Paul.

Stedman Jones, G. (1971) *Outcast London: A Study in the Relationships between Classes in Victorian Society*, Oxford, Clarendon Press.

Stedman Jones, G. (1983) *Language of Class: Studies in English Working-Class History 1832–1982*, Cambridge, Cambridge University Press.

Steedman, C. (1990) *Childhood, Culture and Class in Britain: Margaret McMillan 1860–1931*, London, Virago Press.

Sturt, M. (1967) *The Education of the People: A History of Primary Education in England and Wales in the Nineteenth Century*, London, Routledge & Kegan Paul.

Sumner, C. (1994) *The Sociology of Deviance: An Obituary*, Buckingham, Open Uniersity Press.

Sutherland, G. (ed.) (1972) *Studies in the Growth of Nineteenth-Century Government*, London, Routledge & Kegan Paul.

Sutherland, G. (1973) *Policy-Making in Elementary Education 1870–1895*, Oxford, Oxford University Press.

Sutherland, G. (1984) *Ability, Merit and Measurement: Mental Testing and English Education 1888–1940*, Oxford, Clarendon Press.

Sylvester, D. W. (1974) *Robert Lowe and Education*, Cambridge, Cambridge University Press.

Thompson, E. P. (1967) Time, Work-discipline and Industrial Capitalism, *Past and Present*, 38, pp. 56–97.

Tocqueville, A. de (1945) *Democracy in America*, 2 vols, New York, Vintage Books.

Tocqueville, A. de (1960) *Journeys to England and Ireland*, trans. G. Lawrence, ed. T. P. Mayer, London, Faber.

Tomlinson, S. (1982) *A Sociology of Special Education*, London, Routledge & Kegan Paul.

Tonnies, F. (1955) *Community and Association*, trans. C. P. Loomis, London, Routledge & Kegan Paul.

Turner, B. (1993) Preface in K. Lowith, *Max Weber and Karl Marx*, London, Routledge.

Walkerdine, V. (1984) Developmental Psychology and the Child-Centred Pedagogy: The Insertion of Piaget into Early Education, in J. Henriques *et al.* (eds), *Changing the Subject: Psychology, Social Regulation and Subjectivity*, London, Methuen.

Waller, W. (1965) *The Sociology of Teaching*, New York, John Wiley.

Wardle, D. (1976) *English Popular Education, 1780–1975*, Cambridge, Cambridge University Press.

Weber, M. (1930) *The Protestant Ethic and the Spirit of Capitalism*, trans. T. Parsons, London, Unwin.

Wedge, P. and Prosser, N. (1973) *Born to Fail?*, London, Arrow Books.
Westergaard, J. and Resler, H. (1976) *Class in a Capitalist Society: A Study of Contemporary Britain*, Harmondsworth, Penguin.
Williams, R. (1965) *The Long Revolution*, Harmondsworth, Penguin.
Wormald, J. and Wormald, S. (1914) *A Guide to the Mental Deficiency Act, 1913*, London, King.

Index